IMMIGRANT'S KITCHEN
Italian

IMMIGRANT'S KITCHEN
Italian

Cassandra Vivian
Vivian Pelini Sansone
Elizabeth Parigi Vivian

Trade Routes Enterprises

Dedicated to the Immigrants
Nazzareno Parigi and Carolina Santa Paggini Parigi
Egino "Gino" Pelini and Alessandra "Sandrina" Pitti Pelini

My thanks to Gabriella Durra and Susan Torgensen who set me on the right path at the beginning of this venture.

A note of gratitude goes to the men who shared the secrets of wine and cured meats, without their help these special chapters could not have been written: William "Bob" Pelini, who is carrying on his father's wine-making traditions; Beppe Parigi, our cousin in Italy, who still makes *vin santo;* Pamerino Ciotti, who specializes in *porchetta;* and especially Joseph Stromei, his wife Ida and daughter Lydia. Joe is a fourth generation professional butcher and makes a delicious prosciutto. On our visit to his home he cut a fresh one and let us drink his homemade wine. Taste buds that had been dead for years sprang to life and memories of other times came rushing back. We will be forever grateful.

A very, very special thank-you to Norma J. Iervoline, who tested dozens of recipes with gusto and enthusiasm, and to her family who tasted and commented. And to Joseph D'Andrea, vice consul of Italy, the Rev. Msgr. P. Lino Ramellini, and Janice Guiducci Vairo, who graciously corrected our Italian. Janice is the granddaughter of my grandmother's lifelong friend Amabile Sodi and daughter of Giuliano Aurelio and Rena Sodi Guiducci, with whom we have re-established contact thanks to this book.

Additional thanks to Nigel Ryan, Charlotte "Chuckie" Amico Pelini, Maria Albertini, Helen Shepler, Mary Bitonti, Judith L. Merrick, Rita Mele, Carol Kaufmann, and Lena Poletini Falbo, who all helped in various ways.

Edited by Carolyn B. Reuter
Illustrations by Elhamy Naguib and Louise Hammond
Cover concept and design by Bobbi Monroe and Isabelle Nardelli

Copyright © 1993, Trade Routes Enterprises. All rights reserved.

Publisher's Cataloging in Publication
(Prepared by Quality Books Inc.)

Vivian, Cassandra E.
  Immigrant's kitchen Italian / Cassandra E. Vivian.
  p. cm.
  Includes bibliographical references and index.
  Preassigned LCCN: 93-60497.
  ISBN 1-883509-00-9

  1. Cookery, Italian. 2. Italian-Americans--Pennsylvania--Social life and customs. I. Title.

TX723.V58 1993   641.945
                                      QBI93-688

To order directly from the publisher send $16.95 plus $3.00 shipping and handling to Trade Routes Enterprises, 518 Fourth Street, Monessen, Pennsylvania 15062. Pennsylvania residents add 6% tax.

Table of Contents
Indice

iii

viii

Introduction
Introduzione

There were many ethnic pockets in our community. Almost every block of our small town in southwestern Pennsylvania had a different language and culture, and exotic and wonderful smells wafted from the neighborhood kitchens. There were nearly a dozen Catholic churches, each designated not by its name, but by the origin of its ethnic congregation: the Italian church, the Slavic church, the Irish church. There were Greeks, Finns, African-Americans, Ukrainians, Poles, Serbs, Slavs, Croatians, Russians, Syrians, Belgians, French, and even a Chinese family in our town. In summer, church picnics were held each Sunday afternoon at one of the local parks and each weekend in winter the women prepared meals in the different halls throughout the town: the Sons of Italy, the Italian Hall, St. John's Russian Orthodox Church, the Slovak Home, and the Polish and Sokol's clubs.

Oh, the wonderful dishes we ate. In addition to our own Italian foods we had Greek grape leaves, *moussaka*, *pastitsio*, and *baklava*; Slavic *halupki*, *halushki*, and *paska*; Syrian *kibbeh*, *kofta*, and *shish kebab*; Finnish *nisua*, *hetelma soppaa*, and *sill salla*; and African-American ribs, chops, and sweet-potato pie.

But amid all this diversity, growing up Italian was special. The sounds, tastes, and smells of childhood still surround me as I think back to those wonderful times: of Nonna listening to the Italian radio program on Saturday morning; of Nonno reading the Italian newspaper through his gold-rimmed spectacles; of evenings around the kitchen table playing Italian card games like *tre sette*, *scopa*, and *briscola*, winking at partners to indicate aces, twitching the mouth to indicate threes, touching the ring finger to show diamonds, and always getting caught amid a roar of laughter.

The Italian community was divided into regional groups that held tightly together. Each group had its own style of cooking, its own section of the street, and its own men's club and women's auxiliary. They were not satisfied with any old meeting place, but built huge buildings that were the civic centers of the community, where women would gather to celebrate saints' days and Mother's Day, and men would gather to play *bocce* and *morra*.

I am a grandchild of the immigrant wave that came to America at the turn of the century. These daring men and women were mainly farmers and tradesmen, people who worked with their hands, were close to the land, and kept the traditions of their homeland alive. I remember my first trip to Italy and how shocked I was to discover that everyone there considered me an American. To me, I was an Italian, just as my friends down the street were Greek, Slavic, and Irish. Few of us were American-Americans, we were from another country.

The nonnos and nonnas who raised our families came from the village of Quarata, a small farming community in the glorious Tuscan hills northwest of Arezzo. Nonno and Nonna never let an opportunity pass to tell us we were special, we were Italian, and Tuscan, and should be proud of our heritage.

Just out of their teens these adventurers crossed the ocean in steerage to a new life in a new land. What courage they had. As they approached Ellis Island fearful that they would be turned back, not understanding a word of English, hopeful to find a job, a new world opened for them. Those that had gone before led the way to small towns throughout America. They were the people who were to man the meat-packing plants of Chicago, the steel mills of Pennsylvania and Ohio, and the new auto factories of Detroit.

What it must have been like in that village in Italy as family after family lost children to America. The Bindi, the Poletini, the Ghinassi families, who live beside my uncles and aunts in Quarata, have relatives living down the street from me in America. It made us all responsible to each other, and kept the feeling of family alive. As a member of a family, you were responsible to it for your actions. As a member of the village of Quarata, you were responsible to the other villagers for its reputation, and as an Italian in a town of many ethnic groups, you were responsible for the reputation of all Italians.

Fifty years after my grandparents came to America, I visited Quarata for the first time. As soon as I entered the beige stucco villa at the edge of the small country town and saw my grandfather's brother I knew I was home. Before we sat down my uncle presented me with a glass filled with that magical Italian wine, *vin santo*. The glass was crystal and etched into the side was the word Nazzareno, the name of my grandfather. With tears in his eyes my uncle told me that the last time that glass was used was by my grandfather on the day he departed for America. Then, like now, it was for a toast. Then a *buon viaggio*, now a *ben venuto*. My uncle had cherished that glass and carried it into the hills with him when the town was occupied by Germans during World War II. Who could not cry at such a moment?

Then I sat down at a table in the ancestral home and ate a meal that could have come from my grandmother's or mother's kitchen. I knew every dish. My cousin teased my uncle about his new wine, a conversation I had heard many times back home when the Pelini family would come to visit, or we would visit them. The women were in the kitchen. The men were cutting the homemade prosciutto and preparing the wine for the table. It was home. These were my people. In a small town in southwestern Pennsylvania, the traditions of a small town in northern Italy had been maintained.

2

Nazzareno "Gumbone" Parigi and Carolina Santa Paggini

My grandfather, Nazzareno Parigi, was born March 27 (or 29), 1891, the first of four boys and three girls. His father was Giuseppe Parigi and his mother, Elisa Silvestro Pasquini. Nonno, like his father, was a farmer, a *contadino*, and worked as an overseer, supervising workers from the back of a white horse.

He left his young bride in April and arrived in the United States on May 5, 1913, aboard the steamship *Tormegnia*. He came to the boomtown of Monessen along the banks of the Monongahela River, 25 miles south of Pittsburgh. Why Monessen? Like so many immigrants, the choice was made for him—Domenico (Menco) and Laura (Nonno's cousin) Bindi from Quarata were already there. Mr. Bindi was a straw boss at Pittsburgh Steel and Nonno got a job as a laborer in Bindi's Italian labor gang. Then he sent for his young, pregnant bride.

Nonno worked supervising the horses that were used to haul steel. When the horses were replaced by motorized vehicles he chose not to continue working in that department and instead began to erect fences. He traveled all over western Pennsylvania putting up chain link fences, content to be a laborer, out-of-doors, and refused to be a supervisor or move to another job.

Nonno made the best wine in his family, and, we thought, the best in Monessen. He also made delicious sausage and prosciutto. His wine cellar was a child's dream and I spent many a Saturday morning there with my grandfather.

My Nonno was a red-headed *buongustaio*, a man who liked good food, and he spent his life laboring over the making of excellent prosciuttos, sausages, and wine. I always sat next to him at the table (my Nonna said to protect the guests from his ample distribution of wine), and I think he passed his palate on to me. My eyes twinkle like his when I sit down to a hearty feast. In his waning days he had gout, and, despite its pain, he smiled because he considered it a badge of honor for years of good eating.

Carolina Santa Paggini was born in Capolona, a small village north of Quarata, on April 23, 1891. Her father was Paolo Paggini and her mother, Elisabetta Lesi. She had four sisters and five brothers. She married my grandfather in August of 1911. Carolina was a woman of substance. She taught herself to read and write, paraded for women's suffrage, campaigned for politicians, helped bring the first Italian Catholic church to Monessen, and, until she died at the age of 94, never spent a day when her hands were not busy. I can still hear the clicking of her steel knitting needles. She was so proficient that she would sit on the couch with my head on her lap, and as we watched television the needles would click away. By evening's end a baby's jacket, trimmed with white angora, would be completed.

There is a folk song sung in the villages around Quarata about a young girl and a bandit. While she was sweeping, two men walked past her house in Castelluccio, where the family had moved. Later one returned alone and terrorized the girl to swear she had not seen him. Soon the police came by and asked if she had seen the bandit. Instead of lying, she told the truth and the bandit was caught. The song is about my grandmother.

Along with Sophia Poletini, her lifelong friend, and Anselmo Bonchi, another resident of Quarata who ultimately resided in Aliquippa, Pennsylvania, my grandmother came to the United States in October 1913. They passed through Ellis Island, Nonna 8 months pregnant with what was to be her only child, and terrified that because she was pregnant they would send her back.

It was many years before Nonna applied for citizenship in the United States. On January 5, 1939, the day she was to appear before the judge, a terrible snowstorm gripped northeastern United States. But Nonna insisted she had to go to the courthouse in Pittsburgh. My father drove her and it took them almost four hours to travel the 25 miles. When she entered the courtroom they were closing because of the bad weather. The judge asked her what she wanted and when she told him he smiled, "You must want it pretty bad to travel in this weather. Who is the president of the United States?" She answered. "Citizenship granted," he said. "Now go home."

Nonna always took a *passeggiata* after dinner, and our dog would go with her. They were great friends. Nonna loved fresh fruit and always enjoyed an apple or orange on a winter evening, or peaches, watermelon, or cantaloupe in the summer. She always shared a bit with our dog. To this day whenever a piece of fruit is taken from the refrigerator, Kimba comes running. I often wonder if she thinks of Nonna.

When Nonna's mind was no longer with her, my mother took great pains to keep her physically active. Each morning she would bathe her and move her from the bed to the wheelchair which she would move to the table for breakfast. After breakfast she would place Nonna on the couch and our dog would nestle beside her.

Nonna lived long enough to enjoy five generations in our family. When her great-great-grandchildren, Patty Ann and Mikey, would come to visit, I would sit beside Nonna on the couch and play the old Italian game *bicci-cu-cu*. As I rubbed my hands over their backs and sang the chant, Nonna would come out of her dream world, lift her head, laugh, and join in the fun. It was the only time she responded. I guess the sounds of her own childhood awakened the ancient memories.

My mother, Elizabeth, an only child, was born November 27, 1913, just a month after Nonna entered the United States. Elizabeth married Alfred "Freddie" Vivian, who, despite the name, was pure Italian. They had two children, Alfred and me. My brother, whom we called Bebe, married Margaret Ann Angele and they had four children: Kathleen, Thomas, Michael, and Kristin. All are married. My father died in 1965, my brother in 1989. My mother is now a octogenarian, the matriarch of our family. She has six great-grandchildren (soon seven): Patricia Ann and Michael Karbowsky, Michael, Jr. and Joseph Vivian, Roger Strautmann, and Thomas Vivian, Jr.

Note: The seventh great-grandchild Alan Michael Vivian arrived just in time to add this note.

Egino "Gino" Pelini and Alessandra "Sandrina" Pitti Pelini
by Vivian Pelini Sansone

My father Egino "Gino" Pelini was born in the little hill town of Fillignini, Province of Arezzo, Italy, in the year 1896. Times were tough and the main source of nourishment for the family came from an abundance of heaven-sent chestnuts which were stored on the bedroom floor and meted out as needed. The hardships were many, so at the tender age of 8, Gino, his brother Luigi, and his father Isaia, journeyed to France to work as foresters, for my grandfather was a lumberjack. By being very frugal they saved money and returned home to the family bosom which consisted of four boys, two girls, and my grandmother, Diomira.

My grandparents had three boys before my father's birth and named each Giovanni Battista, but all died within the first year of birth. When my grandmother was pregnant with my father they decided not to name this child Giovanni Battista, but Egino, and broke the chain of tragedy (eventually they did have a son named Giovanni Battista and, praise the Lord, he lived to a ripe old age).

When Gino was 19, the futility of their life and future convinced him and his brother Luigi, who was 23 at the time, to come to America. Since their close *amici* (friends) Gesue (Natalino) and Annetta Chiapparri were already in the mountain state of West Virginia, the Pelini boys followed them. After some time the Chiapparri family moved to New Castle, Pennsylvania, and the boys went with them. They got jobs at the Shenango Pottery Company in New Castle (you can imagine how surprised we were one day when the china set on our breakfast table in Quarata was from Shenango Pottery).

The yearning for home and family kept tugging at them so, after saving enough money, they decided to return to Italy to buy their parents a home and to open a *bottega* (bar and store) in the charming town of Quarata. The home still stands and on our visits to Italy we sleep in Gino's original bedroom.

But success was not that easy. Luigi proclaimed that he, being the eldest, was entitled to remain in Quarata and run the family business while Gino, the younger, would have to leave and fend for himself. Since my father had invested all his savings, all that is but the fare back to America (the ever cautious Gino), he prepared to return to the United States. But he could not return. Immigration was closed. Fate then played its cards.

Alessandra (Sandrina) Parigi Pitti was born in New York City in 1903 to Pietro Pitti and Maria Parigi Pitti. Her father became ill and on his doctor's advisd the Pitti family returned to Italy in 1907 when Sandrina was 4 years old. Gino and Sandrina met, fell in love, and were married in January 1923. In March they sailed to America as newlyweds.

Upon reaching New York they had to go through Ellis Island as Gino was not a U.S. citizen (he became one November 27, 1928). In those days the men were separated from the women and Sandrina, being a very young and sheltered 20-year-old, was frightened to death. By some miracle her prayers were answered and she was befriended by a woman named Mafalda from the south of Italy who helped her. They never saw each other again, but Mafalda became a part of our family lore.

Finally, they arrived in New Castle. They moved in with the Chiapparri family and my father got a job at a cement plant. My mother was pregnant and homesick. My brother Pietro, named after my grandfather Pitti, was born prematurely and died when he was 40 days old, on the exact day he was due to be born. So once again the Pelini *malocchio* (evil eye) convinced my father that none of his children would be named after a deceased person and so neither I nor my two siblings received family names.

In 1926, after staying with a family named Zazzerino, my father and mother built a home on Beckford Street and moved in with their new baby Arnold, who was named after a character in a book my father was reading at the time. When my mother was pregnant with her second son she would often attend the prizefights held each week at the end of their street. She decided to name her new son Bobby, after her favorite prizefighter. But a more knowledgeable friend told her that the proper name for Bobby was William, so my brother William, to this day, is called Bobby. The next generation rectified the long-standing goof by Arnold naming his firstborn son Robert.

Confusion over names was to haunt the young immigrants. When Sandrina went shopping with her friend Dolores "Georgia" Calderini Guiducci, they saw the sign SALE on lawns, in department stores, and everywhere they turned. They were amazed. "Sale" in Italian meant salt, and they could not imagine why so many people in America sold salt.

They did not know the American names for so many of the things they had to buy. So, my mother would act out what she wanted and Georgia would vocalize. When buying diapers in the dry goods store, my mother took a piece of cloth and folded it like a diaper while Georgia cried like a baby.

When the Depression came we would have lost our dream house if it had not been for my father's star boarders, namely his younger brother Oliver and a good friend, Carlo (Cirli) Albertini, who came to his aid until the economy improved.

My mother was a professional seamstress in Italy, and her mother and grandmother did all the cooking. She never liked to cook. When she came to America she leaned heavily on friends until she became the great cook she was. She instilled in me a love of cooking and I enjoy perfecting new recipes and old standbys, much to the joy of my family, especially my husband Tom.

Tuscan Country Cooking
La Cucina della Campagna Toscana

Italians do not need much reason to have a *festa* and, if one does not exist, they invent it to honor a city, a saint, or a food. There are polenta festivals, mushroom festivals, cheese, wine, fish, even a pine nut festival. The first fruit of each harvest is an opportunity to celebrate. Food is so important to Italians that official government boards have been established to supervise the production of cheese, wine, vinegar and other products to guarantee their quality. Italy has a dial-a-recipe service for regional cooking.

Italian regional cooking had its birth in the earth. Whatever the land could produce, the cook used to feed the family. In the richer farm lands of the north, the table was laden with a larger variety of foods than in the poorer mountainous regions of the south. The same basic dish had a host of variations depending on the ingredients the land could provide. Almost every village had its own recipes, and although they were all made with the same ingredients, they tasted different from house to house. It was the pride of the family that good cooks lived among them.

The names of Italian foods are delightful: *diti degli apostoli*, fingers of the apostles; *I calzoni di San Leonardo*, the pants of Saint Leonard; *scarpetta di Sant'Ilario*, Saint Hilary's shoe; *ossi di morti*, bones of the dead; *saltimbocca*, leap in your mouth; *topi*, little mice; *cappelletti*, little hats. Even the cuts of pasta are known by their shape: *rotelle*, wheels; *diti*, fingers; *farfalle*, bows; *acini di pepe*, peppercorns; and *fusilli*, screws.

Tuscany is a region of seaports, mountains, and plains. In ancient times it was the center of the Etruscan civilization, a culture to which ancient Rome is heavily indebted. From the eighth to the fourth centuries B.C., 12 city-states, including Arezzo, created a high culture of seafarers, merchants, and artists, speaking a language it has taken scholars 20 centuries to transcribe.

The modern towns of Tuscany ring familiar in the ear: Pisa, Siena, Florence, and Arezzo. They were the birthplace of the Renaissance, one of the greatest creative periods in man's history. Among the architects, sculptors, painters, poets, and statesmen who lived in Tuscany were Michelangelo

Buonarroti, Leonardo da Vinci, Dante Alighieri, Boccaccio, Giotto, Botticelli, Petrarch, and Piero della Francesa, whose wonderful frescos still grace the cathedral at Arezzo. Tuscany was ruled by the powerful de Medici family and out of this high culture came the Italian language as we know it today.

Catherine de Medici, a member of the ruling Florentine Renaissance family, was a driving force in the early development of Tuscan gastronomy. It was she who introduced the Florentine fork to France, from where it moved to England, and ultimately to the world. When she married Henry II of France, as part of her dowry, she brought her chefs to Paris and delighted the French court with Tuscan dishes of game, sweets, and vegetables. From those early exports, Italian cooking has become an international gastronomy enjoyed by more people than any other ethnic cuisine.

In Italy, Tuscans are known as *Toscani mangiafagioli*, Tuscan bean eaters. They are considered tight-fisted (although you would never know it in my family). The Tuscans use both butter and oil in their cooking for the region is blessed with the olive tree, which exists mainly in the south of Italy, and fine grazing areas for livestock.

Bologna--and its province Emilia-Romagna--has been hailed as home of Italy's finest regional cuisine. Its rich fertile plains yield fruits and vegetables of exceptional taste which are made into delicious dishes by master chefs. Tuscan kitchens have a more simplistic approach to cooking, but their influence over Italian cuisine is equally important.

Tuscan food is wholesome and hearty and usually spiced with rosemary, parsley, sage, or basil. Heavy bean soups, bread without salt, fried bread, flat-bread (the forerunner of pizza), and heaped platters of rabbit, pheasant, duck, and capon are the hallmarks of the cuisine. The *panforte* of Siena is a national sweet of Italy. The grilled steaks of Florence are considered the best in Italy. The wines of Chianti are known worldwide.

The foods of Quarata make good eating and more than a touch of the peasant origins remain intact. Although Nonna had an Italian cookbook, she seldom tried anything new, and her recipes retain Old World flavor and preparation: everything fresh and from scratch. But Nonno's culinary prowess is also represented in *Immigrant's Kitchen*. Traditionally, Italian men were very much involved in producing food. Their gardens and wine cellars brought the food to the kitchen and the women took it from the kitchen to the table.

In this cookbook authentic Tuscan cooking has sometimes taken a strange twist, but all was done with Italian hands and stems from a tradition that was born in the hills of Italy and matured and developed in the valleys of western Pennsylvania.

The Immigrant Year
L'Anno dell'immigrante

People close to the land live by the land and are governed by its moods. On the rich soil of the Tuscan hills the farmer's whole existence is ruled by his farm: spring planting, summer bounty, and fall harvest. The kitchen aromas follow the seasons: the pork and beans of winter, baby lambs of spring, fresh fruits and vegetables of summer, fermenting grapes of the autumn wine, and wild game of the fall hunt.

In Italy, food is ritual. It is impossible to divorce the myths, legends, and superstitions of the Italian people from the foods they eat, for they are one: the lamb of Easter is the Christ, the lentils of the new year, coins of prosperity. The symbolism is a bond between the farmer and the sacrificial animal, which is often honored with a festival in gratitude for sustenance.

In America, immigrants were no longer farmers, but part of the industrial revolution, devoid of ritual. They filled the ranks of steel mills, meat-packing plants, and auto factories: places of technology alienated from both the land and its traditions. The immigrant families fulfilled their need to honor the land by creating a garden, keeping a rabbit hutch or a chicken coop. From the land came special foods to feed the need for things from back home and form a symbolic link to a past steeped in ritual. It was unthinkable to be without pork on Shrove Tuesday, or not to have the ingredients for special dishes for Christmas or Easter. These items had to be provided at all costs, or devastation would follow.

The gift of these ancient beliefs was the united family. Families stayed together in the garden, in the wine cellar, in the kitchen, and in the dining room. Because the holiday meals were complicated, more than one set of hands was needed to prepare the various dishes, and the women shared the chores and the time together. Thus not only did the traditions survive, but so did the family.

January *(Gennaio)*

January, the coldest and least productive month of the year, begins the rituals in an Italian home. On New Year's Day *(Capo d'Anno)* dark and light grapes are eaten for good luck, as are lentils, symbols of wealth. Chicken is never served, for it is believed if one eats chicken on the new year, one scratches backward. Pork is the meat for New Year's Day, and *cotechino* sausage with lentils is the food that fulfills all the promise for the days to come.

The first celebration after the new year is Epiphany *(Befana)*, January 6, when the three wise men visited the Christ child. Epiphany, the twelfth day of Christmas, marks the end of the winter holiday. It is traditionally the day of the *Befana*, an old woman who is considered the mother of Santa Claus. Legend states that the *Befana* was invited to join the wise men on their quest for the Christ child, but she refused. Regretting her decision, she set out alone, got lost, and has been searching ever since. Stockings are still hung in Italian homes for her visit. But the *Befana* is the accountant of bad deeds, and some children fear she will put ashes in their stockings. Arnold Pelini was so afraid of her that each year he was sure to have a stocking full of coal (followed by a gift of course).

In western Pennsylvania, January weather is unpredictable, so life for the immigrants was left to routine. Monday was wash day, and the clothes were boiled in copper boilers *(caldaie)*, run through a hand ringer, loaded into baskets, and hung in the cellar, or carried outdoors. Bushel after bushel the wet clothes were hoisted to blow dry in the breeze. Tuesday those same bushels were piled in the kitchen for ironing. Every Thursday was bread day, and the house was filled with the wonderful aroma of baking bread. By noon, if one was lucky, there was enough dough left over for frying. Once a week the soup pot came out and the broth simmered for hours.

Every Sunday was a holiday in an Italian household. We ate our four course meal at 1 p.m. Although homemade soup began each meal during the week, the first course on Sunday was pasta, and the pots were on the stove as early as 5:30 or 6 a.m. so the sauce would be simmering in time to go to 8 o'clock Mass. When Mass was over, the kitchen was abustle as the rest of the meal was prepared: a stew of beef or lamb served with a vegetable in tomato sauce, then a roast. The last thing to be done was to cut fresh homemade bread and bring the wine up from the cellar. I can still see Nonna as she tucked the bread into the crook of her arm, cutting up toward the shoulder, in what I have discovered is the traditional way to cut Tuscan country bread.

There are few special days in January, but the 17th is the Feast of St. Anthony the Abbot *(Sant'Antonio Abate)*, patron saint of animals. On this day in the hill towns and farms of Italy, animals were brought to the church for blessings and it was the time to begin the harvest of the pig. All over Italy pigs were killed and prosciutto, sausage, salami and other Italian delicacies were prepared. We did not bring animals to the church, but we did dress a pig. Our family spent many hours in the cellar and many months enjoying the foods made from the fresh and cured pork.

February *(Febbraio)*

Linking the year with a series of religious observations, the church played a very important role in immigrant lives. Every month had at least two saints' days, in many instances superimposed on ancient pagan festivals. Saints were linked with animals, grains, fruits, or vegetables and joined to the land, what it produced, or what it fed. Thus the church formed another link to Italian roots. It was a place of refuge where one would go in hope. Nonna never missed a day of Mass: up at dawn for daily devotion, returning to church at night for *novena* and blessings. I often accompanied her to evening *novena*, which would end in an Italian song.

The February feast days begin with Candlemas Day *(Candelora)*, celebrating Christ's entry into the temple of Jerusalem, which falls on the same day and carries the same ancient tradition as Groundhog Day. *Se per la candelora cola, dall'inverno siamo fuora*: "If on Candlemas Day it is dripping, from winter we've escaped." February 3 is the day of Saint Blaise *(San Biagio)* and it was traditionally a time to eat one last piece of the Christmas *panettone,* tucked away for this day and believed to protect from sore throats. Nonno loved it.

Nonno was a steelworker. He went into the mill in 1913 and remained there for more than 40 years. This was when unions were organizing. Working conditions were deplorable. There was no job security. Nonno worked a 12-hour day, seven days a week. There were no vacations, no retirement programs, no health insurance, no compensation for injuries, no safety regulations, and immigrants were paid less money for the same jobs as nationals.

The Great Steel Strike of 1919, the same year prohibition was legislated, was yet another attempt by workers to unionize. They were fighting for an 8-hour day, higher wages, and the dismemberment of company unions. The companies broke the strike with propaganda, strikebreakers, spies, and state and local police. The strike ended on January 9, 1920, simply because the families were starving and losing their homes.

Life must have been impossible. Dominico "Menco" Bindi was a company man and had to go to work. Nonno's loyalty was to him, for Bindi was from Quarata. This must have been a scenario re-enacted throughout Monessen among all the ethnic groups. So, some of the Italian labor gang crossed the picket lines each day and went into the mill. Nonno was given a gun for protection, but he brought it home and hid it. I found it more than 40 years later after he had died and Nonna was coming to live with us. That is when I first heard this story.

In June of 1921, disillusioned with the violence in America, Nonno packed up his family and went back to Italy. But things had changed. Nonna was no longer happy living in an extended family, she wanted her own home and kitchen. Thus, two years later they returned to America. Because my mother was born in the United States and a U.S. citizen, the family was able to return to America without difficulty. They sailed first-class on the maiden voyage of the SS Giulio Cesare on July 1, 1923. Nonno talked about the elegant journey all his life.

March *(Marzo)*

The winds of March brought expectation to Italian immigrant households, signalling preparations for carnival, Lent, and Easter. March 19 is St. Joseph's Day *(Festa di San Giuseppe)* in honor of the earthly father of Jesus Christ, patron of the family. In our household no festivities were connected with St. Joseph's Day, but superstitions and special foods were. It is believed that if you cut your hair on St. Joseph's Day it will grow faster and fuller. In the kitchen Nonna made a rice fritter called Fritters of St. Joseph *(Frittelle di San Giuseppe)*.

In Italy, St. Joseph's Day is a much bigger affair, for he is also the patron saint of pastry chefs and region by region they outdo themselves in his honor. In Sicily, there is a Table of St. Joseph *(Tavola di San Giuseppe)*, an altar of flowers and varieties of breads.

March 25 is the Annunciation *(Annunciazione)* and March 27 was Nonno's birthday. But March also brings carnival, a time of festival, and Lent *(Quaresima)*, a time of fasting and repentance. Many tales are told of the naughty goings on of persons safely hidden behind masks and costumes during the carnivals of the Middle Ages and Renaissance. Along with elaborate and costly costumes, balls, street parades, and buffoonery, food was served on a scale that surpassed almost every other holiday of the year.

By the time I came around, carnival was no longer a wonderful tradition, but my mother remembers the balls held in Italian clubs in our valley. Nonno did not like to go to the dances, so Nonna and my mother went: once as George and Martha Washington, again as a contessa and her lady-in-waiting, winning first prize both times.

Carnival culminates during the week before Lent *(La Settimana Grassa)*, from Maud Thursday *(Giovedi Santo)* to Ash Wednesday *(Le Cenere)*, the first day of Lent. On Shrove Tuesday *(Martedi Grasso)*, the day before Lent, pork must be eaten at all costs. Nonna's meal began with pasta with meat sauce followed by pork chops on a spit, and a salad of endive and celery. This was right in keeping with the traditions of our family in Italy, where the chops were roasted over an open fire in our ancestral home. In 1985, *Zia* (Aunt) *Giuseppina* still used the ancient fireplace in the kitchen of the Parigi home for most of her cooking. Beside it she had a wood-burning stove which she said was only good for boiling water, and a gas stove which she did not use at all. For dessert, in her home and ours, we enjoyed rich, flavorful *fiocchi*, a fried cookie topped with confectioners' sugar.

There are six weeks in Lent, and in the middle, at *Mezza Quaresima*, a rag doll representing an old woman *(La Vecchia)* appears. In Florence she is hung in one of the squares and, amid great ceremony, cut open allowing delicacies to cascade on the waiting children below. My mother remembers attending such parties at the NIPA, the Italian club near our home, but they did not last long as the ceilings were too high and the children could not reach the caches of candy.

April   *(Aprile)*

Busy March is followed by joyous April, a month filled with the rites of spring. April 23, St. George's Day (*San Giorgio,* the patron of dairymen, who ate a rustic bread of corn flour, *pan e mei,* in his honor) was Nonna's birthday; April 25, the Feast of St. Mark (*San Marco,* patron saint of Venice) was celebrated with *risi e bisi,* a soupy risotto of rice and peas.

But April is dominated by Holy Week (*Settimana Santa*) and Easter (*Pasqua*). Palm Sunday (*Domenica delle Palme*) marks the day Jesus Christ entered Jerusalem amid olive branches and palm fronds. The church is draped in purple and each person attending the Mass receives a sprig of palm to take home.

Holy Thursday (*Giovedi Santo,* the day of the Last Supper) must have been the busiest day of the year in an Italian immigrant home. The young lamb had to be slaughtered and dressed, and Easter bread had to be made (Nonna always said the bread would not rise on Good Friday). While she was in the kitchen, Nonno was tilling the land for the spring garden, traditionally begun on Holy Thursday. Onions, parsley, and leaf lettuce were ready for picking within a month, fresh garden vegetables would join the daily menu.

No work was done in an immigrant home between noon and 3 p.m. on Good Friday (*Venerdi Santo*), the time of Christ's crucifixion. Women were at church.

Holy Saturday (*Sabato Santo*) began as a fast day, but at noon, the fast was broken with a meal of blessed Easter bread, blessed eggs (eggs, symbols of renewal, were originally prohibited during Lent), and salami. It was also the day of the *gran fritto misto,* a medley of fried foods that took hours to prepare and an equal number of hours to eat. Chicken, veal, fish, pork, and lamb, sliced into serving pieces and dipped in bread crumbs or flour, then beaten egg, were fried a golden brown. The five varieties of meat were joined by artichokes, beans, cauliflower, mushrooms, and zucchini, also dipped in eggs and flour or coated with a batter. I can still see Nonna at the stove cooking this meal hour after hour with the big black iron skillets sizzling away, filling the house with tempting aromas.

The *gran fritto misto* was arranged on an extra-large platter with each item having a corner of its own. Nonna always laid a flat plate upsidedown in the middle of the platter so the meats would drain and pile high. The vegetables were usually around the edges. The entire masterpiece was trimmed with fresh lemon wedges, their juices dashed over the fried foods to enhance the taste. The melt-in-your-mouth *gran fritto misto* was served with a simple leaf lettuce and onion salad, dressed with oil and vinegar.

On Easter Sunday the table was set with the best china and cutlery (except for Nonno's fork, which he had filed down until each prong was as thin and sharp as a needle). Fresh flowers dressed the buffet, and we all sat around the huge dining room table in my grandparent's home.

To the platters of sliced salami, blessed eggs, and Easter bread was added a large dish of canapes made of milt and chicken livers topped with thin slices of prosciutto. These succulent *crostini* were washed down with white wine. When they were cleared from the table the bowls of *cappelletti* swimming in golden broth arrived. Topped with grated Parmesan cheese, the soup was a meal in itself.

Then the lamb dishes began. Stewed lamb accompanied by spinach cooked in a garlic and rosemary sauce sprinkled with white flecks of grated Parmesan cheese was followed by spiced roast lamb with oven potatoes and a simple salad of garden leaf lettuce and onions in oil and vinegar. Of course the wine was red, and each course had fresh bread as an accompaniment. And amid the dyed Easter eggs and chocolate rabbits were a golden sponge cake *(pane di Spagna)* and rice pudding served with strong Italian coffee and *vin santo*, the best of Italian wines. When it was all over, we were stuffed with good food and filled with good conversation.

For the Pelini family the whole ritual was repeated a week later on White Sunday *(I Bianchi)*, when converts were traditionally taken into the church. The Bonchi's, from Aliquippa, joined them that day for another gigantic feast. Easter was great.

May   (*Maggio*)

Nonno's second spring planting was in early May and green beans, beets, chard, carrots, and celery were planted. At the end of the month the final planting included cucumbers, peppers, tomatoes, and zucchini.

May celebrated the return of spring with the Ascension (*Ascensione*), the fortieth day after Easter when Christ ascended into heaven. Spring brought the immigrant community out-of-doors.

Although the men went to the club (*sala*) all year long, in the spring the gaming area (*pallaio*) came alive with the game of *bocce*. On the first warm days the playing surface was prepared: weeds cut, ground rolled flat, new sand laid down and rolled again, spectator benches repaired and freshly painted. Finally, as the buds of May graced the trees, the first tournament was held. What an event.

The air was filled with shouts as the two teams took turns throwing a small iron ball (*pallino*) down the sand-covered lane. It was the linchpin, and the two teams took turns trying to place larger balls near it. There were "oohs" and "ahhs" as one ball would gently kiss the *pallino*, coming to rest as close as possible, placing a team at the advantage. The opponents would bring out their ace player, who with lightning precision would swack the offensive ball away with the swift exactness of a surgeon, leaving the *pallino* untouched. The game went on all afternoon, and eventually lights were installed in the gaming area so the fun could continue in the evening. No one complained that there was too much noise in the neighborhood.

Nonno went to the *sala* each evening after dinner and many times I would charge in looking for him to beg a quarter. There he would be, pipe in mouth, freshly drawn glass of beer in front of him, sitting in the same place year

14

after year. His face would light up when he saw me and sometimes I would sit long enough to have a soft drink. I can still recall the beery smell that hung in the air, and see the dimly lit hall with the wonderful long wooden and brass bar running its entire length.

Today the club stands empty. Weeds grow in the *pallaio*. The windows are broken. The upstairs hall, where so many Italians had their wedding receptions and older women were crowned with flowers on Mother's Day, gathers dust. Oh, how sad, to leave it all behind. To replace it with fast foods and television. To not have a place for the gathering of the clan. To not hear the lyrical Italian language echo on a Sunday afternoon.

June *(Giugno)*

The third Sunday in June is Corpus Christi *(Corpus Domini)*, in honor of the Holy Eucharist, symbol of the body of Christ. In Italy, streets are festooned with carpets of flower petals as people celebrate a day of color in an *Infiorata*.

June 24, Midsummer Night's Eve, the birthday of St. John the Baptist *(San Giovanni Battista)*, is the time to announce engagements and sprinkle salt at the door to keep away evil spirits. Nonna always made camomile tea on St. John's Day and she would have a dickens of a time getting us to drink it (now I buy camomile in tea bags and wonder why I did not learn to enjoy it earlier).

But June was the time for immigrant weddings. In Italy, couples were married on Monday, and that tradition was transported to America. My mother and father were married on Monday, June 18, 1934. In Italy, the veil of the bride was an heirloom. All the women in our family wore it for communion, confirmation, and marriage: the rites of passage. Nonna's heirloom was in Italy with her family, so my mother had to buy a veil. Sandrina did pass her wedding gown on to her daughter Vivian, but not as a wedding dress. In 1938, Vivian was in a Christmas play at her school. Her parents could not afford a proper dress so Sandrina cut up her wedding gown and made a pleated skirt and long sleeved top trimmed with a red velvet ribbon.

By the time I came along, Saturday had become the traditional day for weddings. Each weekend the hall at the NIPA was festooned with crepe paper and the kitchen was filled with dozens of hands preparing a feast for the guests. Of course there was pasta. But the pastries were special, with mounds of *brigidini, biscotti,* and anise cookies topped with pastel icing. There was always an Italian band and the highlight of the evening was not the bride dancing with the groom, but a woman dancing with a broom, an Italian square dance called the *quadrella*, and the most famous of all Italian dances, the *tarantella*.

The *tarantella* is a story set to dance. Originally it was the story of a young boy and his mother. Bitten by a tarantula he was told to dance faster and faster to rid his body of the poison. Over the years it became a dance of seduction, danced by a man and woman.

All of the rites of passage for Italians were ritualized. Baptisms occurred, of course, year round, but communion and confirmation ceremonies, both

15

accompanied by processions, were performed in the spring. When my mother was born they thought she was going to die so the two women who assisted at her birth wrapped her in a blanket and walked to St. Leonard's Church to baptize her. But the priest refused to name her Darna, the name my grandmother had selected. The women were afraid to walk back to my grandparent's house and back to the church for fear my mother would die, so they named her Liza Betta, after her two grandmothers. Her American birth certificate reads Elizabeth, and that is what she is called.

July (Luglio)

Family picnics are a summer favorite and as early as 1925, when few city or county parks existed in our area, the farms of friends became sites of festivities each Sunday. The women would begin preparations on Wednesday or Thursday, making bushels of *biscotti* or *fiocchi*, and gallons of sauce for homemade pasta. By Friday and Saturday they had moved on to prepare the fresh spring chickens for the spit.

No store-bought chickens here: the chickens were bought live and carted home in a crate. The women would gather in the basement of one of the homes and began by wringing the necks of the chickens and hanging them from the rafters to settle the blood. Then, in assembly-line fashion, they would continue to clean the chickens. One by one, they would dip them into scalding water and remove the feathers. When the chickens were cleaned, each would be passed to a second group who would slit the abdomen below the breast to remove the innards, and remove the head and neck. The final group of women would wash the springers inside and out, drain them, and place them in a bushel basket. They were now ready for the spit.

The spit was made to order in the foundry of the local steel company. It was a square rod 1-1/2 inches thick and 50-inches long, and held 20 chickens. Pointed on one end for the skewering, it had a flat, round 6-inch disk at the other end to hold the chickens firm. Beside the disk was a grooved wooden wheel to which a 60-foot rope was attached. This created the pulley. Once the fire was laid and the chickens were in place, it was the job of the children to take turns working the pulley and rotating the chickens. The spit was supported by two iron pegs, 20- to 24-inches long, which were pounded into the ground. One peg had an eye to thread the spit, while the other had a cradle to hold it in place. Four thin sticks, the length of the spit (usually made from the wood of a 20-pound spaghetti box), were placed on either side of the chickens to keep them in place. Thin wire was wrapped around the sticks.

The fire, built 6- to 8-inches upwind from the spit, was made from dry fruitwood, preferably cherry wood, usually found on the farm. While the women were putting the chickens on the spit, the men would prepare the fire. Once the chickens were ready, the spit would be hung in a tree until it was time to place it on the fire. The meal was served on white tablecloths with china dishes and proper glasses.

16

It was Prohibition, but the wine from the various wine cellars was also bottled, packed, and transported. Nothing stopped these celebrations: rain, mist, or fog. A favorite story is of Nonna walking in front of the car down a country lane because the fog was so dense it was impossible to see.

August   *(Agosto)*

August brought hot, humid, lazy days: a time for eating fresh garden tomatoes, delicate zucchini flowers, and green peppers; and time for planting the winter garden of endive, escarole, and savoy cabbage.

August 15 is the celebration of the Feast of the Assumption of the Virgin Mary *((Ferragosto)* and throughout the United States there are still dozens of street fairs held in her honor. Each celebration is bound to have an Italian band for an immigrant summer was not complete without bands, so popular throughout western Pennsylvania.

An Italian band from Monessen was the Order of the Sons of Italy Band organized in the early 1900s by John Janotta. It later became the Monessen Fireman's Band, then the Monessen Civic Center Band, and today has been revived as the MARS Community Concert Band for the Mon Valley Association of Retired Steelworkers, who helped the band stay together. The MARS band performs regularly at cultural heritage festivals and summer park concerts.

The Red Coat Band *(La Banda Vestita di Rosso)* of New Castle (Mahoningtown) was organized in 1898 by Feliciano DeSantis who taught music. It was also known as the Duke of Abruzzi Italian Band and later divided into two bands, the Red Coat Band and the Blue Coat Band (these unusual names were given because of the color of the uniforms. The official name of the Blue Coat Band, for example, was *La Banda Vestita d'Azzurro di Santa Margherita, Mahoningtown,* "The Band Dressed in Blue of St. Margaret Mahoningtown).

Whatever the names, the bands of western Pennsylvania provided hours of entertainment and they were formed along ethnic lines. In addition to the Italian bands there were bands from almost all ethnic groups and it was important to all of them that they had glorious uniforms to accompany their distinct, ethnic music.

It seems as if the "good old days" were wonderful. And they were--in their innocence and simplicity.

September   *(Settembre)*

September is a month of dividends and returns for all the hard work of summer. The first Sunday in September is the Joust of the Saracen *(Giostra del Saracino)* in Arezzo, a jousting tournament rooted in the city's medieval tradition. Arezzo is the hub of a number of small hamlets in south central Tuscany including our small village of Quarata, which is only a few miles to the northwest. The game originated during the Crusades and was revived in 1931, too late for Nonno and Nonna to enjoy it.

The *Giostra* is held twice a year and on one of my visits to Italy I was lucky enough to see it. Teams made up of people from the different gates of the walled city, dressed in traditional medieval costumes, compete with each other to attack the Saracen (Arab). The Saracen in this case is a stationary figure with a shield in his left hand and a whip tipped with lead balls in his right. A horseman, complete with a long jousting stick, attacks the Saracen. As he hits the statue he must get away without receiving a hit from the lead balls which whip around as the Saracen turns from the force of the blow.

The game was wonderful as were all the beautiful costumes and festivities, but the most thrilling part for me was to see the antique clock high on the walls of one of the squares of the city. It was the moon of Arezzo (*Luna di Arezzo*), the term by which my Nonno and Nonna called *panforte*, that delicious medieval fruitcake we enjoyed so much on holidays.

But Arezzo and its tournament were too far away for us to enjoy. One Saturday in September we would head for the Salotti farm. It was time to pick the fresh fruit waiting for us in the hilly Pennsylvania orchards. Eventually it was a chore for Nonna and me. Off we would go, our baskets piled high and empty in the back seat of the car. What a day we had climbing the trees and selecting the fresh fruit. The farm boys would be there to help, but Nonna liked to do it herself, climbing the ladder in her black wide-heeled shoes and cotton dress. Eventually they would leave us to it, and grandmother and grandchild roamed the hillside looking for trees heavy with ripe fruit.

Nonna would spot a tree and up she would go, her skirt flapping in the wind (I never saw her in pants). I always wanted to shake the tree and let the apples fall to the ground, but that was sacrilege, not to be done. We picked a variety of apples and then we hit the pear trees. By the end of the day we were exhausted, but there was always time to visit the owner in her rambling farmhouse filled with hidden stairways and mysterious rooms. It was so Victorian and spooky that I would tingle with excitement as I crossed the threshold. On the way home we barely had room to sit. I can remember going apple picking from the time I was 7 years old.

In later years, when Nonna was too old to climb trees, we still went out to the farms each October, but now we selected from the bushels of fruits already picked by the farmers. The Salotti farm was sold, Nonna's friend gone, and few farmers permitted people to pick their own. But Nonna was just as fussy and spent hours poking into each basket until she made her choice.

October   (*Ottobre*)

As spring was busy with sowing, fall was busy with reaping, and in most years the bounty was plentiful. There were fruits to be picked, festivals to enjoy, and wine to be made. And we did them all.

The first Sunday in October is the *Festa di Quarata*, the festival of the village in Italy where most of our family still lives. In addition to pasta, the menu includes duck: roasted in *porchetta*, stewed with fried celery in red sauce, and simmered in pasta sauce. Nonno always said that if you raised ducks you had to have a pond or running water so they could swim or the flesh would taste of mud.

Above all, October was the month to make the most important product of the year, the new wine. If Nonno had settled in California instead of Pennsylvania we could have been a dynasty of wine makers. His wine was known far and wide, including back home in Italy, as delicate, clear, and powerful. During Prohibition more than one person came to Nonno to ask him to start a bootleg wine business. But Nonno always refused.

In Italy the grapes were harvested in September and early October, and Tuscany, home of Chianti, was the center of great wine making. It was a grand affair with grape festivals and gigantic meals served to the pickers in the fields.

To me, this time of year always has a faint smell of new wine and memories of Nonno's wine cellar. What a special place: drying sausages hung from the rafters beside curing prosciuttos and hundreds of green or brown wine bottles filled the shelves along the walls. At least three oak casks were set on their sides filled with wine—two for red, one for white--and for a little while each fall, another for half wine (*mezzo vino*).

How many hours I spent in the wine cellar with my grandfather I'll never be able to count. He would sit in his black, overstuffed rocking chair, pipe in mouth, and I would crawl up on his lap and beg him to tell me stories. My favorite was always a trip to Italy. The closer we got, the bigger the fish in the sea and the bigger the smile on my Nonno's face. We went by train and boat. As the train approached Arezzo we ate a picnic lunch of prosciutto and drank good red wine. The first time I visited my family in Italy I went by train from Rome and relived those hours with my grandfather in his wine cellar.

My brother, seven years older than me, preceded me in the wine cellar. He would beg for a sip of wine and Nonno would eventually give it to him. As he tasted it, he would smack his lips, and Nonna, ever vigilant from her kitchen, would yell down, "Nazzareno, don't give that boy any wine." My brother would look up at Nonno with his big blue eyes and say, "How did she know, Nonno?"

I cannot leave October without recalling one Halloween. I was in kindergarten and was dressed as Robin Hood. We had a grand parade around the grounds and the teacher awarded prizes. I did not win, but when I came out of school Nonna was waiting for me with a wonderful leather pencil box with several drawers and a dozen multi-colored pencils.

November   *(Novembre)*

November 1 brings All Saint's Day *(I Santi)*, and on that day it is traditional to eat roasted chestnuts and wine. Chestnuts are a staple of the Tuscan countryside. They are roasted, baked, made into cakes and sweets, and ground into flour. Throughout Italy, fairs in honor of the chestnut are held and *castagnaccio*, a cake of raisins, pine nuts, and rosemary, sometimes called the *panforte* of the poor, is served.

November is the month of ghosts and goblins, and the traditional festivals reflected the atmosphere. All Soul's Day *(I Morti)*, November 2, is a day set aside to remember the dead. In Italy, it is believed that on the night of November 1st the dead return to the world and walk the streets searching for gifts for children (like our Halloween). Thus it is another day of gift-giving. Among the dishes to grace the table and tempt the palate on this scary night are *ossi di morti*, bones of the dead, and chestnuts roasted or made into a pudding.

The 11th of November is St. Martin's Day *(San Martino)*, an important day for winemakers (see page 59 for details). The saying goes: *Per San Martino si chuide la botte e apre il vino*, "For St. Martin's Day one closes the barrel and opens the wine." It is also the time to harvest and press the olives.

The first Sunday in November Gino, Cirli (Carlo Albertini), and Pino (Giuseppe Guiducci) would take to the forests and fields of Pennsylvania in search of rabbit, pheasant, and quail. The second Sunday in November they headed to Monessen, game well cooled, to celebrate the autumn hunt.

A trip between New Castle and Monessen was quite an event in those days. There were no interstates, no turnpike, and routes 19 and 51 did not exist. Travel was via routes 88 and 906. My grandfather never learned to drive. In fact, we had a hard time getting him into a car at all and he only agreed when it was absolutely necessary, like going to Pittsburgh for grapes to make wine and going to New Castle (Nonno did not like the telephone either and seldom used it). Gino had a Jewitt car and would crank it up at 4 a.m. to arrive in Monessen at 11:30. In 1937, he bought a used 1936 Plymouth which he bargained down from $250 to $190, and kept it until 1947 when he finally sprang for a new Plymouth.

The road was always an adventure filled with flat tires, wrong turns, and picnic lunches. One time the Pelini family, along with our friend Annetta Chiapparri, headed for Monessen in Annetta's Grand Paige. After a flat tire and a lot of tension, they ended up in Donora. The journey north was also an adventure. My mother, riding in a two-car caravan with Tom and Elvira Cherubini Celli and my grandparents in one car, and Arturo Moncini driving Alfredo and Amabile Sodi and their daughter Rena in his Ford coupe (yes, four people in a one-seat car), ended up near Washington, Pa, after having taken the wrong turn onto the newly constructed Route 19. It took them eight hours to get to New Castle that time (today we make the journey in less that two hours, but we do not make it as often).

One can imagine how many times during those journeys the favorite Italian sayings of *per bacco, mannaggia cane, accidenti, porca miseria*, and *figure* were used. These sayings, whose original meanings are lost in time, are the same as the American "you're kidding," "gosh darn," "damn," "can you figure it," etc.

We were Americanized into Thanksgiving, but November also saw the beginning of Christmas preparations in our home. The first item to be made was the fruitcake. This required a trip to Pittsburgh to buy candied fruit at Donahue's on Fifth Avenue. The Friday after Thanksgiving we walked down to the bus station and took the early bus. We shopped all day, saw a movie that evening, and took the last bus home. We would come home weary from shopping and carrying pounds of candied cherries, pineapples, and mixed fruit, and additional pounds of the finest unshelled nuts money could buy. How many nights we spent cutting the fruit and chopping the nuts I do not remember, but the warm kitchen, table filled with shells and chopped nuts, is etched into my memory.

December *(Dicembre)*

We had plenty of birthdays in December and these were augmented by night after night of Christmas baking. Nonna had a handmade *brigidini* iron with her initials pressed into the center. It was long-handled so one did not have to stand too close to the open flame and as each spoon of batter was placed on the hot iron, it would sizzle. You had to judge the cooking time just right, turning the iron so both sides browned evenly. Soon mounds of delicious anise-flavored wafers topped the kitchen table: soft at first, they hardened as each day passed, tasting more delicious with age. They were good in coffee, dipped in red wine, or, a favorite of the children, in milk.

Although we shopped at the Italian food store year round, the Christmas trip was special. The very smells that offended other nationalities still fill me with joy. Barrels of olives fermenting in tangy juices lined one wall: green olives; wrinkled black olives; shiny, plump, black olives. Our shopping list included cod (*baccalà*), *panforte*, *amaretti*, sweet tobacco for Nonno's pipe, and tightly wrapped DiNobile cigars that looked like little twigs and smelled of strong tobacco. (Recently, as I was checking out at an Italian store, I picked one up and could not put it down. I paid for it and took it home.)

As long as Nonno was alive we did not have to buy prosciutto, since a fresh one was taken from its peg in the wine cellar and cut for Christmas. The same was true of sausage and wine. Our wine cellar was bursting with bottles, some from the first batch of wine Nonno made in America. In fact, I never really learned to buy good wine until I was an adult and Nonno was gone.

Although December is dominated by Christmas, there are other days of celebration as the four weeks before Christmas are part of Advent. Where Lent is a time of fasting and penitence, Advent is a period of renewal. It marks the beginning of the ecclesiastical year.

But joyous and glorious Christmas *(Natale)*, the festive day in mid-winter, is the focal point of December. Christmas Eve *(La Vigilia)* has its own special foods. Traditionally the meal consists of either seven or nine courses (for the 7 sacraments and the triple trinity), all centered around the fish.

Our traditional table was heavy with good foods, but with such a small family, Nonna did not follow the appropriate number of courses. She began with chickpea soup and wide egg noodles, followed by boiled cod in oil and chickpeas, and cod and onions in tomato sauce, or cod with garlic and sage in tomato sauce. The salad was always lettuce and celery. How excited I would get when the cod was put to soak in the cellar. The anticipation would last all week.

The next day was a feast to lay low even the heartiest of appetites: liver canapes covered with prosciutto, cappelletti in broth, macaroni in meat sauce, beef in red sauce with celery, roast capon with oven potatoes, and a leafy green salad. The desserts would tempt the gods themselves. Nonna's wonderful dark fruitcake, over which we had labored since Thanksgiving, was joined by *panforte* from Siena, *torrone* from Cremona, and *amaretti*. We had white wine to begin the meal, red wine with the macaroni, white wine with the capon, and in the end *vin santo*, holy wine, with the sweets. When it appeared as if the meal was over out would come a medley of fresh fruit, nuts and cheeses, accompanied by more *vin santo*, *espresso*, and *sambuca*. Both Nonno and Gino always said, "If the serving trays were empty at the end of the meal, the cook did not prepare enough food."

My mother says she never received gifts at Christmas, but at Epiphany, 12 days later. Instead, at Christmas it was traditional to kick the yule log for the candy and fruit inside in hopes of good gifts on Epiphany.

Epilog
(Epilogo)

Thus the time passed. Year after year of growing up in an Italian family. Today so many of these wonderful traditions are gone. Nonno and Nonna are dead. So are my father and my brother. When they were alive my mind did not understand so many things I want to share with them now. Of the family that enjoyed these times only my mother and I remain. Now as the year passes we fail to remember St. Joseph's Day. We no longer enjoy the largess of the *gran fritto misto* or a *pane di Spagna* in the oven for Nonna's friends. The prosciuttos no longer hang in the cellar and only one or two bottles of my Nonno's precious wine remain.

The joy my mother and I have shared in reliving these days cannot be measured. It has brought us closer together, it has brought the spirit of family back into our lives. Now it is recorded. And because of the pages of this book, and the fact that you have shared it with us, it will not be lost.

It is also a penance, since I am of the generation that broke the link with the past. I ate a food because I liked it, not because generations of my ancestors had eaten the same thing, at the same time of year, for the same reason, for hundreds and hundreds of years. I left the family for college, then to live in a foreign land, where I studied and wrote about other people's traditions and left my own. I was not there as the family began to dissolve and disappear. I chose not to marry and have children to keep alive our ancient link to the past. Thus, as humble as it is, this is my legacy, my contribution to the clan, to the past, and hopefully, to the future, when we turn once again to claim our heritage.

Cassandra Vivian, Monessen, Pennsylvania, 1993
with text on Egino "Gino" Pelini and Alessandra "Sandrina" Pitti Pelini by Vivian Pelini Sansone.

22

Shopping all'Italiana
Far la Spesa all'Italiana

It was not easy for immigrants to find the foods and equipment needed to maintain their traditions. A few immigrants carried precious seeds or prized kitchen implements to help with their gardening and cooking as they traveled across the Atlantic, for to try to find items on the American market that suited an Italian household was next to impossible in the early part of this century.

As the skills of the Italian communities grew, Italian carpenters came to the rescue. They made pastry boards, rolling pins, wooden spoons, and molds. Metal workers forged cookie irons and spits. Even Italian crockery became available in America.

Eventually some Italian men became peddlers, visiting neighborhoods by horse-drawn cart loaded down with Italian goods. They sold 20-pound boxes of spaghetti, Italian tuna, *toma* cheese, anchovies in salt, and cookie and cake items at Christmas. It was just like home.

As time passed the traveling merchants became stationary and established stores in Italian neighborhoods. In Monessen we had the Italian Food Store run by our friends, the Colangelo's. There was also DeSua's, Moio's and DeNunzio's. In New Castle, it was Graziani's, Frediani's, Saccomani's (in Mahoningtown), and Troggio's.

When our families became more adventuresome they journeyed to the Strip District in Pittsburgh to do some of their shopping. Here were stores that maintained they could provide any Italian product, and they did.

Today, neighborhood Italian food stores are almost a thing of the past, but the demand for Italian specialties in western Pennsylvania is so strong that it is not hard to find the special ingredients needed for the recipes in this book. In addition, ethnic foods have become the province of the gourmet, so many of the items can be found in gourmet shops.

Over the years the quest for unusual ingredients has become a joke in our family. Where once butchers threw away meat organs and good soup bones, and would gladly give them to us for nothing just to get rid of them, today these same items are considered delicacies and command high prices in food stores.

Anchovies

The anchovy is a small silver fish easily stored in oil or salt and used in breads, pizzas, and canapes. Anchovies are available filleted in oil in 2-ounce tins or salt packed. The latter is the best buy, for the anchovy is whole and retains its taste.

To use a salt-packed anchovy, soak it in a bath of 4 parts water to 1 part vinegar for a few minutes. Wash under running water, place on a cutting board, split down the center, and remove the spine.

To store, wrap entire opened tin in plastic and keep in a cool, dark place (cellar, refrigerator). Do not disturb the individual salt-packed anchovies until you are ready to use them. If anchovies are not whole when can is first opened, return the tin for the salt has consumed them.

Bread Crumbs

Never buy bread crumbs when they are so easy to make yourself, especially if you have a grinder or food processor. Keep them unseasoned to use in different dishes.

Capers

The caper, found in ancient Roman recipe books, grows wild in Italy. In America, capers are readily available packed in brine in 3.5-ounce jars found in most supermarkets.

Although a caper must retain the tangy taste of the brine, wash it generously under running water and squeeze gently before using.

In Nonna's day one could buy capers under salt, but we have not seen them on the market for a long time.

Cheese

Formaggio, the Italian word for cheese, comes from the word *forma*, referring to the wicker baskets in which ancient cheeses were stored to dry. Cheese is so valued in Italy that in addition to festivals celebrating the cheeses, laws exist to ensure the quality of at least 13 specific types of cheese, including Asiago, fontina, Gorgonzola, Parmigiano Reggiano, and pecorino.

The process of making cheese is an Italian institution dating back to the Etruscan era, before ancient Rome. There are over 500 varieties of cheese in Italy and most small villages have their own specialty, made from the milk of carefully tended goats, sheep, cows and even buffalos. The cheese from each herd has its own distinct taste, depending on the food eaten by the animal that produces the milk.

Cheeses should be stored in a cool place, or in the refrigerator. Never store different types of cheeses in the same container, but always cover each cheese separately in foil or plastic. Store mozzarella in the freezer.

Asiago

Produced at the foot of the Alps Mountains near Venito in the village of the same name, Asiago is a straw-yellow cows' milk cheese, which comes in several varieties. The *mezzanello*, or *Asiago di taglio*, has a short aging period, remains sweet, and is good as an eating cheese, especially for dessert. The *Asiago vecchio*, aged 12 months, is also for eating, but has a tangy taste. The *Asiago stravecchio*, aged 18 months, is used as a grating cheese.

24

Fontina

An eating cheese favored in fondue, fontina dates to ancient Rome and is produced in the Val d'Aosta from pure-bred Valdostana cows. It is made in summer when the cows are grazing high on the mountain. Aged four months to a straw-yellow color, the longer it ages, the sharper the taste.

Gorgonzola

Gorgonzola, or *stracchino Gorgonzola*, is a cows' milk cheese made since the Middle Ages in the town of Gorgonzola, Lombardy. It is soft, creamy and flecked with specks of green or blue mold. Creamier and milder than most blue cheeses, it is either *dolce*, sweet, or *piccante*, sharp.

Gorgonzola con Mascarpone

This delicate and delicious layered torte of Gorgonzola and mascarpone cheeses is a true masterpiece. Unfortunately, it spoils quickly and must be eaten the day you buy it to achieve the ultimate taste. We never refrigerate it.

Mascarpone

A very rich triple cream cheese made in 24-hours, which must be consumed in a relatively equal time or it will go bad, mascarpone is used in place of whipping cream in Italy.

Mozzarella

Originally a water buffalo cheese from southern Italy, today, with demand all over the world, it is made from cows' milk. The rare *mozzarella di bufala* is a pungent, tangy, delicacy never wasted on a pizza, but served as an appetizer. Ricotta from *mozzarella di bufala* is another delicacy.

Parmigiano

Boccaccio wrote that paradise was a mound of grated Parmesan cheese surmounted by pasta makers. Today Parmesan, the king of cheeses in Italy, maintains its high appeal and is recognized worldwide for its delicate color and flavor.

Parmesan was originally made during winter (November 15 to April 15) in only five villages in Parma, Italy. Stamped with the name *Parmigiano Reggiano*, it is so valued that it has been stored in bank vaults and traded like gold.

Made mostly by individual farmers, 600 quarts of milk are needed to produce one 75-pound wheel of *Reggiano*. The milk is left overnight and the cream is skimmed and stored. It is the skimmed milk that begins the process. Blended with whole milk, the two are heated and allowed to coagulate. The curd is stored in cheesecloth and the whey (watery part of milk) given to animals that in turn produce milk for cheese. When the whey is drained, the fresh cheese is lowered into *fascera*, wooden forms, that press it into shape. Once formed, the cheese is submerged in brine for 25 days, then bathed in the rays of the sun and stored for two to three years.

Parmesan is married to Italian sauces; however, eaten as is, it is a delicacy in its own right. Never buy Parmesan (or any cheese) already grated. You can get good Parmesan, imported or domestic, at Italian food stores and gourmet shops.

Pecorino Romano, Pecorino Toscano, or Caciotta

A specialty of Tuscany, probably dating to their illustrious ancestors, the Etruscans, pecorino is the oldest known cheese in Italy. As its name implies, it is made from sheep's milk. Made in 40-pound wheels, it can be eaten fresh, but is most often aged for grating.

Once a year, on the first Sunday of September in the Renaissance village of Pienza, there is a fair devoted to pecorino.

Provolone

Provolone is from southern Italy. It is dipped alternately in boiling water, then cold water, and left to age for two to five months. There are three varieties: *provolone dolce*, sweet, aged three months; *provolone piccante*, sharp, aged longer; and *provolone affumicato*, smoked, aged two months. It is an eating cheese.

Ricotta

Ricotta is not cottage cheese and the latter should never be used as a substitute. Rather, it is a delicate, highly perishable, creamy white cheese made from the whey of the second curd when making other cheeses like Parmesan. It is sold fresh on the market and not permitted to age; therefore, it does not store well.

Chestnuts

Chestnuts ripen in the fall. When Gino Pelini was in Italy, they were the staple of the family diet. In addition to the traditionally roasted chestnut, necessity created a host of uses, including finely ground flour used in cakes, polentas, pastas, and puddings.

Chestnut flour is available on a hit-or-miss basis in gourmet shops and Italian food stores.

Cured Meats

The wonderful cured meats of Italy are not only sold, but also produced, in more countries of the world than any other type of cured meat. The best buy is always the original for the animal's environment cannot be reproduced: the water and feed an animal ingests and the air it breathes are also ingredients that create the ultimate flavor.

Most ethnic food stores have a variety of cured meats, both imported and domestic, and making a selection is not easy. Since Italy is undergoing a health awareness, we can expect a "lite" (less fat, fewer calories) variety of cured meats to reach the market.

Bresaola

Originating in the Lombardy district of Italy, this is a salted, air-dried beef which is served like prosciutto.

Mortadella

A specialty of Bologna, *mortadella* is a big, fat sausage that has been ground, mixed with pieces of fat, pistachios or olives, stuffed into a bladder, and boiled. The imported brands can be as large as 16 to 18 inches in circumference, enough to feed the appetite of a king. *Mortadella* should be sliced as thin as possible and never stored in a refrigerator where it loses its delicate taste. Mortadella is the father of American bologna (baloney).

Pancetta

Pancetta is a cured meat like prosciutto; but, where the prosciutto is the hind quarter of the pig, the *pancetta* is the belly, or the bacon.

Once *pancetta* was difficult to find, but it is now prepared like a small slab of bacon, neatly packaged, and laid beside the bacon in most supermarkets (in Italian stores *pancetta* is rolled, complete with rind).

Pancetta lasts a long time and only a small quantity is needed for cooking, so it is best to buy it in small pieces of a half pound or less. It is easily stored in the refrigerator wrapped in foil or plastic.

Prosciutto

The king of Italian cured meats, prosciutto is the salted and aged hind quarter of a pig under 2 years old. It is not smoked; however, one variety called *speck* is a cured, smoked ham. The most famous prosciutto in Italy is *prosciutto di Parma*, originating in the same area as Parmesan cheese. The pigs are fattened on the whey of the famous cheese and produce a sweeter meat. It is this prosciutto that is best served as an appetizer with melons or figs.

Prosciutto di Parma is one of three brands of prosciutto that have been given the prized DOC rating in Italy. The other two are *prosciutto San Daniele* and *prosciutto Veneto*. But almost every village in Italy has its own variety of homemade prosciutto, and they are all delicious.

Today you can buy prosciutto deboned (it helps with the aging) and by the pound. First, it should be sliced paper thin. Second, prosciutto slices should never be stacked, but laid one beside the other and covered with tissue paper before placing the next layer. Third, if possible, it should not be stored in a refrigerator, but in a cool place. Never wrap in plastic.

Salami

The true name of this excellent cold cut is *insaccato*, meaning "things put in a sack," and the varieties are endless. The thickness or thinness of the grind, the amount of salt, the type of pork, and the individual spices vary from village to village and region to region.

Probably the most famous salami in America is Genoa salami, but to the Italian connoisseur *salame Fabriano* is the best from central Italy, and *salame Felino*, from the same area as *prosciutto di Parma*, is considered the best, period.

There are excellent salamis found in small mountain villages where the inhabitants have never tried to enter the commercial market. A Tuscan variety, which my family has made for centuries, is called *finocchino* and is flavored with fennel.

Almost any food store in the United States sells some type of salami, but to have an interesting selection one must go to an Italian food store. There the array is overwhelming: imported or domestic, hard or soft, lean, cooked, or aged. You can buy salami freshly sliced, in a piece, or whole.

Flour

American white flour is of a better quality than Italian flour. When baking breads use all-purpose flour. Always sift flour for pastry, but never for bread.

Corn flour, *farina di grano turco* (Indian corn), is ground finer than cornmeal, but is even better when stone-ground, thus rough. Cornmeal, again stone-ground, is grittier. Buy regular, not degerminated.

Garlic

Garlic, a member of the lily family, is synonymous with Italian food. It is also good for you, helpful for a bevy of ills. In some cultures people wear a piece of garlic on their person, not only for its curative powers, but to keep away evil spirits.

Although always popular in ethnic America, the soldiers returning from Europe after World War II helped make garlic an acceptable ingredient in American foods.

If you grow your own garlic, store it in a brown paper bag in a cool room. If you buy garlic, look for small, firm bulbs and buy small quantities. Although it is picturesque to see garlic bunches hanging in kitchens, for a longer life and fresher flavor, store the garlic in the refrigerator.

In our kitchen we peel cloves of garlic to chop or fry, but do not peel garlic when it is pounded or crushed. Garlic salt or powder will not do when making good Italian dishes.

Herbs and Spices

Trade routes that linked Asia and Africa to Europe via the Middle East were a lifeline of exotic treasures during the Middle Ages. Spices, important to that trade, dominated the economy of the medieval world. And the Venetian merchants who brought the spices into Europe, dominated the European market.

When spices arrived in Italy, the Italian chefs were quick to incorporate them into recipes. One can usually tell a recipe that originated at that time, like *panforte*, for the ingredients include a number of different spices.

In addition to salt and pepper, the four main spices in Tuscan cooking are basil, parsley, rosemary, and sage. Secondary are nutmeg, thyme, and fennel.

The modern cook is lucky for not only do supermarkets offer spices and herbs in neat little boxes and jars, but fresh spices are available in the produce departments of most supermarkets. For the recipes in this book, use fresh spices whenever possible.

Spices lose their fragrance so it is best to buy small quantities and once a year clean out your spice cupboard.

Anise Seeds

Blooming in July and August, the licorice-flavored anise seed (*semi di anice*) is not only flavorful in cooking, but is good for digestion. In Tuscan cooking, it is used to flavor sweets eaten at the end of the meal.

Basil

There are a variety of basil (*basilico*) plants on the market: lemon-scented, tall, with purple leaves, full-leafed, and the most common, sweet basil. Served in a salad with fresh home-grown tomatoes steeped in oil, basil is ambrosia. It is also good for you. Basil clears congestion and cures headaches.

Fennel

Fennel (*finocchio*) has a licorice taste and comes into season in the fall. Florentine fennel is sold like celery, fresh on the stalk. The seeds of common fennel, another variety of the plant, are dried and used as a seasoning.

28

In our kitchen we ate Florentine fennel raw or cooked in a stew and used common fennel as a flavoring for chicken, duck, and pork.

Oregano

Until pizza took over the world, oregano was seldom used in an American kitchen, or in ours. In addition to pizza, it is also good on roast chicken.

Parsley

Always use the flat-leafed Italian parsley *(prezzemolo)* for the recipes in this book. Save the curly parsley to decorate the dinner plate as a garnish. Never, never, never use dried parsley--you might as well add a piece of paper to your recipe.

Rosemary

Called dew of the sea, rosemary *(rosmarino)* is recommended for failing eye sight and headaches. It is also delicious.

Dried rosemary loses its fragrance after a year and must be thrown away. There is nothing as good as fresh rosemary, but it is difficult to grow. We tend our plants carefully, but have lost them time and time again. We use rosemary to flavor beef, lamb, and pork.

Saffron

Saffron *(zafferano)* is the stigma of the crocus flower and is mostly imported from the Middle East. It is extremely expensive and difficult to find and substitutes are often used. You can buy saffron in small quantities in pharmacies and gourmet shops.

Sage

The Italian word *salvia* (sage) means to heal, and, true to its name, the herb is good for everything from bad breath to bruises.

Fresh sage is best for Italian cooking. Sage thrives well in a garden and we have always had a plant growing in the back yard. Whenever we want to make a dish with sage, we pick it fresh from the plant. We use it in sauces and to flavor poultry.

Thyme

Thyme *(timo)* is often used in the bath to give courage. It is excellent to flavor meats and the best thyme recipe in this book is the stew of veal and peas found on page 141.

Mushrooms

The most flavorful mushrooms in Italy are the *porcini*, named after the pig *(porco)*, and found growing wild in the autumn fields. They have a musty taste and are very expensive in the United States. A few *porcini* added to the readily available white mushrooms of Pennsylvania will add good flavor to a dish at one-fourth of the cost. *Porcini* are available in gourmet shops and Italian food stores.

Oil

We use two types of oil in our kitchen: corn and olive, the first for most cooked dishes, the latter for salads and specialties.

The best Italian olive oil in Italy is the rich, fruity, Tuscany oil. The variety of olive oils available on the American market is growing. Our old staple tends to be less pungent and is an accustomed ingredient in foods. Extra-virgin olive oil is from the first pressing of the olive (which normally goes through three pressings), and is usually darker in color and has a strong flavor. The type of oil you use has to be determined by your palate.

Pasta

Although most European cultures have some type of pasta, the word and the food are synonymous with Italian cooking. There seems to be an infinite number of pastas, with new cuts being added to the American food scene yearly.

Traditional cuts and shapes of pasta have a distinct purpose and we have arranged them on the following pages according to their use.

Pastas for Soup
Pastina

Chioccioline
"small shells"

Ditallini
"little thimbles," small and tubular

Orzo
" barley," shaped like barley or rice

Acini di pepe
"peppercorns"

Quadrucci
"little squares"

Anellini
"little rings," with or without grooves

Stelline
"stars"

Tripolini or farfalline
"small bows," egg bows

Gemelli
"twins," 2 strands twisted together

Long Pasta

Spaghetti is "a length of cord or string," and the various names for the pasta are determined primarily by the thickness.

Spaghetti
"cords," thin, round, long pasta

Bucantini. (Roman)
Perciatelli (Neapolitan)
long, thin, tubular pasta with a hole, *"buco,"* in the middle

Spaghettini
"little cords" a thinner spaghetti

Tagliolini
ultra thin, long, flat noodles sometimes used in broth

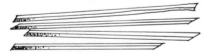

Linguine (small tongues) or **Bavette**
flattened spaghetti 1/4-inch wide

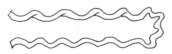

Fusilli
"twists," twisted spaghetti

Vermicelli
"little worms," thin, round, long, pasta

Long Flat Pasta

Fettuccine, Tagliatelle
"small ribbons," 1/8-inch wide

Conchigliette
"tiny shells"

Mafaldi, Pappardelle
1-inch wide and fluted on the edges

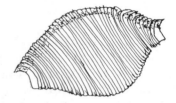

Conchiglie or chiocciole
" shells"

Lasagna
"pots," a broad, thin noodle usually 2
to 3 inches wide

Diti
"fingers," short, fat tubular pasta

Short Pasta

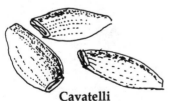

Cavatelli
dumplings made of semolina and flour
from the south of Italy

Farfalle
" bows" or "butterflies"

32

Tortiglioni
"springs," a twisted pasta

Rotelle
" wheels," a circular pasta wheel

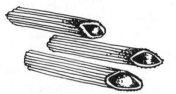

Gnocchi
potato, ricotta, or semolina dumpling

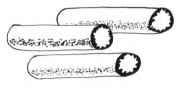

Ziti
similar to *penne,* but cut straight

Penne
" quills," cut on the slant and ridged

Stuffed Pasta

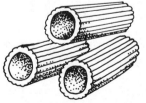

Pennette
" small quills"

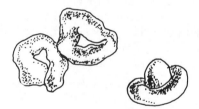

Cappelletti (Tortellini)
"small hats" or "belly buttons" like a
ravioli

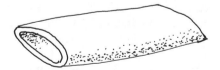

Rigatoni
thick tubular pasta 2 inches long

Cannelloni
"large reeds" or "canes" same as
manicotti, "small muffs," 3 to 4-inch-
long tubular pasta for stuffing.

33

Ravioli
2-inch squares of dough filling with stuffing

Rice

Never, never, never prepare the dishes in this book with minute rice. American long-grained rice works well, but imported *arborio*, a flat, fat rice, is better.

Arborio rice is found in Italian food stores and specialty shops. Read the instructions for cooking *arborio* rice carefully, for it can become a glutinous mass if cooked improperly.

Salt

Many ingredients in Italian cooking are already salty, so use salt sparingly, and not at all when using anchovies, salted cod, and cured meats like prosciutto and salami.

Most of our stews and sauces call for *soffritto* which contains enough flavor to carry the sauce so salt need not be added to the simmering tomatoes. The best way to decide if you want to add salt is to taste before adding. In our home we have a heavy hand and measurements in this book reflect our preference. If anyone picks up a salt shaker at our dinner table the cook has failed to prepare the dish properly.

34

Sausage

The varieties of sausage from central and southern Europe are amazing. They come in all shapes and flavors. From blood sausage made with, of course, blood, to *cotechino*, often made with pork rinds, sausage is a staple of Italy and has become an American institution. There is sweet sausage, garlic sausage, hot sausage, dried sausage, and today turkey and chicken sausage where the traditional pork is replaced by a lighter meat.

We always make our own and prefer garlic sausage. In addition to eating it fresh, we enjoy tasty dried sausage, which we cut and eat like salami.

For more information on sausage consult pages 152 and 160.

Tomato

The tomato is the most noble of Italian vegetables and is amply represented throughout this book, especially in the preparation of sauces. Take heed! No tomato sauce in this book should look bright red—it should be deep red, leaning toward brown. If red, the sauce has not simmered long enough. A sauce with tomatoes must simmer until the oil separates from the tomato and rises to the top. Then the sauce is done.

When buying fresh tomatoes leave the hothouse varieties for someone else. Until scientists solve the problem of tasteless winter tomatoes, in the winter use good canned tomatoes.

In summer, when in season, select firm tomatoes with deep color for salads and fresh tomato recipes, but for stews and sauces look for soft, very ripe tomatoes. Never select a tomato with broken skin.

We plant a garden and use every tomato the garden gives us. All summer long, in addition to eating fresh tomatoes, we are freezing them for the winter. When the last green tomatoes are on the vine and a frost is coming, we pick all of them, wrap each one in newspaper and store them in the cellar. They will slowly ripen and we have fresh tomatoes as late as November.

We plant extra tomato vines expressly to freeze them for winter. We use tomatoes in soups stews, and sauces.

To freeze a tomato is easy. Wash each tomato carefully and allow it to dry. Place on a cookie sheet and freeze. When frozen, remove from cookie sheet and place in a plastic bag. Store in freezer.

When ready to use, remove from freezer. If you want to remove the skin, place the frozen tomato under the water faucet and the skin will peel off easily.

Vinegar

Ordinary wine vinegar will do for the recipes in this book, but we also use balsamic vinegar for a delicate, mellow taste. *Aceto balsamico*, traceable to medieval times, is made from fresh grape juice boiled into a concentrate in a copper kettle and aged in casks of various woods for 12 years. As the liquid evaporates the vinegar is transferred to various casks of chestnut, cherry, or juniper wood. Each cask is smaller and the smallest contains the best vinegar.

Balsamic vinegar is considered one of the treasures of Italy and, like wine, its production is controlled by the government to insure its high quality. It is available on the American market in Italian food stores and gourmet shops.

Notes

Our Italian Kitchen
La Nostra Cucina Italiana

Eighty years of good Tuscan cooking has taught us that there are four basic recipes that must be mastered to have a good Italian kitchen: a good *soffritto* (*battuto*), a tasty bread stuffing, a basic soup stock, and a rich, deep red *umido*, form the base of 80 percent of Tuscan main courses.

Although we give these warnings at the beginning of each recipe, the points are so important to the final outcome of the dish we want to stress them here. We cannot repeat enough the proper way to prepare these basic ingredients. If they are right, the dish is right. If they are not, to our way of thinking, the dish is a disaster.

Battuto means something that is chopped into small pieces. When it is fried in oil it is called *soffritto*. Both are used universally as a base for soups, stuffings, and sauces. They are a combination of onion, celery, parsley, carrots, salt, pepper, garlic (sometimes), and *pancetta* (see basic recipe on page 163). In soup stock, then called *battuto*, the mixture is boiled with the meat. Once the broth is properly simmered, the mixture is passed through a sieve and added to the finished broth. It provides flavor, color, and texture.

As a base for stuffings and stews, *soffritto* is ground in a meat grinder and fried in oil. There are two important points here. If ground in a meat grinder, the juices add richness and moisture to the final dish. When fried, *soffritto* must simmer until it is well-blended, the ingredients turning dark. In the final minutes it wants to stick to the pan. That is when *soffritto* is at its best. It is so flavorful no additional salt or flavoring need be added to the final recipe.

The basic bread stuffing begins with a good *soffritto*. We use it as a stuffing for meats, poultry, and vegetables. It must be moist. If dry to the hand, it will be dry to the palate. It can be made with bread crumbs or bread cubes, and some additional spices may be added. But a good basic stuffing needs no help. It is delicious with just the *soffritto*, bread, eggs, and soup stock (see stuffing recipe on page 67).

There are also a few basic "must dos" for soup: fresh ingredients, adequate simmering, and the proper use of water. Soup must simmer for 3 to 4 hours until the meat falls from the bone. Never, never add additional water once the soup begins to boil and always cover the pot with a lid. Finally, as mentioned previously, pass the vegetables through a sieve into the broth (see soup recipes beginning on page 237).

Of all the sauces in Italian cooking, tomato sauce dominates the cuisine. When making a stew of meat or vegetables, a pizza topping, or a pasta sauce, the main point to remember is that the sauce must simmer until the tomatoes turn a rich red-brown and separate from the oil. If they are the same color as when they first hit the skillet, the sauce has not simmered long enough and the dish will have a heavy tomato taste. When tomato sauce is properly cooked, the oil should float on top of a thick brown-red sauce where it can easily be drained.

The most difficult part of assembling these recipes was not the organization or the testing, it was the perplexing question of how to turn each recipe into an entity unto itself. In Nonna's kitchen everything was integrated. If it was bread day she used a bit of the dough to make a pizza, a *schiacciata,* or fried dough. If it was soup day she added a potato and made potato salad and used the meat from the soup for several different dishes of the *misto bolitto.* When making pasta dough she made a large quantity of cappelletti, a smaller quantity of ravioli, and cut extra pasta into noodles for sauce or for soup.

Quantity also became an issue. "Cappelletti for four?" We never heard of it. Nonna made cappelletti by the hundreds and used them immediately. My mother also makes hundreds, but she freezes them. In Nonna's day, the amount of each ingredient in a dish was usually a little of this, a handful of that. Not so when preparing a cookbook.

Authenticity, too, reared its ugly head. Some of the recipes in this book, sin of sins, are not Tuscan. Where and how Nonna and Sandrina first made them, we do not always know. But it is obvious that the melting pot of America had its hand in the stew, so to speak. With so many Italian families from so many different Italian provinces living together in the same small town, a little recipe sharing was bound to go on. However, recipes that were sacred, part of provincial pride and heritage, were never altered.

The most gratifying part of creating this book was that our kitchen became an Italian kitchen once again. And it is going to stay that way.

Kitchen Aids

Cheese grater. Any variety of cheese grater will do as long as one remembers to grate the cheese fresh each time you use it. Grated cheese dries out and loses its flavor.

Store cheeses in a cool place. Some cheeses can be placed in the freezer.

Colander. No kitchen should be without a colander and especially a kitchen where pasta is made. For soups and sauces you need a fine mesh colander, for pasta a thick mesh.

Garlic press. Found in most kitchen departments, this handy gadget is used exclusively for crushing garlic to obtain the juice. If a recipe calls for crushing garlic in a press there is a reason, trust us.

Meat grinder. Recipes that call for minced foods suggest a meat grinder. This is the old-fashioned type of grinder with a hand-operated handle and a variety of templates of different sizes. They are available in Italian food stores and gourmet shops.

Although we have said you can use a food processor, the consistency will not be the same. The grinder grinds the food into fine pieces and releases the juices to keep the mixture moist.

My niece once ate stuffing at a friend's house. She told my mother, "She puts celery in her stuffing; I saw big chunks of it," and wrinkled her nose.

My mother laughed. We put celery in our stuffing, too, but it is so finely ground, it blends with the bread.

Pots and pans. In most recipes requiring a pan you will note that the recipe calls for a black iron skillet. We have used these skillets in a variety of sizes as far back as I can remember. We seasoned them once, when they were new, and never had to do it again.

Some cooks never wash these skillets, but merely wipe them clean after use. We have always washed and dried them immediately. You may use other types of pans to prepare these recipes, and the food will taste delicious because the ingredients and foods are of fine quality, but Elizabeth will swear that she can taste the difference and Nonna will turn over in her grave.

Iron skillets are available in a variety of sizes in hardware stores at reasonable prices, or in gourmet shops at higher prices.

If you have old iron skillets from your grandmother, do not throw them away. They are worth their weight (and they are heavy) in gold.

Pasta machine. A crank pasta machine is the best one for the recipes in this book, but we also have a pasta machine that mixes the dough and makes various cuts of noodles, and we find it satisfactory when in a hurry. They are available in most gourmet shops and department stores.

Pastry board or (*spianatoia*) is almost mandatory if you are going to make pasta. When in need of a large work space we recommend a hardwood, preferable cherry wood, bread or pastry board.

Ours is wooden and we have been using it, like our pans, for 80

39

years. Needless to say, it was so worn that we had to have the wood turned about 20 years ago.

Today modern nutritionists do not recommend wooden boards for they maintain that food remains in the wood and can cause poisoning. We have never been poisoned. No one has ever been sick after a meal in our home. If you are concerned, use a plastic bread or pastry board. Sorry, Nonna.

Rolling pin or *matterello*. Our families *matterello* was made by a friend who made all the wooden utensils for the Italian cooks in our area.

It is now an heirloom handed down through three generations and still going strong. Made of hardwood it is 32-inches long and 1-1/4-inches thick.

Stoves. Nonna cooked on a gas stove. It is still in our basement. My mother prefers an electric stove. During the process of creating this cookbook we had to buy a new one. Our wonderful porcelain-finished, 30-year-old stove just could not be mended anymore. It now shares space with Nonna's stove in our basement.

When our new stove arrived we were appalled to discover that times, especially in roasting and baking, varied. Take heed! There is no replacement for the cook. The final decision as to when a dish is finished remains with the person preparing the meal, not with the times listed in recipes.

Times. After we wrote all the recipes, we tested them following our own written instructions. Well, we had to alter quite a few recipes to achieve the taste that was equal to our traditional foods. That is when we added many of the times listed in the recipes that follow.

The times only serve if the heat is the same. If your idea of simmer is faster than our idea of simmer, then the times will vary for stews and sauces.

If you make a cookie larger or smaller than we do, the time will not be the same.

If your oven heats hotter than ours, that is also a problem. We used an oven thermometer in both our old and new stoves, but the new oven bakes and roasts faster than our old oven.

Our outside testers working in their own kitchens found our times accurate, but our advice is: use our carefully calculated times as a gauge, an approximation, and use your eyes and taste as the final judge.

If we have brought back memories of your own heritage, let us hear from you. We would love to share your experiences. There was more than one immigrant kitchen and, we will prepare more than one immigrant cookbook.

We wish you good cooking and hours and hours of good eating, wonderful conversation, and genuine friendship enjoying the special foods in this book.

Buon Appetito!

Appetizers
Antipasti

For an Italian, the flavor that begins a meal (*anti pasti*, "in front of the meal") must blend with the dishes that follow. It is the true beginning of an Italian meal and is always eaten at table, never served with cocktails but with good wine. The only exception to this rule in the recipes that follow is *bagna calda*, a salty dish often served at stag parties accompanied by gallons of homemade Italian wine.

Nonna's favorite antipasto was a milt with chicken liver canape which was served so often we simply called it *crostini*, the Italian name for all canapes. Today milt is next to impossible to find and I have been told by several butchers it is illegal to sell milt in the United States. In Nonna's day we went to the slaughterhouse to get it, and, because they threw it away, it was free. Today, when we are lucky, we make the chicken liver canape with milt; when we are not lucky, we make it without. Both recipes appear in this chapter.

Most Italian appetizers tend to be salty, offering an invitation to eat and drink abundantly, and the ones listed in this chapter are no exception. But throughout this book are additional recipes that can be turned into appetizers by adjusting the size or the cut: stuffed escarole, Italian meatballs, sweet farina, fried anchovy puffs, anchovies with onions and parsley salad, anchovy and butter sandwich, *polpette*, headcheese, stuffed Italian peppers or tomatoes, and any *schiacciata* or fried vegetable.

Today, traditional antipasti have turned into the meal itself, and are an exciting addition to any buffet. They have also become popular as snacks. Anyway you serve them, they are exciting.

Antipasto

1/4 pound each thinly
sliced salami, prosciutto,
mortadella, mozzarella,
pepper cheese,
and provolone
6 oz. black olives
4-5 celery ribs

Pick your favorite serving tray. Arrange meat and cheese to taste: either in rows or in segments, flat or rolled. Garnish with celery and black olives. Serve with *bagna calda* (recipe below) or fresh Italian bread.

Serves: 12-15.

Hot Bath and Vegetables
Bagna Calda e Vegetali

Delicious *bagna calda* was prepared by Nonna Parigi whenever Nonno's friends came to visit. It was never eaten as a family meal, which is very much in keeping with the origin of this delicious appetizer. Centuries old in Italy, *bagna calda* was traditionally served as part of the workers' meal during the autumn grape harvest. When the meal was almost finished, the grape pickers often added an egg to the remaining liquid and scrambled it over low heat.

You eat *bagna calda* like a fondue: pick a vegetable, dip it into the hot bath, and eat. It is tangy and delicious, a meal in itself. If you find the artichokes too much of a bother, eliminate them. Simply add more of the other ingredients, or include green onions and Florentine fennel.

2 fresh artichokes
1 tsp. lemon juice
Pinch salt
2 cups water
1 tsp. olive oil

1 bunch cardoons*
3 celery hearts
2 green peppers
2 red peppers
4 carrots
7-8 radishes

3/4 cup olive oil
3 T butter
2 tsp. chopped garlic
8-10 flat anchovy fillets
1 tsp. salt
1 tsp. pepper

Wash all artichokes. Remove outer layer of hard leaves (for illustrations see pages 260-61). To loosen the leaves hit each artichoke on a drain board three or four times, then hold the artichoke by the head and spread the leaves to expose the center. Remove pointed and hairy parts in center of artichoke with a small knife. Then cut away the tips of the remaining leaves with kitchen shears or scissors. Wash by placing in fresh water to which lemon juice and salt have been added and allow to soak for half an hour. Drain upsidedown on drain board. Dry each artichoke.

Stand artichokes upright in a deep saucepan. Cover the bottom of the pan with water and sprinkle a little oil over each artichoke. Cover and steam cook for 1 to 1-1/2 hours. Check water level every 15 minutes and, if necessary, add more hot water. Artichokes may also be served uncooked. They must be cleaned the same way.

42

To eat artichokes with *bagna calda* tear off a leaf, dip into the bath, place between the teeth, and pull out of the mouth, eating only the tender heart of the leaf.

Clean the cardoons and celery hearts and chop each rib into 3-inch pieces. Wash peppers and carrots and dice into 3-inch strips. Wash radishes, remove stems and roots; if small, serve whole, if large, cut in half. Allow all vegetables to drain before arranging either in individual dishes or on one large platter.

Heat the olive oil and butter in a 6-inch iron skillet over medium-high heat. When the butter is thoroughly liquefied and begins to foam, add the garlic and saute briefly. Lower heat. Do not brown the garlic. Chop the anchovy fillets, add to skillet and dissolve them into a paste by mashing with a fork. Add salt and pepper to taste (note that anchovies are already salty, so use salt sparingly). Stir.

Pour the hot liquid into a chafing dish and bring to the table. If possible place on a warming rack, for *bagna calda* must stay warm. Arrange the vegetables around the chafing dish. To eat, select a piece of vegetable, dip it in the *bagna calda*, and eat.

Variation: This is *bagna calda* all dressed up with cream and ready for a party. Prepare as in recipe above. When anchovies have completely dissolved, remove from heat. Let stand a few minutes, then blend in 1 cup clotted cream (can use sour cream).

Serves: 4.

Notes: *Cardoons are not readily available in the United States and when you do find them in a specialty store they are often bitter and not as nice as those in Italy. They are also seasonal, appearing in the late fall and winter. You may wish to eliminate the cardoons and double the quantity of celery.

Vegetables can be prepared ahead, then placed in a bowl of cold water with the juice of a lemon. Just before serving, drain and allow to dry.

Blue Cheese and Green Olive Spread
Condimento di Gorgonzola e Olive

7 oz. green pimento
olives
1/3 pound blue cheese

With both ingredients at room temperature, blend in a meat chopper or food processor. Remove and mash with a fork until well blended. Form into a ball and serve with crackers.

Serves: 15-25.

Chicken Liver Canape
Crostini di Fegatini di Pollo

This recipe is a variation of the milt and chicken liver recipe found on the next page. It was served often in the Pelini household.

6 fresh chicken livers
2 slices prosciutto
1 small onion
1 T fresh parsley
3-4 anchovy fillets

1 T butter
Pepper
1/4 cup dry white wine

10-12 slices day-old
bread
1/2 cup broth
3 oz. capers

Be sure livers are fresh. Wash livers and remove all large veins. Chop as fine as possible. Remove all fat from prosciutto and chop lean portion into tiny pieces. Wash and dice onion and parsley. Drain anchovies and chop fine.

Place a small-size iron skillet over medium-high heat. Melt butter and add diced onion. Saute until onion is transparent. Add chopped livers, prosciutto, and parsley and continue to cook, stirring often. When mixture is almost cooked, add anchovies and a little pepper (the anchovies should produce enough salt, but you may wish to add a little). Finally, add the wine and let the mixture come to a boil. Boil for 3 minutes or until most of the wine is absorbed. Let cool.

Slice 10 to 12 thin slices of day-old bread. Cut into wedges. Place on a tray and dry in a 250-degree oven until golden on both sides, about 15 minutes. Place broth in small wide-mouthed bowl. Dip one side of bread lightly in broth. If the bread turns soggy you have used too much broth. Spread liver mixture on dampened toast wedges. Top with a few capers. Place on garnished flat dish and serve immediately.

Yield: 40-48 pieces.

Note: *Crostini di fegatini di pollo* are also good topped with thin slices of prosciutto and can be served on thin slices of French baguette.

Milt and Chicken Liver Canape
Crostini di Milza e Fagatini di Pollo

Crostini always began a holiday meal in the Parigi household. We used *milza* (milt, or beef spleen) in addition to the chicken livers and had to purchase it from the slaughterhouse. Now it is almost impossible to find on the market.

1 small beef spleen (milt)

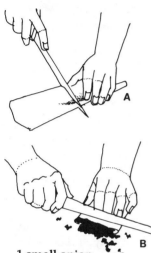

1 small onion
2-3 sprigs fresh parsley
3-4 celery leaves
2 tender celery ribs*
1/4-inch-thick
slice *pancetta*
4 fresh chicken livers

1-1/2 T butter
2 T broth
Peel of 1/2 lemon
1 tsp. tomato paste

2 oz. anchovies
3-1/2 oz. capers

10-12 slices day-old bread
6 oz. dry white wine
12 thin slices prosciutto

Wash milt in warm water. Place milt on a board and cut in half (see A). Using back blade of a butcher knife (not the cutting edge), scrape milt to loosen the pulp inside (see B). Hold milt at top and scrape away from you until all pulp comes out. Discard outer membrane. Set pulp aside. Repeat with second half.

Place onion, parsley, celery leaves and tender ribs, and *pancetta* in a meat grinder or food processor and grind fine. Place chicken livers in a meat grinder or food processor and chop until fine. Set both aside.

Place small-size iron skillet over medium-high heat. Heat to warm. Add butter and melt; add onion mixture and saute onions until transparent (about 15 minutes). Add chicken livers. If mixture begins to dry, add 1 tablespoon broth. Once all is brown (about 7 minutes), add milt and cook for 10 minutes.

Slice lemon peel into 1/4-inch strips and add. Cook 5 minutes. Add 1 tablespoon broth to tomato paste to soften, then add tomato paste to mixture. Cook 30 to 35 minutes. Remove from stove and cool.

Drain anchovies and capers. Place on bread board. Chop with knife into fine pulp. Blend into cooled milt mixture (can refrigerate up to 2 days).

To serve: Remove mixture from refrigerator. Bring to room temperature. Cut thin slices of bread into wedges (see Chicken Liver Canape). Toast in broiler until golden on both sides. Place wine in wide-mouthed bowl. Dip one side of toast lightly in wine (if soggy you have added too much wine). Spread mixture on dampened toast. Top with 1/2 slice of prosciutto. Place on flat dish and serve. Do not stack.

Yield: 40-48 pieces.

Note: *Celery ribs should be from center of plant and less than 2 inches long.

45

Hard-boiled Eggs with Anchovy and Caper Sauce
Uova Sode con Acciugata

Traditionally served with *bollito misto* (boiled mix), eggs with anchovies are good anytime. We eat them on days when fresh broth is made, spooning the anchovy sauce generously over the boiled chicken from the soup, as well as the eggs. Added to a buffet, this recipe presents a colorful, tasty dish.

1 cup *acciugata*
6 eggs

Prepare anchovy and caper sauce *(acciugata)* on page 230. Boil eggs to taste. Cut lengthwise, arrange on dish, and cover with sauce. Serve with Italian bread.

Yield: 12 pieces.

Stuffed Mushrooms
Funghi Ripieni

This recipe, a favorite of the Pelini family, is always a sensation when presented to guests.

20 large fresh mushrooms
8 oz. Italian sausage
1/2 clove garlic
1 T fresh parsley
Salt and pepper

1/3 cup bread crumbs
1/4 cup freshly grated
Romano cheese

Take one mushroom at a time, cut off the stem and remove blemishes on crown (you may wish to peel the top layer off crown). Rinse and brush clean. Dice stems into small pieces. If sausage is in a casing, remove the casing. Peel and mince garlic. Mince parsley.

Place a small-size iron skillet over medium-high heat. Do not add oil. Add sausage meat, breaking it up with a fork. When sausage has been frying for 5 minutes, add chopped mushroom stems, garlic, and parsley. When completely cooked, add salt and pepper (the cheese has enough salt to our taste). Remove from heat and add bread crumbs and cheese. Stir well.

Lay a mushroom cap on a flat surface. Fill mushroom with mixture. Repeat. Place stuffed mushrooms on an oiled baking pan. Add a little water to the pan and bake in a 350-degree oven for 25 minutes (do not add water until ready to bake or mushrooms will absorb it).

Yield: 20 pieces.

Marinated Green Beans, Artichokes, and Mushrooms
Fagiolini Freschi, Carciofi, e Funghi alla Marinati

In addition to being served as an appetizer, this marinated dish is at home at a buffet or on a picnic. Its variations are endless.

6 oz. tuna (Italian style)
2-3 cups cooked fresh
green beans
6-1/2 oz. artichoke
hearts in brine
2 oz. anchovies
2-3 T capers
1 can button mushrooms
(can use fresh)
2 T grated onion

dressing:
2/3 cup olive oil
1/4 cup vinegar
2 T water
1 envelope dry Italian
salad dressing
seasonings

Drain tuna and break into chunks. Cut cooked beans into 1-1/2-inch pieces. Cut artichoke hearts in half. Drain anchovies and cut in half. Rinse capers under faucet, squeezing out excess moisture. Combine ingredients in large mixing bowl, add mushrooms and onion, and toss.

In a 10-to-12-ounce lidded jar combine oil, vinegar, water, and seasonings. Mix and pour over mixture. Toss and refrigerate for a few hours to marinate. Serve with fresh Italian bread.

Serves: 8-10.

Variations: Add 2 cups cooked cappelletti and you have an excellent pasta salad.

Note: May be stored for 3 to 4 days in refrigerator. The longer it marinates, the better it tastes.

Oil, Salt and Pepper Dip
Pinzimonio

We have individual crystal bowls approximately 1 inch in diameter for *pinzimonio*. They sit to the right of the dinner plate at each place setting. *Pinzimonio* is a cold Tuscan variation of *bagna calda* (see pages 42-43).

1 cup cauliflower
1 cup broccoli
1 heart of celery
5 radishes
5 green onions

1/2 tsp. salt
1/2 tsp. pepper
3-4 T olive oil

Use 1/4 of a cauliflower or buy pieces at a deli. Wash cauliflower and broccoli and break into florets.

Clean celery heart and chop into 3-inch pieces. Wash and trim radishes. If large, cut in half. Clean and peel green onions. Drain vegetables and arrange on platter.

In a small bowl mix salt, pepper, and oil. Place on table near vegetables, or in individual bowls. Select a vegetable, dip in *pinzimonio*, stir, and eat.

Serves: 8-12.

Prosciutto with Cantaloupe or Figs
Prosciutto con Melone o Fichi

This excellent appetizer, now a favorite in Italian restaurants, attests to the fact that salty ham is not only good in savory items, but can also garnish sweets. The best prosciutto to use for this dish is the sweeter *prosciutto di Parma*.

1 wedge of cantaloupe
or 1 fig
2 slices prosciutto
Parsley to garnish

Slice a wedge of melon, remove rind and chill. Lay a slice of freshly cut prosciutto on top of the melon, garnish with a sprig of parsley and serve on an elegant plate. For figs, slice a fig in half and top with prosciutto.

Serves: 1.

Tomato Canape
Crostini di Pomodori

6 very ripe
fresh tomatoes
(or 12 oz. canned)
2 T capers
3 anchovy fillets
1/2 clove garlic

1/4 tsp. black
peppercorns
1 T olive oil
Salt (optional)

6-8 slices day-old bread
cut into wedges

Lay tomatoes on a pastry board. Peel, remove as many seeds as possible. Rinse capers under cold water and squeeze out excess moisture. Chop capers and anchovies very fine. Peel garlic and chop into fine pieces or press through garlic press.

Place a medium-size iron skillet over medium-high heat. Add tomatoes, bring to a boil, lower heat and cover. Allow to simmer, crushing with a fork to reduce pulp, until most of the liquid is gone. It should reduce to a puree. Add anchovies and capers to the tomato mixture. Allow to simmer 5 to 10 minutes. Add garlic to simmering mixture. Add peppercorns, a little olive oil, and some salt (if needed) and continue to simmer until thick and spreadable.

Cut 4 or 5 thin slices of day-old bread (or use a baguette) into wedges. Place on a tray and dry in a 250-degree oven until hard, about 15 minutes. Spread tomato mixture on toast. Top with a few capers (or parsley). Place on garnished flat dish and serve immediately.

Yield: 1 cup or 25-30 canapes.

White Canape
Crostini Bianchi

The first time Vivian Sansone tasted these luscious *crostini* was on a trip to Italy in the '70s. While being entertained in a relative's home, a variety of *crostini* was served, including several represented in this chapter.

4 oz. butter
3-1/2 oz. tuna
in olive oil
Juice of 1 lemon
Salt (optional)

5-6 slices day-old bread
10 marinated artichoke
hearts

Make sure butter is at room temperature. Place in a medium-size bowl and cream. Drain tuna and add to butter. Mix by hand until smooth and creamy. Add lemon juice and a little salt if necessary.

Slice 5 to 6 thin slices of day-old bread (or use a French baguette). Cut into wedges. Place on a tray and dry in a 250-degree oven until hard, about 15 minutes.

Spread tuna mixture on bread wedges. Cut artichoke hearts into halves. Top each canape with a slice of marinated artichoke heart.

Place on garnished flat dish and serve immediately.

Yield: 20-25 pieces.

Notes: Tuna mix can be frozen. Bring to room temperature and mix before serving. French baguettes may be substituted for day-old bread.

Notes

Beverages
Bevande

Italian beverages are as famous as Italian foods. It would be difficult to find a person in Western culture who has not heard of espresso or cappuccino, the strong Italian coffees. Fewer people may have knowledge of the medicinal teas concocted by thousands of peasant women in the hills and valleys of Italian provinces, but most of the world concedes that wine is Italy's most famous and greatest gastronomic treasure.

When an Italian meal is prepared the choice of wine is just as important as the cut of meat or the blend of spices, and that choice traditionally belongs to the man. Red meats require dry red wine. White meats, including pork, poultry, and fish, dry white wine. When a meal is as abundant as a proper Italian meal, a different wine is served with each course. Wine often accompanies the antipasto, the first course of a grand meal, but is removed from the table for the soup course, and reappears for the rest of the meal.

A few specialty wines were made in Nonno's wine cellar. Their lives were short, but their arrival at table was anticipated each year. They included *mezzo vino*, a half wine and half water by-product of the new wine, and *puntello*, a sweet wine using water and sugar. Holy Wine, *vin santo*, a sweet wine made from raisins, was the wine of wines as far as we were concerned.

Italians also have excellent liqueurs. *Anisetta* is a licorice-flavored drink that can be sipped slowly for the full bouquet of its heavy taste, or added to coffee. *Amaretto* is an almond-flavored liqueur. The most famous commercial brand of *amaretto* is *Amaretto di Saronno* first created in the 16th century. *Sambuca* comes from the elder tree, and is most often served with a coffee bean and called *sambuca con la mosca*, "sambuca with a fly." *Galliano*, easily recognized by its tall slim bottle and yellow color, is another licorice drink.

Two other types of spirits that we did not make but deserve mention here are *grappa* and *Marsala*. *Grappa* is distilled from crushed grapes after wine has been made, aged for two years in an oak cask, and usually served in morning coffee. *Marsala*, originally made in Sicily, is named after the town in which it was first produced, and is a cooking wine.

Coffees
Caffè

Coffee was introduced to the world from the Yemen on the Arabian peninsula during the Middle Ages and, thanks to the Venetian traders who almost monopolized Eastern trade at the time, it soon (between 1585 and 1615) reached Italian shores.

Espresso

Strong rich espresso is traditionally served after a large meal in an Italian home. In Italy they say it helps to digest food. One way to make espresso is to use an espresso machine that forces steam through the coffee. Espresso machines, used in a *bottega* (coffee shop) in Italy and in upbeat restaurants and coffee shops in America, are also available for the home.

In an Italian *bottega* one has choices: *un caffè* or *un espresso* is a standard, demitasse cup; *caffè doppio* or *caffè alto* is a double portion; *caffè macchiato* is coffee with a dash of milk; and *caffè corretto* is espresso with *grappa* or brandy.

But you do not need to go to a coffee shop or buy an espresso machine to make a good cup of espresso coffee. An Italian coffeepot produces the same results. There are two types of coffeepots: the Napoletana (A), a drip coffeepot, and the Moka (B). The latter is named after Mocha, the seaport in the Yemen where coffee was first exported.

Espresso coffee is finely ground. It can be purchased packaged in Italian food stores or in various blends at gourmet shops where any flavor, including the decaffeinated brands, can be ground for espresso. It is served in demitasse cups.

1 T espresso grounds
1/4 cup water
Sugar to taste

Prepare coffee as per instructions on your coffee machine. Usually 1 tablespoon of espresso needs 1/4 cup water.

Serves: 1.

Variation: Run a piece of lemon over the lip of the cup and dip the rim in sugar. Add coffee and sip through the sugar.

Cappuccino

Once, after a meal in Italy, I asked for a cappuccino. The restaurant owner refused to make me one. He said cappuccino is good in the morning, or as an afternoon pick-me-up, but after lunch or dinner only espresso would be served.

Varieties of cappuccino include the standard half steamed milk-half coffee; *cappuccino senza spuma*, coffee with hot milk that has not been steamed; and *caffè con panna*, coffee topped with sweetened whipped cream.

If you have trouble making a good foam for a cappuccino, use skim milk. Heavier milks and creams sometimes refuse to foam.

1/2 cup skim milk
1 T espresso
1/2 cup water
Sugar to taste

Cinnamon
Chocolate
Cloves
Or flavor of choice
as garnish

Place the milk in a steel cup and set it in the freezer while you prepare the coffee. The metal helps to chill the milk.

Prepare espresso according to instructions on your machine.

If you have an espresso machine, when the brewed espresso reaches the steam level, remove the skim milk from the freezer, place it under the steam nozzle with the nozzle barely below the surface of the milk. It will begin to foam immediately. Allow to foam for 30 seconds to a minute. Be sure to use a potholder to hold the metal container or it will become too hot to handle.

Pour the espresso in a cup. Add sugar, stir. Spoon steamed milk over the espresso. Garnish with cinnamon, chocolate, cloves, or any flavor of choice.

Serves: 1.

53

Teas
Te

Nonna, like so many immigrant mothers, was a storehouse of medicinal knowledge. When I had my first two-wheel bike, one day I flew over the handlebars and landed on my right knee. I could not walk. Nonna made a poultice of melted soap and rags which hardened into a protective cast. Sandrina also had her remedies -- she boiled wine to drink for coughs and sore throats.

Whenever a woman in our town was pregnant, our local doctor would say, "When it's time, call Mrs. Parigi to assist me." Children were born at home at that time and my Nonna was there when my brother was born, and seven years later when I came along. But she also helped with operations. During the Depression one of the men in our neighborhood injured the heel of his foot and it was badly infected. The doctor operated at home and Nonna assisted. Well, the man began to wake up before the operation was over and Nonna had to run out into the street to get men to hold him down while the doctor finished.

Nonna was the seventh child of the seventh child, and whether you believe in the superstition that that child has psychic powers or not, I know my Nonna was uncanny in her warnings. She always knew when something was wrong, or about to go wrong. One evening she came running to our house and asked where my brother was. My mother said he was at his friend's house. Nonna said, "Call and tell him to come home." At that moment the phone rang, our dog howled, and my mother was told that the car my brother was working on had fallen on him. It was a terrible time in our family.

We never believed in psychic powers and Nonna never tried to develop her abilities, but I believe that she possessed them. Psychic or not, she always had a remedy whenever anyone was not up to par, and the remedy was often a tea.

Camomile Tea
Te di Camomilla

Once a year Nonna brewed up a pot of camomile. Camomile is a daisy-like flower that blooms in June and Nonna used it for its calming properties. Today one can buy camomile tea all nicely packaged, but if you want to do it Nonna's way, here's how:

Be sure you have the proper flower. Gather bunches from the field. Lay them flat in a cool dry place, and allow to dry. Do not stack too high or they will rot. Once the flowers are dry, store them in an airtight sack but never in plastic wrap.

1-2 flowers, stems and all	Combine flowers and water. Steep to taste. The longer you steep, the stronger the taste.
1 cup of boiling water	Camomile tastes good with sugar, lemon, or honey. **Yield:** 1 cup.

Wine
Vino

In Italy, the Etruscans nurtured the grape and made wine in the Tuscan hills 4,000 years ago. Ancient Italy had a reputation among its neighbors for its wine, and the Greeks called their Italian colony *Oenotria*, the land of wine.

Although French wines appear to dominate the market in modern times, Italian vintners have regained the title of the best of the winemakers and Italy exports more wine than any other country. Wine is so important to the Italian economy that its production is supervised by the government and each vintner must conform to strict regulations. Supervised by the *denominazione di origine controllata* (DOC), 220 wine growing areas producing 800 types of wine have been approved by the Italian government with six wines distinguished as *denominazione di origine controllata garantita* (DOCG), or guaranteed authenticity. These are *Barbaresco, Barolo, Brunello di Montalcino, Chianti, Vino Nobile di Montepulciano,* and *Albana di Romagna.*

Tuscany is the home of three of the DOCG wines: *Brunello di Montalcino, Chianti,* and *Vino Nobile di Montepulciano.* The most popular is *Chianti;* the most prestigious is *Brunello di Montalcino* produced south of Siena.

I grew up on wine. Not the wine of *Brunello di Montalcino* nor *Chianti,* but the wonderful reds and whites of my Nonno's cellar. We had wine for dinner everyday and on Sundays and holidays a different type of wine for each course. Two things are always placed on an Italian table: bread and wine, symbolically, the body and blood of Jesus Christ.

Wine can be stored indefinitely and we believe it continues to age in the bottle. In fact, Nonno Parigi always saved a few bottles of a special year and when my brother got married we drank the wine from the year he was born. We still have a bottle of wine from 1933, the year my mother graduated from high school (which we will open the day this book is published). It, like all the bottle-aged wine that came before, stands on the shelf, as opposed to lying on its side. When Nonno opened one of these aging bottles, he was very careful not to disturb it too much. Once he delicately uncorked the bottle, he very cautiously inserted a special stick *(tromba)* and tilted the bottle, pouring out the contents in one continuous, slow-pouring flow. The sediment remained in the bottle. Then he rebottled the wonderful wine and brought it to table.

Wine should be kept out of bright sunlight and in a cool room between 50 to 60 degrees in temperature. If the storage area is too warm the wine will not be good.

Equipment

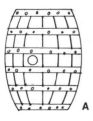

Barrels. To make wine you need at least three 45-to-50 gallon wooden barrels (see A): two for mash and one for storage. The mash barrels are open on one end,

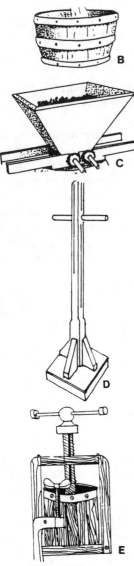

while the storage barrel must be closed at both ends to allow aging and have at least one, if not two, openings, both plugged by a bung (*spina della botte*), a wooden cork. All barrels must be leak-proof. To assure that the barrels are leak-proof, with the tap bung in place, swell the wood by filling the barrels with water. Allow barrels to set overnight.

Half barrel. Catches the wine (see B).

Grinder. A grape grinder (*mostatoio* or *pigiatrice*, see C) replaces the ancient method of stomping the grapes and mashes them to begin the fermentation process.

Plunger. A plunger (*pistone*, see D) is used to push the mash down each day during fermentation.

Press. After the wine has been removed from the barrels, the residue of mash is passed through the press (*strettoio* or *torchio*, see E) to extract the juices for half wine or other specialties.

Grapes. When trains no longer delivered grapes to our town, Nonno went to the Strip District in Pittsburgh. Then he would wait patiently -- maybe not so patiently -- for the grapes to be delivered. Our neighborhood would be filled with anticipation as day after day trucks would arrive with grapes for the anxious men. Some experts maintain shipped grapes are too old and do not produce good wine. They should have tasted Nonno's wine, or talked to the men in our town. Nonno insisted on California grapes from the Kokomonga region.

Our wines have no additives: no sugar (except *Puntello*), no chemicals, no yeast. They are pure, uncontaminated, and delicious.

Table Wine
Vino da Tavola

Gino's Red Wine
22 cases zinfandel

Nazzareno's Red Wine
20 cases zinfandel
4 cases muscat

Gino's Mixed Wine
14 cases alicante
8 cases muscat

Preparing the Work Space

Traditionally the process of making wine should commence on October 15. Create ample workspace when making wine. Twenty-two cases of grapes at 36 pounds each take a lot of space. Stack crates no more than six high near the mash barrels within easy reach.

Grapes must be clean and cool when you begin. Remove only the excess heavy stems and any leaves. The remainder goes in the mash.

Preparing the Equipment

All equipment must be free of contamination. Wash each wooden tool 3 times in lukewarm water combined with 1 cup baking soda, rinse 5 to 6 times in boiling clear water, and check barrels for leaks. Set aside to dry for several days. Some winemakers buy new barrels every year, but Nonno and Gino used the same barrels year after year and their wine never turned to vinegar.

Mashing

To mash grapes you can use any non-porous material (including your feet). Nonno always used a grape grinder (*mustatoio*, see B); however, many home brewers, even today, feel that using the feet is the best way to get a good crush, and Gino followed this method. Eleven cases of mashed grapes should fit into one barrel (approximately 50 gallons).

To grind the mash: Place grinder on open end of first barrel (see F). Pass 11 cases of grapes through grinder, crushing them and allowing juice to fall into barrel. Crush remaining grapes in second barrel.

To stomp the mash: Remember grapes are very susceptible to bacteria and everything that touches them must be absolutely clean. Gino had a pair of rubber hip boots he used exclusively for stomping and he cleaned them in hot sudsy water, then rinsed them 5 or 6 times in boiling clear water and hung them to drip dry (wiping would contaminate). They must never touch the ground, so it is not easy.

Place 1 case of grapes into each vat. Enter vat and lift feet up and down until grapes are well crushed (about 5 minutes for each vat). Remove grapes to mash barrel (mind your boots), step into second vat, add fresh grapes, and continue until all are crushed and both barrels are full.

The grapes have now become a *mosto*, or must (or mash), and they should be covered to protect the must from fruit flies and other bacteria that will spoil wine. Cover with barrel lid, a clean, heavy cloth, or even a newspaper.

Fermentation

After grapes have been mashed and barrels are full and covered, allow to stand for 4 to 8 days. If

Nazzareno's White Wine

12 cases muscat

You will need:
1 50-gallon mash barrel with lid
1 50-gallon storage barrel with 2 holes and 2 bungs
1 grinder (or a pair of boots)
1 plunger
1 large funnel
1/2 barrel
1 wooden spigot
2 vats (if stomping)

F

G

H

I

J

weather is warm it will probably take 4 to 5 days; if cold, 6 to 8 days. Check grapes everyday and when liquid begins to swell and grapes rise to surface they are fermenting. They must be punched down each day. With a plunger (*pistone*, see G and H), push grapes to bottom of barrel. Do this 5 to 6 times, twice a day. Punching down eliminates cap on surface, allows oxygen to enter mixture, and aids processing. If mash turns sour wine is spoiled.

Fermentation ends when must stops bubbling and rising to top, or rises very slowly. Do not plunge or push mash down after bubbles subside or it will become cloudy and cloud finished wine. Allow wine to set for 24 hours to clear the wine. In addition to taste, clarity is a requirement for good wine.

Removing the wine

Now it is time to remove the wine from the fermentation barrels and transfer it to the storage barrels. If the storage barrels are new, or have not been used yearly, in addition to washing and rinsing in boiling water, they must be sweetened (any new barrel must be sweetened). To sweeten mix 6 quarts of must with 3 to 5 gallons of boiling water in a plastic pail or wooden tub. Strain and pour juice into storage barrel. Roll all around the storage barrel, empty, and rinse with warm water. Place upsidedown to drain for several hours.

All storage barrels should have a permanent tap on the side, which has been plugged up during fermentation (see notes that follow).

Place a wooden tub or 1/2 barrel under the opening of the mash barrel to catch wine (see I). Let juice flow until it stops. At this point wine is not clear because of the fermentation process.

If you are not making *mezzo vino* or *puntello* remove mash from barrel, place in press (see J), and press mash. Add to wine. If you are making additional wine, eliminate this step.

Storing the wine

Place storage barrel on its side, in permanent location. It must be absolutely level. Transfer wine using a funnel. After transfer, wine is still foaming. Do not seal opening. Filled to top and as wine foams impurities will spill over sides. Top barrel with wine every day. Allowing the wine to breath and foam is the most important step in making good wine.

On November 11, Saint Martin's Day (if begun on October 15), seal barrel by hammering a bung into opening. Dampness from barrel will swell and seal it. Wine must be in air tight barrel (Nonno and Gino placed fresh cement over the bung to ensure no air would enter and ruin the wine).

Stored for 6 months or more in a cool, dry place. This continues fermentation. Sediment will settle to bottom and juice will become a clear wine.

Tapping the wine

After 6 months (around Easter), during dark of moon (from full moon to new moon), tap new wine. Boil spigot (see K) in clear water and with hammer or wooden mallet pound it into bung on front side of barrel. Move quickly and accurately. Bung is soft and spigot will swell to seal opening.

You may place wine in prepared clean 5-gallon, 1- gallon, or quart containers, or leave it in the barrel. You may cover the wine with a little oil and seal with a press cap (like Gino) or cork the wine and cover the cork with melted wax seal (like Nonno).

A Few Warnings

If fermentation does not start, the must could be too cold or too hot. If fermentation does not stop, let it continue, the longer it processes the more sugar will be converted into wine. It makes it stronger. If the final wine is vinegary, it has been contaminated and must be discarded or used as vinegar.

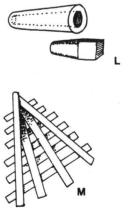

Notes: Buy a spigot or, as Gino did, make your own. The spigot is made of wood (usually from a grape box or broom handle). Drill hole through the center of wood and make plug to fit into hole (see L). The plug must be tapered. It is placed into hole to stop flow of wine and removed to allow liquid to flow.

Gino also placed a handmade wooden sieve (see M) inside the barrel above the spigot opening. This prevented grape seeds, skins, and stems from coming through the spigot with the grape juice.

Twelve cases grapes produce 25 to 30 gallons wine, or 2-1/2 gallons juice from 1 case grapes.

Half Wine
Mezzo Vino

Mezzo vino is a special type of wine enjoyed after the new wine is set to age. It is a combination of water and the used mash from the new wine. In addition to good drinking, it indicates the success or failure of the new wine now aging in barrels. It shows the clarity and previews the bouquet.

Old mash
2 cases new grapes
10 gallons water

15 gallon barrel
with spigot
1 mash barrel
1 grinder
1 press
1 plunger
1/2 barrel
1 large funnel

Prepare equipment and be sure it is clean (see page 56). Pour boiling water and 1 cup of baking soda into the 15 gallon barrel and rinse with hot clear water. Repeat 3 times. Do not wash mash barrels.

Make wine as described on pages 57 to 59. After all wine has been drained from the mash add 10 gallons of water to 1 mash barrel. Grind 2 new cases of grapes into barrel, remove mash from second barrel and add.

Ferment for 2 days, punching down with plunger if mash rises to the top or begins to bubble. Drain as described on page 58. Place in a 15 gallon barrel and seal as described on page 59.

If this is last wine, press mash and add to barrel before fermenting. If not, save mash for Prop Wine.

Yield: 15 gallons.

Prop Wine (Raisin Jack)
Puntello

Used mash

3 gallons water
5 pounds raisins
or 1 pound sugar
15 gallon barrel with
1 press
1/2 barrel
1 large funnel

Be sure all equipment is sterile and all liquid is drained from the mash. Make wine and half wine as described on pages 57 to 60. After half wine has been drained from the mash, grind raisins over mash, add water and stir. Add sugar if desired.

Cover and allow to ferment one day. Tap and pour into freshly cleaned and boiled barrel or clean glass gallon jugs. After all wine has been drained from mash, remove mash from barrel. Place press (see J) over barrel, and press mash so juices flow into barrel. Remove juices and add to *puntello*.

At this point the *puntello* will be cloudy. Allow to rest for a day to clear. It is ready to drink.
Yield: 6-8 gallons.

Holy Wine
Vin Santo

Vin santo was the wine of wines in our home. My mother maintains Nonno never made it in America. I insisted he did. None of us recalls grapes hanging in the cellar to age, but we all remember drinking *vin santo*. I finally had to concede that his white muscat wine, made with the same grapes (not allowed to age to raisins) and served only on special occasions is what I remember.

Vin santo is a specialty of Tuscany. It is a wine of ritual. The wine is given to anyone who is ill and served to the new bride as a symbol of welcome by the father of her husband as she enters her new home for the first time. In the month of June during the wheat harvest, called *la battuta del grano*, *vin santo* is served before the huge breakfast given to the people who would go out into the fields.

On my second visit to Italy in 1967, *Chianti* had just begun to make a commercial *vin santo*. My Cousin Lydia's husband, Narciso, brought a bottle to my Uncle Gino's table. What a hullabaloo. And it was not a momentary thing. The discussion and the tasting went on all day with men from other homes coming to taste. It endeared my uncle to me, as it was the same back home when men came to visit my Nonno. Wine, prosciutto, and salami: these were the topics. No sports. No cars. Food was the topic. Each man priding himself on his ability and many kept the ingredients or the recipe a secret.

The following method for making *vin santo* comes from our cousin, Beppe Parigi, Uncle Gino's son. Beppe grows his own grapes for this wine. When they are ready for harvest he handpicks them, and carefully sews the clusters together to hang in rows on the rafters of our ancestral home. He refuses to add central heating to the house, which is heated by fireplaces, because he feels central heat will harm the *vin santo*. In fact, when the grapes are drying he keeps the house shuttered against the fumes of modern day automobiles.

3 cases
white muscat
You will need:
1 15-gallon
mash barrel
with lid
1 1/2-barrel
1 5-gallon
storage barrel
with spigot
1 grinder
(or a pair of boots)
1 press
1 large funnel
1 vat (if stomping)

Pick one bunch of grapes at a time, remove excess leaves and hang grapes on a nail. Allow to age in a cool dry place for 6 to 8 weeks until they become raisins. The wine making process usually begins around Christmas.

Read all instructions for making table wine on pages 56 through 59. Prepare all equipment as described. You will need smaller barrels for this wine.

Once all grapes have aged and all equipment is sterilized remove excess leaves and stems from the grapes and crush grapes in a grinder or by stomping.

Place the grinder on the open end of the first barrel (see F). Pass the raisins through the grinder, crushing them and allowing the juice to fall into the barrel.

Cover the must to protect it from fruit flies and other bacteria that will spoil the wine.

Let stand for 4 to 5 days; if cold, 6 to 8 days. Check grapes daily and when they begin to rise to the surface fermentation is under way.

Plunge mash down with plunger (*pistone*, see G and H), pushing the grapes to the bottom of the barrel. Do this 5 to 6 times, twice a day. Punching down eliminates the cap on the surface, allows oxygen to enter the mixture, and aids processing.

Fermentation is over when must stops bubbling and rising to top, or rises very slowly. Do not plunge or push mash down after bubbles subside or it will become cloudy and cloud the finished wine.

After fermentation is over allow the wine to set for 24 hours to clear it. In addition to taste, clarity is a requirement for good wine.

Remove from barrel transfer and seal as described on pages 58 and 59.

After sealing, *vin santo* is stored in a cool place for a minimum of 2 years, and preferably 4 to 5 years. It is not tapped until the wine has reduced to half its original size. The keg is tapped around Christmas. It is put into dark glass bottles, sealed, and opened as needed.

Yield: 6-8 small bottles.

Breads, Schiacciate, and Pizzas
Pane, Schiacciate, e Pizza

Senza il pane tutto diventa orfano, "without bread, everything is an orphan," goes an Italian saying. Bread is the staple of the Italian kitchen, and hundreds of varieties of it are produced in Italy where restaurants have begun to serve a different bread with each course of the meal. Attempts have been made to officially classify and control the production of bread, like wine, to insure the quality and accuracy of its many forms and tastes.

Today, Italian bakeries, *panetteria,* make long loafs, flat loafs, brown bread, white bread, stuffed bread, sweet bread, breads of rice, corn, or potato flour, and even saltless bread, a specialty of Tuscany. Bread is called by dozens of different names: *corona,* the crown; *mattone,* the brick; *pagnotta,* round; *panino,* rolled; *schiacciata,* flattened; *sfilatino,* long and thin; and *treccia,* braided. The flat bread of Sicily is called *carta di musica,* sheet music bread, and there is even *pane dei morte,* bread of the dead. There are breads for special days: All Soul's bread, Saint Anthony's bread, the sourdough bread of Saint Blaise (*panicelle di San Biagio*), and Easter bread (*panina di Pasqua*).

Bread is used for everything from sandwiches to an ingredient in salads. It is taken to the church for blessing, given by the church in the name of a saint, and it is a sin to throw it away. In medieval times it was used in place of the fork and spoon, served as a napkin to wipe the mouth or clean the knife, and, allowed to age into a thick slice, was used as a dish or serving tray.

When Nonna was a girl the brick bread ovens of the village were fired up daily, but each family had access only once a week. By the end of the week the bread had turned quite hard and a host of recipes were devised to use it: bread in soup, bread in salad, bread as stuffing, and bread as crumbs.

The most famous bread of Tuscany, *pane Toscano o pane sciocco,* is a saltless bread. Tradition has it that Tuscans, ever mindful of their purses, refused to pay the salt tax in the Middle Ages and had to cook without salt. When my grandmother told her father that she was going to America with her husband he said, "You'll learn the price of salt." The implication went over her head and she wrote back to him from America, "Salt is only five cents."

Homemade Bread
Casareccio

Every Thursday was bread day in Nonna's kitchen. Out came the *spianatoia* (bread board), on went the apron, and the kitchen would be tied up for hours. The aroma promised a treat to please the most critical gourmet.

Almost everything affects the final outcome of a loaf of bread: the type of water, the kind of day (damp days are the worst), the altitude, and probably the temperament of the baker. Patience is the name of the game when making true Italian bread: patience and a lot of time. Nonna used the whole day and baked copious amounts; today my mother bakes a few loaves at a time.

This recipe is a fourth of what Nonna prepared. And, unlike the typical Tuscan bread, our recipe contains salt. We do not know if Nonna, having been warned of the value of salt, added it once she came to America, but we never made saltless bread.

10 cups white flour
3 cups water, divided
1 oz. dry yeast
1/4 pound (1 stick) margarine or butter
1/4 cup granulated sugar
2 tsp. salt
1/4 cup white flour for kneading, or as needed

4 bread pans

A

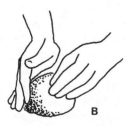

B

Put flour into a large mixing bowl. Heat 1 cup water to 90 degrees. Add dry yeast, dissolve, and set aside (be sure yeast water is not over 90 degrees or it will cook the yeast and the bread will not rise).

To 2 cups of water add margarine, sugar, and salt and heat until dissolved (be sure this water is warmer than yeast water, from 115 to 120 degrees).

Make a well in the center of the flour (see A) and slowly add the lukewarm yeast water. Mix with a fork. When yeast water has been absorbed into the flour, slowly begin to add the warmer sugar water. Keep mixing until all the liquid is absorbed.

Prepare a large work space (2 by 3 feet), preferably a large pastry board, and dust it with flour. Use flour sparingly as it is only a bonding agent. If dough is already firm, limit the extra flour. Turn dough onto board, and begin to knead (see B).

Kneading is a long process and one must work the dough for half an hour, adding flour as needed to keep the mixture from sticking.

Once the dough has been kneaded, place it in a large mixing bowl (Nonna always blessed the bread 3 times with the sign of the cross at this point), cover with at least one clean cloth and 2 to 3 blankets (bread must be kept warm and we always used blankets), and let rise about 1-1/2 hours until double in size.

Uncover the dough and punch down 10-to-12 times. To punch down (see C), form a fist and beat the bread like a punching bag (get out frustrations). Flip dough over, cover, allow to rise an hour.

When dough is almost ready, prepare 4 baking pans greased with a little shortening so the bread will not stick. Begin to pan the loaves immediately, filling each baking pan to little more than half full. Then cover with cloth and blankets and allow to raise for 1 hour. Ten minutes before uncovering, heat oven to 350 degrees.

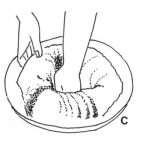

Bake the loaves for 50 to 60 minutes, or until golden (see note). Remove from oven, place on a wire rack to cool, and cover with a thin cloth.

Yield: 4 loaves.

For sandwich buns: Prepare bread as above. When ready to pan take enough dough to make one roll the size of a hamburger bun (at this point dough is half of the final size and the size of the sandwich roll is up to the chef). Roll the dough between your hands into a round ball and place on a greased cookie sheet. Six breads should fit on a sheet. Continue until all dough is rolled. Cover bread and allow to rise for 1 hour. Bake in 350-degree oven for 45 to 50 minutes.

Yield: 24 buns.

Note: To check bread remove from pan and tap the bottom with your fist. If it sounds hollow, the center of the bread is well done.

To make less than 4 loaves:

1/4 recipe (1 loaf):	1/2 recipe (2 loaves):
2-1/2 cups flour	5 cups flour
1/4 cup water	1/2 cup water
1/4 oz. yeast	1/2 oz. yeast
1/2 cup water	1 cup water
2 T margarine	4 T margarine
2 T sugar	4 T sugar
1/2 tsp. salt	1 tsp. salt
1/8 cup flour	1/4 cup flour
1 pan	2 pans
Knead: 15 minutes	Knead: 20 minutes
1st rise: 30 minutes to 1 hour	1st rise: 1 hour
2nd rise: 30 minutes to 1 hour	2nd rise: 1 hour
(must double at each rise)	

Garlic Bread
Fett'unta

Called *bruschetta* in Rome and *fett'unta* in Tuscany, garlic bread is an Italian export made popular in America by returning GIs during World War II. As famous as pizza, one can find garlic bread in any Italian restaurant and it is enjoyed as an accompaniment to pasta and salad, or as a snack.

True Tuscan *fett'unta* is made with olive oil, not butter, and crushed garlic cloves, not garlic salt or powder. The olive oil and fresh garlic produce a stronger taste, but to our palates, the stronger the better.

4 slices Italian bread
8 tsp. olive oil
4 cloves garlic
Salt, pepper

Place bread slices in a broiler or, preferably, a charcoal grill. Brown one side until golden (see note).

Drizzle 1 teaspoon of oil over untoasted side of each slice. Press garlic in a garlic press and spread juice and pulp generously on each slice (the amount of garlic is a matter of taste, but fresh garlic is stronger than powders or salts).

Add salt and pepper to taste and pour additional teaspoon of warmed olive oil on each slice. Return to broiler and brown garnished side until golden.

Serve immediately.

Serves: 2.

Note: Before second broiling, sprinkle freshly grated Parmesan cheese over each slice.

Variations: For lunch Nonna would sometimes cut a thick slice of homemade bread and drizzle oil and vinegar over it. This simple fare, topped with salt and pepper to taste, is excellent.

Another variation is the *Struffa Struffa* open-face sandwich found on page 275.

Bread Stuffing
Ripieno di Pane

Bread stuffing forms the base of dozens of recipes in the *Immigrant's Kitchen* and is one of the four most important recipes mentioned in the chapter "Our Italian Kitchen." It is good with game, poultry, meat, and vegetables.

1 onion
1/4-inch-thick slice
pancetta
1 celery rib with leaves
1 small carrot
1 tsp. fresh parsley

1/4 cup corn oil
1 tsp. pepper
1 tsp. salt

4 cups bread cubes
3 eggs
4 T freshly grated
Parmesan cheese
1 cup broth

Peel and wash onion, cut into wedges. Dice *pancetta*. Peel celery and carrot, wash, and cut into 1-inch pieces. Chop parsley fine. Combine all and grind in a meat grinder or food processor (the grinder is better because it releases the juices).

Place a medium-size iron skillet over medium-heat. Heat to hot. Add oil. When oil is warm add chopped ingredients, pepper, and salt, and saute until onions are transparent, stirring often. The longer you cook this mixture the better the stuffing will be. When it begins to stick to the skillet (15 to 20 minutes) it is done.

Place bread cubes (see note) in a large bowl. Remove onion mixture from heat and add to bread cubes. Then add eggs and cheese. Mix. Add broth and mix again. If cubes are moist, stuffing will be moist, so be generous with broth.

Serves: 4-5.

Notes: You can substitute bread crumbs for cubes. For some dishes garlic is added.

Sweet Breads
Pani Dolce

Easter Bread
Pane di Pasqua o Panina

Nonna's kitchen was ahummin' on Holy Thursday as Easter bread filled with plump raisins was mixed, panned, and baked. This is a bountiful recipe--a good way to give an Easter present to a friend. In our family, every Holy Thursday promptly at 4 o'clock Tom Cherubini Celli would appear at Nonna's door to collect his Easter Bread. This tradition is still maintained at Vivian's home -- but the delicacy is Sandrina's oiled *schiacciata* (see recipe on page 75).

3 T Spanish saffron*
1/2 cup boiling water

1-1/2 pounds raisins
Hot water

3 eggs
3 T olive oil
1 tsp. salt

2 sticks (8 oz.) margarine
or butter
1 cup granulated sugar

1 cup water
1-1/2 oz. rapid rising
dry yeast

5-6 cups flour

3 (8-inch) pie plates
Shortening

A

Add Spanish saffron to 1/2 cup boiling water, stir, and set aside to brew and come to room temperature. Beat eggs in mixer, slowly add olive oil and salt.

Place raisins in a bowl. Add hot water to cover and allow to set. This plumps the raisins.

Place a small-size iron skillet over medium-high heat. Cut margarine or butter into 1-inch squares and place in skillet. Do not allow to brown. When butter is partly melted add sugar. Stir slightly, turn off burner and allow to remain on cooling burner until needed.

Heat 1 cup water to 90 degrees. Dissolve dry yeast in water and set aside. If yeast water is above 90 degrees the bread will not rise.

Put 5 cups white flour on a board or into a large mixing bowl. Make a well in the center (see A). Add 1 to 3 tablespoons of flour to the yeast mixture until it begins to hold some shape. Pour yeast mixture into the well and begin to pull flour from the sides of the well until yeast mixture is absorbed.

When yeast water has been absorbed, strain saffron tea that has cooled to room temperature. Be sure this water is no hotter than 115 to 120 degrees or it will cook the yeast and the bread will not rise. Add saffron tea to dough and keep mixing until all is absorbed. Add egg mixture. Drain raisins and add to dough. Continue to pick up flour until all is well blended.

Prepare a large work space, preferable a large pastry board, and dust it with flour. Turn dough onto board and begin to knead (see B). This is a long process and one must knead the dough for 1/2 to 3/4 hour, adding flour as needed to keep mixture from sticking. Return the dough to a clean mixing bowl, cover with at least one clean cloth and two blankets, and allow to rise for 2 hours (sweet bread is slower to rise than regular bread).

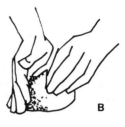

B

Remove covers and punch dough down 10-to-12 times. To punch down form a fist (see C) and beat the bread like a punching bag (get out all your frustrations). Flip dough over. Cover again and allow to rise an additional 1 to 1-1/2 hours.

When dough is almost ready prepare 3 baking pans. Grease all pans with a little shortening so the baking bread will not stick to the sides. Pan bread immediately, filling each baking pan to little more than half. Cover once more with cloth and blankets and allow to raise for 1 to 1-1/2 hours. Ten minutes before uncovering, heat oven to 350 degrees.

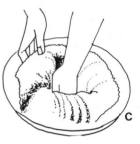

C

Place bread in oven and bake for 45 to 60 minutes. When done (see note) remove from oven, remove from pan, place on wire rack, cover with a thin, clean cloth, and allow to cool.

Yield: 3 loaves.

Notes: *Spanish saffron can be purchased in pharmacies or in gourmet shops.

To check bread, remove from pan and tap the bottom with your fist. If it sounds hollow, the center of the bread is well done.

Snack Idea: Easter bread makes wonderful toast and is especially delicious topped with cream cheese. It is also nice served with salami for a sweet and savory snack.

Panettone

In Italy, *panettone* is a Christmas bread. There are many stories as to the origin of *panettone*, most about the poor who enjoyed it only once a year as a special treat. One story tells of a poor baker whose beautiful daughter caught the eye of a rich man. He sent the baker, named Tony, oranges, lemons, and other delicacies that Tony baked into his bread. Of course his bread was wonderful, the rich man married his daughter, and the bread of Tony, *pane di Toni*, became famous. Today in Italy *panettone* is tall and cylindrical (see illustration), a form popularized after our immigrants were in America.

Sandrina got this recipe from her mother and when she came to America and made it for her family, she used certain bowls and pans which were the right size for all the ingredients. Those same bowls are still used by Vivian, who converted all the measurements for this book.

2/3 cup raisins
1 cup hot water

1/4 cup butter
1 egg and 2 egg yolks
1/2 cup granulated sugar
2-1/2 cups flour
1/2 cup milk
1/4 tsp. salt
1-1/2 tsp. cream of tartar
1 tsp. baking soda
1/2 cup candied fruit

1 T soft butter
1 T flour
1 T granulated sugar

Place raisins in bowl, add hot water, and allow to plump. In medium-size bowl stir room-temperature butter and eggs until smooth. Slowly add sugar, flour, milk, and salt, alternating and stirring constantly. When smooth, add raisins, cream of tartar, baking soda, and candied fruit. Turn onto floured board. Knead 5 minutes, or until dough is soft and sticky. If too sticky, add a little flour.

Grease round pan or 1-quart casserole with tablespoon of butter. Combine 1 tablespoon each of flour and sugar and dust interior of pan. Distribute evenly, especially up sides, or bread will stick. Place dough in pan. Do not allow to rise. Heat oven to 350 degrees; bake 1 hour or until top is golden. Remove from oven and allow to cool on a rack.
Yield: 1 loaf.

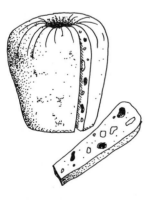

Variation: To make high *panettone* use 1/2 oz. dry yeast, 5 T sugar, 1/4 cup warm water, 3 cups flour, 1/4 cup water, 3 eggs, 2 yolks, 1/2 tsp. salt, 3/4 cup soft butter, 1 T vanilla, 1 T grated lemon peel, 1/3 cup citron, 1 cup raisins. Dissolve yeast in 1/4 cup warm water and 1 T sugar. Let foam and add 1/2 cup flour. Form ball, slash top, cover, rise to double. Combine all but butter, citron and raisins and knead. Add butter and knead 10 minutes. Add citron and raisins. Cover, rise for 1-1/2 hours. Punch down, cover, refrigerate overnight. Remove, punch down, place in high pan, set 4 hours until double in size. Brush with beaten egg. Bake at 400 degrees for 10 minutes and 350 for 40 minutes or more.

Fried Dough with Sugar
Pasta Fritta con Zucchero

While the bread was rising in the pans, Nonna prepared left-over dough as a wonderful sweet snack. This is our answer to the doughnut. We eat fried bread so fast that when the last one is frying it belongs to the cook. The rest are gone.

1/2 homemade bread
recipe*
1 cup corn oil
1 cup granulated sugar

Prepare the dough as described in the homemade bread recipe on page 65. If making only enough dough for this recipe divide the recipe in half. After the last rising, knead, and divide dough into 16- to-20 pieces (size is a matter of choice).

Place a medium-size iron skillet over medium-high heat. Heat to hot. Add oil. Stretch each piece of dough to look like a veal cutlet. Drop into hot oil. It will puff up immediately. Brown one side, turn, and brown on second side.

Remove from oil and place on a paper towel. Sprinkle with sugar to taste, and eat. Continue until all the bread is fried.

Eat at once, for fried dough is best served piping hot.

Yield: 16-20 pieces.

Note: *You can buy fresh bread dough from a bakery or pizza parlor. You can also buy frozen bread dough, but it tends to lack substance.

Stuffed Breads
Pani Imbottiti

Fried Anchovy Bread
Pane Fritto con Acciuga

From the kitchen of Bob Pelini's mother-in-law, Mrs. Amico, this recipe was a Christmas Eve specialty in her home.

3 oz. anchovies

3 cups flour
1 tsp. granulated sugar
Pinch salt
1/4 oz. dry yeast
1 egg
2 cups water
1 T olive oil

3 cups corn oil

Drain anchovies and cut each fish into thirds. Set aside. Combine flour, sugar, salt, and yeast in a bowl. Beat egg and combine with water and 1 tablespoon oil. Add egg mixture to flour and mix until blended. Dough should be soft and runny. Place in a bowl, cover, and let rise for 1 to 1-1/2 hours.

When dough is double original size, remove from bowl and set on pastry board. Pinch off 1 teaspoon, flatten in palm of hand, and place anchovy in center. Seal the anchovy inside the dough and roll.

If dough is too soft to handle allow it to remain in bowl. Keep a little extra flour on hand. Take a teaspoon, dip into dough, pull up enough dough to fill the spoon. With flour on fingers trim off hanging dough. Place anchovy in center of dough and fold dough over it. Do not place on board, but drop directly into hot oil, coaxing dough from spoon with a floured finger. You may want to fill several spoons before dropping into oil to keep the pot full.

Place a 2-quart pot over medium-high heat. Heat to hot. Add oil. Allow to heat. Drop anchovy balls into hot oil. They will puff immediately. Allow to brown. Turn. Remove and drain. Eat warm.

Yield: 35-40.

Notes: Anchovy puffs are best eaten immediately, but they can be zapped with the microwave for 30 seconds to warm. They can also be frozen and zapped for 30 seconds.

Variations: You can eliminate the anchovy, fry the dough, and coat it with sugar or honey. If you add corn, you have corn fritters.

Sausage in a Blanket
Involtini di Salsiccia

When the dough is ready to rise the battle is on: Should we have fried dough, anchovy bread, or sausage in a blanket? When Nonna was baking, fried dough usually won, but sausage has always been my favorite.

8 fresh sausage links
1/4 of homemade bread recipe
Vegetable shortening

Place a medium-size iron skillet over medium-high heat. Do not add oil. Add the sausage links and fry about 10 minutes, turning once. Drain on paper towel.

If panning bread, set the dough for one loaf aside. If making dough for this recipe, simply make 1/4 recipe on page 65. After the second rise, divide dough in eighths and wrap each piece around a cooked sausage (see A and B). Seal well.

Grease cookie sheet with a little shortening. Set each sausage roll on cookie sheet and cover. Allow to rise about 1 hour, or until double in size. Place cookie sheet in oven and bake at 350 degrees for about 25 minutes, or until done.

A

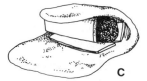

B

Serves: 8.

Notes: You can buy fresh bread dough from a bakery or pizza parlor. You can also buy frozen bread dough, but it tends to lack substance.

Variations: Sausage with cheese: The sausage filling can be dressed with a number of ingredients. In the center of each blanket place 1 cooked sausage, 1 slice mozzarella, 1 slice of salami, and 1 slice provolone (see C). Fold over the ends of the dough to wrap the filling firmly inside. If not sealed well, cheese will leak. If you wish, you can chop sausage, salami and cheeses together and spoon onto dough.

C

Sausage with escarole: A Pelini family favorite, this combines 1/2 pound sausage, 1 cup cooked chopped escarole, 1 onion, and 2 cloves garlic. Peel and dice garlic and onion. Saute in corn oil until soft. Wash and boil escarole, cook until done. Break up sausage meat and cook. Combine and continue as above.

Serves: 4.

Schiacciate

Schiacciata (*stiacciata* in Quarata), also known as *focaccia*, and called pizza in Naples, is a flattened bread made in Tuscany. The size of the *schiacciata* can be anything from a large 18-inch rectangle to a tiny 2-inch pie, and the toppings are just as varied. Probably the fried dough with sugar (see page 71) that we enjoy so much is a version of *schiacciata*.

You can buy fresh bread dough from a bakery or pizza parlor. You can also buy frozen bread dough, but it tends to lack substance.

Classic Schiacciata
Schiacciata Classica

This *schiacciata* is as Tuscan as it gets: good bread, good olive oil, fresh rosemary and course salt. Nonno loved it, and I can still see him sitting under the grape arbor enjoying a *schiacciata classica* for lunch.

1/4 homemade bread recipe
1 T olive oil
1 tsp. course salt
1 T rosemary

Prepare 1/4 of the bread recipe as described on page 65.

After the last rising, knead, place into an oiled cookie sheet or pizza pan and flatten the dough to cover the bottom of the pan. Brush with olive oil and sprinkle with salt and rosemary.

Bake in 400-degree oven for 15 to 20 minutes, or until brown.

Serves: 6-8.

Variation: Sprinkle with pressed garlic or cheese.

Schiacciata with Grapes
Schiacciata con Uva

Schiacciata with grapes was a specialty of the grape harvest each October. At noon, the owner of the vineyard served up this delicious meal.

1/4 homemade bread recipe

1 pound red seedless grapes
1/4 cup granulated sugar
2 cups walnuts
1 T fennel seeds
3 pats butter
1 T olive oil

Prepare 1/4 of homemade bread recipe on page 65. After last rising, knead, and flatten the dough on oiled cookie sheet or pizza pan. Cut half the grapes in half and combine grapes, sugar, nuts, and fennel. Top dough with mixture. Cut up butter and top. Drizzle olive oil over all. Bake in 400-degree oven for 25 to 30 minutes or until brown.

Serves: 24 (1-1/2-by-3-inch) pieces.

Sandrina's Oiled Schiacciata
Schiacciata Unta alla Sandrina

This recipe is a specialty of Holy Week in the Pelini home. With variations, it is the traditional *schiacciata di Pasqua* to which *vin santo* and anise seeds are sometimes added.

1/2 oz fresh (cake) yeast
1 cup warm water
3 cups flour
1 T vegetable shortening

1/4 pound diced
*pancetta**
1 (4 oz.) stick butter at
room temperature
Rind of 1 orange
Rind of 1/2 lemon
Juice of 1/2 lemon
1 tsp. lemon extract
1 tsp. vanilla
1 tsp. salt
5 large eggs

1 cup flour
3/4 to 1 cup lard**
1-1/2 cups granulated
sugar

Dissolve yeast in 1/2 cup warm water. Sift flour into a large pan (approximately 8-quart). Make a well in the flour and add the dissolved yeast, remainder of warm water, and shortening. Mix into flour to form a dough and knead for 10 to 15 minutes until no longer sticky, adding small amounts of additional flour if needed.

Remove dough from pan. Clean pan and grease with a little shortening. Place dough into the pan. Cover, and let rise 1-1/2 hours. Punch dough down. Add *pancetta*, butter, orange rind, lemon rind and juice, lemon extract, vanilla, salt, and eggs at room temperature. Mix well and then add 1 cup flour to stiffen the dough and hold it together. Remove from pan, clean and grease pan with shortening, then return dough to pan and cover. Allow to rise for 2 hours.

Grease six or seven 9-inch cake pans and cut the dough into an equal number of parts. Spread dough like pizza over bottom of each pan. Cover and let rise for 1-1/4 hours. Uncover and with fingers make indentations in the dough. With a butter knife put a small piece of lard (reason it is called *unta*) in each indentation. Sprinkle entire pie with sugar.

Heat oven to 400 degrees. Place in oven and bake for 20 to 25 minutes or until golden brown. Do not over cook.

Yield: 6-7 loaves.

Notes: *Because we made this *schiacciata* during Holy Week, we omit the *pancetta*. If using *pancetta*, then dice it into small pieces, place in a small-size skillet over medium-high heat, and cook until well rendered. Drain and add as indicated above.
**Lard is available in supermarkets (use vegetable lard on fasting days).

Pizza

Pizza is Naples' gift to the world. Today it is one of the most popular foods in the United States, but as its twins, *schiacciata* and *focaccia*, it was once the bread of the poor, topped by whatever ingredients were fresh, cheap, and available.

Classic Pizza
Pizza Classica

dough:
2-1/2 to 3 cups flour
1/4 oz. quick rising
dry yeast
1 cup warm water
1/2 tsp. salt
1 T granulated sugar
1/4 cup corn oil

1 tsp. olive oil or
cornmeal

sauce:
1 clove garlic
1 T corn oil
1/4 tsp. salt
1/8 tsp. pepper
1/2 tsp. dried oregano
2 cups whole canned
tomatoes
1/4 cup broth

toppings:
16 oz. mozzarella cheese
4-6 T freshly grated
Parmesan cheese
1 stick pepperoni

Put flour (reserve 1 cup) into large bowl and set aside. Combine yeast and water and dissolve yeast. Make a well in the flour and add yeast, salt, sugar, and oil. Mix until all is dissolved, turn onto floured pastry board, and knead for 10 minutes. Gradually add reserve flour until dough is no longer sticky. Dough will be soft. Place in a greased bowl cover, and let rise for 1-1/2 hours. Punch down, cover, and let rise for 45 minutes.

Take a 12-inch circular or rectangular pizza pan or pie plate. Coat the bottom with a little olive oil or cornmeal. Place a ball of dough in the center of the pan and begin to stretch it until all the pan is covered. If you like thick pizza (Sicilian style) use more dough. If you like thin pizza, stretch paper thin and cut off remaining dough. Use the tips of your fingers to push the dough toward the edge of the pan.

Let dough rest for 20 minutes.

Sauce

Cut garlic into small pieces. Place a medium-size iron skillet over medium-high heat. Heat to hot. Add 1 T corn oil. When oil is warm, add garlic, salt, and pepper, and saute until garlic is brown. Press with a fork into tiny pieces. Add oregano.

Add tomatoes, rinse tomato can with broth or water and add to mixture. Reduce heat and simmer for 30 minutes, or until reduced.

While sauce is simmering, grate mozzarella into course pieces and Parmesan into fine pieces. Slice pepperoni thin or thick to taste. Set on pastry board in individual piles.

When pizza is rested, spoon on sauce to completely cover the dough. Top with shredded mozzarella cheese, sprinkle the Parmesan cheese over the mozzarella, and finally add the pepperoni.

Bake in 425-degree oven for 15 to 20 minutes or until done. The thicker the crust the longer it will take to bake.

Yield: 1 (12-inch) pizza.

Topping Combinations

Traditional Pizza. Any combination of sausage, pepperoni, anchovy fillets, chopped green peppers, sliced canned or fresh mushrooms, sliced black olives (Italian or Greek variety) added to the tomatoes and cheese.

Seafood Pizza. This is a cheeseless pizza. Bake the pizza shell for 10 minutes. Remove from oven. Top with pizza sauce. Select 6 pieces each of crab, shrimp (whole), scallops (whole), squid rings, and cod (cut into small pieces) and marinate for at least half an hour in 1 teaspoon olive oil, salt, pepper, and garlic chopped into small pieces. Stir 4 to 5 times. Drain. Arrange around pizza. Top with additional sauce (and cheese, if desired). Sprinkle with basil and oregano. Bake an additional 10 minutes or until seafood is done.

Vegetable Pizza. Top with tomato sauce and any combination of raw or cooked broccoli, cauliflower, zucchini, green peppers, mushrooms, onions, black olives, tomato slices, and marinated eggplant. You may add additional sauce (and cheese).

White Pizza
Pizza Bianca

Long before we made what is known as pizza, we made white pizza and so did most Italians. Our recipe includes cheese, but many variations did not.

dough:
2-1/2 to 3 cups flour
1/4 oz. quick rising dry yeast
1 cup warm water
1/2 tsp. salt
1 T granulated sugar
1/4 cup corn oil

1 tsp. olive oil or cornmeal

topping:
4 cloves chopped garlic
1-1/2 T chopped basil
6 oz. shredded mozzarella
4 oz. thinly sliced fontina cheese
1/4 cup freshly grated Parmesan cheese
1/2 tsp. pepper
2 T olive oil
Coarse salt

Sift flour into large bowl, reserving 1 cup, and set aside. Combine yeast and water and dissolve yeast. Make a well in the flour and add yeast, salt, sugar, and oil. Mix until all is dissolved, turn onto floured pastry board and knead for 10 minutes. Gradually add reserve flour until dough is no longer sticky. Dough will be soft. Place in a greased bowl, cover, and let rise for 1-1/2 hours. Punch down, cover, and let rise for 45 minutes.

Take a 12-inch circular or rectangular pizza pan or pie plate. Coat the bottom with a little olive oil or cornmeal. Place ball of dough in the center of the pan and begin to stretch it until all the pan is covered. If you like thick pizza (Sicilian style) use more dough. If you like thin pizza, stretch paper thin and cut off remaining dough. Use the tips of your fingers to push the dough toward the edge of the pan. Let dough rest for 20 minutes.

Peel and chop garlic and basil. Shred mozzarella. Slice fontina. Grate Parmesan.

Combine basil, pepper, garlic, and olive oil. Spread over stretched dough. Top with mozzarella, fontina cheese, and Parmesan cheese. Sprinkle with coarse salt.

Heat oven to 350 degrees. Bake pizza for 15 to 20 minutes or until cheese is bubbly and crust is brown around the edges.

Yield: 1 (12-inch) pizza.

Note: If you do not want to make pizza dough you can buy dough from bakeries, pizza shops, or in the frozen foods section of your super market.

Variation: Our original white pizza did not have cheese. Spread oil mixture over dough, add course salt and bake. We cannot make up our minds, so we often do half the pizza with cheese and half without.

Another choice is to use only Parmesan.

78

Desserts
Dolci

The Italian dessert is a delight. Cookies tend to be hard, equally at home dunked in good wine or cold fresh milk. Cakes are either rich and chewy, filled with nuts and candied fruit and laced with spices, or light and airy and layered with cream. And when one is sated with rich desserts out comes a medley of fresh fruits and cheeses to equal the most elaborate torte.

The hardness of some Italian desserts (like the cured meats) reaches back to Roman, and probably Etruscan, days, when storage was a problem. A hard cookie or cake lasted longer and could accompany a traveler, including an army, on difficult journeys.

Spicy Italian desserts had their birth in the Middle Ages when Venetian merchants first brought back spices from Africa, the Middle East, and Asia. As Italian cooks discovered the rich taste of these spices they used them abundantly, often combining half a dozen flavors in one delicious dish. *Cavallucci* and *panforte*, two of our favorites, are representative of this type of dessert.

One of the specialties of Tuscany is the chestnut. It is ground into flour, used in breads and polentas, chopped like a nut as a filling for sweets, boiled in milk, candied, dried, or roasted. The chestnut staved off famine in the Middle Ages, when in some Italian villages it was the only food available. In this century chestnuts did the same for Gino's family.

Chestnut flour *(farina dolce)* is not easy to find in the U.S. market and there is no good substitute. Look for it in specialty or gourmet shops. Not all people will like *castagnaccio*, the unusual chestnut cake blended with rosemary and pine nuts, but for those who do, it is a delicacy.

Citron is another Tuscan specialty used in desserts. Grown for its rind, which is then candied, it looks like a lemon, but is longer in shape. It can be found in candied form in Italian food stores and gourmet shops.

Candy
Caramelle

Almost every province in Italy has a candy making center like Perugia, in Umbria where a variety of sweets are made. Our favorite candy is *confetti*, a sugar-coated candy with an almond, licorice, or liquor center, which always appears at weddings. We never made *confetti*, but we do make another non-Tuscan treat, *torrone*, a chewy nougat that is a favorite at Christmas and Easter.

Italian Nougat
Torrone

Torrone has been a specialty at Christmas since it was first made in the town of Cremona in Lombardy (home of Stradavari violins) to celebrate a royal wedding in 1441. On that occasion is was shaped like the city bell tower.

3 T pistachio nuts
1/2 cup hazelnuts
2 cups almonds

2 cups water
1/3 cup honey
1 egg white
1/8 tsp. salt

1/2 cup granulated sugar
1 tsp. vanilla or orange extract
2 T water

2 sheets wafer paper (*ostie*)*

Peel and chop nuts into desired thickness. Set aside. Fill bottom of double boiler with water and place over medium heat. When water comes to a boil, place top of boiler over water and add honey. Stir constantly with spoon until honey forms a hard ball (265-270 degrees on candy thermometer).** Add salt to egg white, beat until stiff, and fold into honey.

Place small saucepan over medium-high heat. Add sugar, vanilla, and water. Stir constantly until it reaches crack (275-280 degrees on candy thermometer). Blend two mixtures into saucepan and continue stirring until thermometer reaches 280 degrees. Remove from heat, add nuts, and stir well.

Line the bottom of a loaf pan or an ice cube tray with a layer of paper thin wafers (*ostie*). Pour mixture into pan, smooth out top, and cover with additional wafer paper. Press down with palm of hand until firm and smooth. Allow to cool.

Once cool, remove from pan and cut into 1-1/2-inch-by-2-1/2-inch rectangles. Wrap each in foil. Store in a covered jar in a cool place.

Yield: 10-12.

Notes: *Ostie* are wafer-thin sheets of edible paper found in confectioners' stores.

**If you do not have a candy thermometer, test nougat with cold water. Drop a pinch of nougat into cold water. If it forms hard ball, proceed.

Cakes
Torte

Light and airy or hard and spicy, Nonna always had a delicious cake on hand for holidays. They are all favorites, but each belonged to a special season and appeared only at that time. Like most of our foods, the ingredients were not available year round and each season dictated what was to appear at our table.

Today, availability is not a problem, but we still make each cake or treat on its special day.

Chestnut Cake with Rosemary and Pine Nuts
Castagnaccio

Castagnaccio is a Florentine specialty sold by street vendors in the autumn when chestnuts are in season. Its origin has been lost, but its unusual blending of chestnuts, pine nuts, and rosemary creates a sweet and tangy taste. The chestnut is sweet enough without adding sugar, but the flavor of this cake is definitely an acquired taste.

2 T white raisins
1/4 cup water

1-1/2 cups chestnut flour
1/4 tsp. salt
2 T corn oil
1 cup water

2 T pine nuts
1 tsp. rosemary

Place raisins in 1/4 cup water and allow to soften for at least half an hour. Drain and set aside.

In a mixing bowl combine flour, salt, corn oil, 1 cup water, and raisins. Mix until smooth and pour into a well-oiled 8-to-9-inch pie pan.

Sprinkle the top with pine nuts and rosemary and bake at 350 degrees for 45 minutes, or until the top begins to crack.

Yield: 1 (9-inch round, 1-inch-high) cake.

Notes: Chestnut flour is already sweet, but for a sweeter cake add 1 tablespoon of sugar.

Chestnut flour is sometimes available in gourmet and health food stores.

Medieval Fruitcake
Panforte

Of all Italian desserts, this rich, chewy cake filled with spices, candied fruit, and nuts, is the epitome of things Tuscan. Its origin is obscure: it may have come from the kitchens of Sienese monks. But we do know it accompanied medieval knights on crusade.

Panforte (strong or pungent bread) is a specialty of the Tuscan city of Siena where each baker has guarded the ingredients, especially the spices, for centuries. It is the best and most famous torte of Italy and is shipped all over the world, especially at Christmas. In our family it is a must at Christmas, served at the end of the meal along with coffee and the fruitcake on the next page.

1 cup hazelnuts
1 cup almonds
1-1/4 cups candied fruit
1 tsp. candied lemon peel
2/3 cup flour
1 T cocoa
1 tsp. cinnamon
1/4 tsp. coriander
1/4 tsp. cloves
1/4 tsp. nutmeg
1/8 tsp. white pepper
1/2 tsp. vanilla

1/3 cup granulated sugar
1/2 cup honey

Confectioners' sugar
1 parchment sheet (optional)

Spread hazelnuts and peeled whole almonds on separate cookie sheets. Toast at 350 degrees for 5 to 6 minutes. Remove, rub hazelnuts in a towel, removing skins. Chop nuts in half (can remain whole). Chop candied fruit and lemon peel into chunky pieces. Combine all in a large bowl and add flour, cocoa, cinnamon, coriander, cloves, nutmeg, pepper, and vanilla. Toss.

Grease bottom of 9-inch springform pan and line with parchment paper (optional). Grease paper.

Place sugar and honey in saucepan and heat to 242 degrees (use a candy thermometer) until it becomes a clear syrup. If it bubbles, remove from heat and stir until bubbles subside. Pour over fruit-nut mixture, stir, pour into springform pan. Smooth top with a floured spatula.

Heat oven to 300 degrees, bake 35 minutes. Remove sides of pan. Allow to cool 1 hour. Add enough confectioners' sugar to make it pure white. Press down firmly. Allow to cool another hour.

Turn upsidedown (will be soft at this point). Remove parchment paper and bottom of springform pan and cover second side with confectioners' sugar (if pan resists, run a dull knife between it and the cake). Allow to set another hour. Wrap in plastic and store for 1 month before eating (most of the time we cannot wait and eat it the next day).

Serves: 10-12.

Notes: Can be stored in freezer. You may wish to make small cakes and hang them from the Christmas tree, or simply give them as presents, just as they did in 16th century Tuscany.

Fruit and Nut Cake
Torta di Frutta Candita e Noci

I almost gave up hope when trying to find if Nonna's fruitcake was truly Italian. I could find no equivalent until I presented it as a gift to one of the translators. His eyes lit up in recognition.

Fruitcake took a month to make, and added to the anticipation of Christmas. Shelling and chopping nuts was a family affair. After dinner each evening we would sit at the kitchen table and eat more nuts than we chopped.

1 pound almonds
1 pound Brazil nuts
1 pound walnuts
1 pound hazelnuts
1 pound dates
1/2 pound red candied cherries
1/2 pound candied pineapple
2 pounds mixed candied fruit
6 T flour

4 cups flour
1 tsp. salt
1 tsp. cloves
1 tsp. nutmeg
2 tsp. cinnamon
1-1/2 cups butter
2-1/4 cups brown sugar
6 eggs
2 tsp. vanilla

1/2 cup molasses
2-1/2 tsp. baking soda
2 shots whisky or rum

1-2 cups strong black coffee

Shell and chop nuts into large chunks. Blanch almonds in hot water, remove skins, cut lengthwise. Cut Brazil nuts, walnuts, and hazelnuts sideways. Set aside. Cut dates in thirds, cherries in half, pineapple slices in eighths. Add candied fruit and combine all in a large bowl or pot. Add enough flour to coat and keep from sticking together (4 to 6 tablespoons). Set aside (may be stored covered for several days).

Sift flour, salt, cloves, nutmeg, and cinnamon together. Set aside. Cream butter on medium speed, slowly add sugar; cream. When well mixed add eggs, one at a time, then vanilla.

In separate bowl combine molasses with baking soda. Stir. When bubbly alternately add it and sifted ingredients to the butter mixture. Mix. Add whisky or rum. Remove from mixer and add to dry ingredients in a large bowl or pot. Mix with your hands. Use enough strong coffee to wash out the mixing bowl (1 to 1-1/2 cups), and add to the combined batter. The consistency should be very thick.

You will need 4 to 6 baking pans depending on size. Put similar sizes into oven together. Line all pans with wax paper. Fill each to 1 inch from top. Push exposed fruit and nuts into batter. Rinse empty bowl with more coffee and pour onto panned cakes covering the top evenly. Trim excess wax paper.

Bake in 300-degree oven for 1-1/2 to 2 hours. When cool, de-pan and remove wax paper. Allow to set for a day. Wrap in foil. Store in cupboard or freezer. Two days before serving remove, unwrap, and cover with a cloth saturated with rum or whisky.

Yield: 4-6 cakes.

Sponge Cake
Pane di Spagna

As its name implies, *pane di Spagna* came to Italy from Spain, arriving with the Spanish conquest of Italy in 1412. On holidays the women of Quarata still take turns beating an enormous *pane di Spagna* by hand (including the egg whites), quickly passing the bowl so as not to miss a beat.

When Nonna was in her 80s, she played cards once a week with her friends. Along with the ice cream and coffee, a *pane di Spagna* was always served. *Pane di Spagna* was a ritual in the Pelini home, too. Whenever someone was not feeling well, Sandrina would whip up this pleasing cake. This is her recipe.

6 egg yolks
1/2 cup water
1/4 cup corn oil
1-1/2 cups granulated
sugar
1/2 tsp. almond extract
1/2 tsp. lemon extract
1 tsp. vanilla
1/2 tsp. salt
1-1/2 cups sifted cake
flour

6 egg whites
3/4 tsp. cream of tartar
Confectioners' sugar

In a large bowl separate yolks from whites. Beat yolks for 10 minutes until they become lemon colored. Slowly add water and oil, and beat until thick, 20 minutes. Add sugar a little at a time. Add all extracts. Combine salt with flour, mix, and slowly add to batter. When well mixed remove from mixer.

Place egg whites in a large bowl and beat slightly with mixer. Add the cream of tartar and continue to beat until stiff. With a large spoon fold beaten egg whites into batter.

Preheat oven to 325 degrees. Pour batter into ungreased tube pan and bake 1 hour or until golden (see note). Remove from oven and invert, placing hollow of tube pan over a bottle. Allow to stand until cool. Remove from pan and dust with confectioners' sugar.

Serves: 6-8.

6 large eggs, separated
1/4 cup cold water
1 tsp. vanilla
1 tsp. almond or
lemon extract
1 cup cake flour
1-1/4 cups granulated
sugar, divided
1/2 tsp. salt
1/2 tsp. baking powder
1/2 tsp. cream of tartar

Variation: Every kitchen had a slight variation of the traditional *pane di Spagna*. My Nonna's and ultimately my mother's recipe varied from the Pelini recipe slightly.

No vegetable oil was used. Beat yolks, cold water, vanilla, almond or lemon extract until lemony.

Sift flour. Combine with 1 cup sugar, salt, baking powder. Add to yolk mixture little at a time.

Combine cream of tartar with egg whites, beat slowly adding remaining sugar. Fold batter into whites. Bake at 325 degrees for 50 to 60 minutes.

Note: *For 60 years we baked this cake for one hour. In our new stove it bakes in 45 minutes.

Sponge Cake with Cream
Zuccotto

Finally, the queen of Tuscan cakes in our home, *zuccotto*. The first time I ate this cake was in my *Zia Ada's* home in Italy where it was made with *mascarpone* cheese. We did not have *mascarpone*, so we used whipping cream.

Zuccotto, named for pumpkin squash, or *zucco*, is also said to resemble the orange-colored cupola of *Il Duomo*, the famous Florentine cathedral.

1 *pane di Spagna*
7 oz. semisweet chocolate
2 cups whipping cream, or 6 cups *mascarpone* cheese
3/4 cup confectioners' sugar
1 cup chopped hazelnuts
1 cup chopped almonds
8-10 maraschino cherries

1 T cocoa
3 T confectioners' sugar

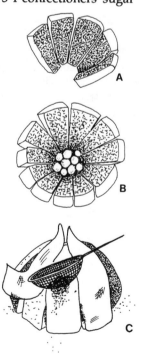

Prepare a sponge cake according to recipe on page 84. Divide chocolate in half. Place half in double boiler and melt until smooth, stirring occasionally. Allow to cool. Grate remainder into slivers.

Place whipping cream (or cheese) in a blender and whip. Once cream peaks, slowly add confectioners' sugar and continue to blend. Divide into two portions. Into first half fold melted chocolate and hazelnuts. Into second, almonds and chopped chocolate. One half should be dark, the other white.

Select a 7-to-8-inch deep bowl that is narrow at bottom, wide at top, and 6-to-8-inches deep. Line with wax paper.

Cut sponge cake into 10 to 11 oblong pieces (1-1/2-inches wide, 4 to 5 inches long) resembling ladyfingers (you can substitute ladyfingers for the sponge cake if you desire).

Place cherry juice in a wide-mouthed bowl. Dip each cake finger into juice, abundantly wetting one side.

Place each piece of sponge cake into wax-paper-lined bowl vertically (see A), lining entire perimeter, with saturated side facing inside of bowl.

Place 8 to 10 cherries in bottom of the bowl (enough to fill the hole, see B). Top with the almond mixture, then hazelnut mixture. The bowl should be full. Cover with foil and chill for several hours.

Remove from refrigerator, turn upsidedown on a serving platter, and remove bowl (slips out easily). Remove wax paper. Place a strip of foil on either side of a finger of sponge cake. Sprinkle cocoa through a sieve on uncovered finger (see C). Skip next finger and repeat, alternating coatings around cake. Once cocoa is completed, repeat with confectioners' sugar.

Serves: 6-8.

Cookies
Biscotti

You cannot "eat just one" of these delicious Italian cookies. They are all chewy and dunkable, and absolutely delicious. The *cavallucci* are intentionally hard, made to last a long time.

Almond Cookies
Ricciarelli

A specialty of Siena, *ricciarelli* are made of almond paste and have a chewy marzipan flavor. They were originally a Christmas cookie, but we serve them all year long. You will, too, once you taste the rich flavor and see how easy and quick they are to prepare.

1-1/2 cups almonds
3 cups almond paste
3 egg whites
3/4 tsp. baking powder
2 tsp. vanilla
Confectioners' sugar
Flour as needed

Place small pot over medium-high heat and add water. Heat to boiling. Pour over almonds. Cover and allow to set for 20 minutes; peel almonds. Allow almonds to dry and then grind in a meat grinder or food processor until powdery.

Combine almonds with almond paste. Mix by hand, add egg whites (do not beat whites); mix by hand until soft. Add baking powder, vanilla, and mix by hand. Dough should be firm and a bit sticky.

Sprinkle a little flour on a pastry board. Add dough. Divide dough into 4 to 5 batches. Roll out each batch until 1-inch thick. Cut with a floured knife into 1-1/2-inch rounds. Roll in confectioners' sugar (if dough is too sticky, flour your hands to roll out).

Lay each piece flat and flatten with hand to half the thickness. You can press a whole, peeled almond into the center of each cookie if you wish.

Place on slightly greased cookie sheet and let stand at least 2 hours, but preferably overnight.

Heat oven to 300 degrees and bake for 20 to 25 minutes or until beige. Do not allow to brown. Cookie should be chewy, not crunchy.

Yield: 3-4 dozen.

Notes: It is important to cut cookies into 1-1/2-inch pieces or the baking time will be too long and the cookie will be hard instead of chewy.
Can be frozen.

Anise Cookies
Biscotti all'Anice

Anise cookies are traditionally served at Italian weddings where they are arranged on silver trays, their pastel icing of yellow, blue, pink, or green gleaming enticingly.

8 cups flour
2 cups granulated sugar
1 heaping T baking powder
1-1/2 cups shortening
3 tsp. anise seeds

12 large eggs
3 T vanilla or lemon extract

icing:
2 egg whites
1 box confectioners' sugar
1 tsp. vanilla or lemon extract
Dash milk (optional)

Red, green, blue, and yellow food colorings

In a medium-size bowl sift together the flour, sugar and baking powder. With a pastry cutter (*mezza luna*), cut in shortening and anise seeds until the consistency of pie dough (there is no liquid in this cookie so the texture is dependent on the proper amount of shortening, be generous).

In a mixing bowl blend eggs and vanilla or lemon extract. Add egg mixture to the dough. Mix with hands into a tender, but not sticky, dough. Add more flour if necessary.

Remove from bowl and place on pastry board. Dust hands with flour. Pinch off piece of dough and roll into ball. Place balls on ungreased baking sheet that has been dusted with flour. Fill sheet and bake 10 to 15 minutes at 375 degrees or until lightly brown. Repeat until all dough is used. Allow to cool and ice.

Make icing by beating egg whites with confectioners' sugar, vanilla or lemon extract. If too thick, add a little milk to soften. Divide into 3 or 4 bowls. Add scant drop of the different food colorings to individual bowls (too much and icing will be too dark). Mix well. When cookies are cool, place a dab of icing on each cookie and spread with a spatula.

Yield: 10-12 dozen.

Note: This cookie can be frozen.

6 eggs
2/3 cup corn oil
1 T lemon or anise extract
1 cup granulated sugar
2 cups flour
3 T baking powder
Pinch salt

Variation: The Pelini *biscotti* are slightly different. Beat eggs, add oil and extract. Continue to beat, add sugar gradually, then flour, baking powder, salt. Dough will be soft. Heat oven to 350 degrees. Drop teaspoonfuls of cookie mixture onto greased sheet. Bake 10 to 12 minutes. Cool and ice.

Yield: 7-8 dozen.

Biscotti

Biscotti are the most popular Italian cookies. In fact, the name *biscotti* is often used for any type of cookie. *Biscotti* are dipped in coffee for breakfast, in wine at the end of the meal, and are served on all holidays. No Italian wedding is complete without a mound of *biscotti* waiting to be served. Children love them dunked in milk. *Biscotti* are cooked twice, *bis cotto*, so they can be stored, almost forever. To Gino a meal was never complete without 2 or 3 *biscotti* and he always reminded Sandrina when the store ran low.

The first time I made *biscotti* Nonna was well into her 80s. One day when we were home alone she said, "I think I'll make *biscotti* today." Then she proceeded to say, "Get this, get that. Sift the flour, grate the lemon, etc." By the time we were finished I made the cookies; she sat at the kitchen table giving instructions. I think it was her way of teaching me how to make them.

4 tsp. baking powder
1/2 tsp. salt
4 cups flour, sifted

2/3 cup shortening
6 eggs
2 cups granulated sugar
Grated rind of one lemon
2 tsp. vanilla
Juice of one lemon
2 tsp. lemon extract

2/3 cup pine nuts or
chopped toasted almonds

topping:
3 egg yolks
3 T granulated sugar

In a small bowl combine baking powder, salt, and sifted flour. Set aside. In another bowl, cream shortening, add eggs one at a time alternating with sugar. Allow to blend. Add lemon rind, vanilla, lemon juice and extract. Blend well. Add nuts and dry ingredients. Blend.

When dough is firm, but soft, turn onto floured board. Knead. If dough is too sticky add additional flour, up to 1/4 cup, until firm. Knead for 20 minutes. Cut dough into four pieces. Form each piece into a 12-inch-by-3-to-4-inch loaf which is higher in the center and tapered at the sides. Length is not important. Place on a greased cookie sheet.

Bake at 375 degrees for 20 minutes or until light brown. Remove from oven. Let sit for a few minutes. Combine yolks and sugar and brush top of each loaf. Cut into 1-inch thick cookies. Lay each cookie on its side on cookie sheet. Return to oven, toast until light brown on each side.

Yield: 15 cookies per loaf, or 60 cookies.

Note: The Pelini variation includes 6 tsp. baking powder, 5 cups flour, 1-1/2 sticks margarine (replacing shortening), 1-3/4 cups granulated sugar, no lemon rind or lemon juice, no pine nuts, but toasted almonds. Bake at 350 degrees for 30 minutes. The remaining ingredients are the same and so is the process.

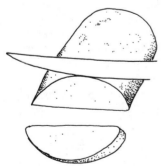

Bows
Fiocchi

The shape determines the name of this tasty fried cookie made especially for carnival in northern Italy. Called *bugie* (little lies) in Piedmont, *chiacchiere* (gossips) in Lombardy, and *lattughe* (lettuce) in Emilia-Romagna, they have three different names in Tuscany: *cenci* (rags), *guanti* (gloves), and *fiocchi*, (bows).

We serve *fiocchi* on *Martedi Grasso* (Shrove Tuesday) ending a meal of homemade pasta, pork chops on a spit, and endive salad with celery.

4 eggs
6 T granulated sugar

4 cups sifted flour
1 tsp. baking powder
3 T corn oil
1 shot whisky
1 tsp. lemon extract
1 tsp. vanilla

1 cup corn oil
4-5 T confectioners' sugar

Beat eggs and sugar in a large bowl until lemon yellow in color. Gradually add flour (reserve 1/4 cup), baking powder, oil, whisky, extract, and vanilla, mixing until blended and manageable (not sticky). Turn onto a floured board and knead into a very soft dough for about 20 minutes, adding remaining flour as needed. Form into a ball, cover with a small bowl, and set to rest for half an hour.

Break dough into 6 pieces and work 1 piece at a time. Roll the piece out gently to the thickness of pie crust (if using a pasta machine roll to #4 thickness-- see note). Cut into 1-inch-by-6-inch strips. Place each strip flat on the board. Cut a 2-inch slit (see A). Bring the bottom of the strip up and through the slit (see B). Place on clean piece of cloth. Do not stack.

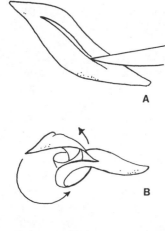

Place a large skillet on high heat and fill with corn oil. Bring to high heat for *fiocchi* must fry quickly. When hot, drop the *fiocchi* into the fat one at a time. Do not crowd (see C). They will puff up immediately and increase slightly in size. Fry to a golden color (about 30 seconds on each side -- see note). Turn only once. Remove and lay on paper towel. When slightly cooled, sprinkle with confectioners' sugar.

Yield: 7 dozen.

Variation: In the Pelini version the procedure is the same, but the ingredients are: 3 cups flour, 4 eggs, 2 tsp. baking powder, 1 T corn oil, 2 tsp. lemon extract. Cut into strips. Now tie the dough into a bow, just as you would a ribbon. Fry as above.

Notes: If rolled finer than #4, fiocchi are fluffier. If they fry too fast, lower heat.

A

B

C

89

Brigidini

Almost every European ethnic kitchen has some variation of this sweet waffle (see C). Also known as *gallets*, *brigidini* were first made in Italy in the convent of Saint Brigida in Pistoia. They are made with a waffle iron. Our original iron was created in the foundry of the local steel mill and we used it for decades. Cooking was a long process as dozens and dozens of *brigidini* were made in a single evening and once the iron was hot, it was non-stop until the last bit of batter was gone. Today, we use an electric iron.

3 eggs
3/4 cup granulated sugar
3/4 cup melted butter
1 tsp. vanilla
1-1/4 cups flour
1 tsp. baking powder
1 dash salt

Beat eggs in a large bowl. Add sugar a little at a time. When eggs and sugar have been blended, add melted butter and vanilla, then flour. Beat by hand until smooth. Add baking powder and a pinch of salt. Mix well. Dough is not firm, but runny.

Chill dough 2 hours or overnight to enrich flavor. To use, dough must be at room temperature.

A

Using a hand iron: Clean iron (see A) and grease slightly with butter or corn oil. Heat burner on stove to high. Place 1 teaspoon of mixture in center of warm iron. Close lid and secure. If batter spills over side clean it off. Place iron over heat for 25 to 30 seconds. Turn. Cook other side for additional 25 to 30 seconds. Open iron and remove waffle. It should be golden brown. The amount of time needed to cook each waffle may vary with type of iron.

B

Using an electric iron: An electric iron (see B) is easier because it makes 2 or 4 waffles at the same time. Each type of iron varies slightly, but the procedure is the same. Add 1 teaspoon of batter to the center of each rosette, close the lid, and allow to cook for about 1 minute. Electric irons do both sides at the same time.

Yield: 5-6 dozen.

C

Variations: The Pelini version of this cookie substitutes 1/2 cup corn oil for butter, 2 tsp. lemon for vanilla and uses only 1-1/2 cups flour and no baking powder.
Anise flavored: Add 1 T anise seeds.
Chocolate flavored: Omit anise, add 1/4 cup cocoa or 1/2 square melted semisweet chocolate, 1 tsp. vanilla.

90

Italian Macaroons
Amaretti

A sure bet to be on the table during holiday seasons, *amaretti* are a tangy, crisp, bitter (*amaro*) almond-flavored cookie. The original *amaretti* cookie contains bitter almonds which are illegal in the United States because they contain lethal prussic acid when raw and are considered toxic (the acid disappears once the pit is heated). American recipes substitute peach or apricot pits that have been blanched and toasted in a 250-degree oven for 10 minutes, or until pale gold. Peach and apricot pits also contain prussic acid, which is also destroyed by heating, but they are legal in the United States.

1 full cup almonds
3 T bitter apricot pits
or 1 tsp. almond extract
3/4 cup confectioners' sugar
1 tsp. flour

2 egg whites
1/3 cup granulated sugar

Place a small pot over medium-high heat and add water. Heat to boiling. Pour over almonds. Allow to set for 20 minutes, then peel almonds. Repeat for apricot pits. Allow both to dry and then grind in a meat grinder or in a food processor until powdery. Add confectioners' sugar and flour to nuts.

Beat egg whites until soft peaks form and add the sugar a little at a time until stiff. Fold nuts into mixture. If substituting almond extract, add it now.

Spoon into a pastry bag with a plain 1/2-inch tip. Squeeze 1-1/2-inch mounds onto a greased cookie sheet. If you do not have a pastry bag, shape cookies into patties 1-1/2 inches wide and 1/4 inch thick. Sprinkle with granulated sugar and let stand for 2 hours.

Heat oven to 400 degrees. Bake 10 to 15 minutes until light brown.

Turn off oven and allow cookies to dry for additional 20 minutes. Enjoy.

Yield: 30-36 cookies.

Little Horses
Cavallucci

Cavallucci are a special Christmas cookie filled with spices. Known in Italy since medieval times, they are named after *cavallari*, horse drivers, who ate them in copious quantities at *osterie*, or country inns. The best way to eat these wonderful hard, hard biscuits is to soak them in coffee or milk or a good glass of *vin santo*.

Cavallucci are served on All Saints' Day and Christmas. For years at Christmas the Pelini family received a holiday package from Italy. Among the precious cargo was a handful of *cavallucci*. Each child got one cookie and sucked on it all day. Their father Gino said, "*Cavallucci* sharpen the teeth."

1 cup water
1-1/4 cups granulated sugar

1/2 cup candied orange peel
1/2 cup walnuts
1 tsp. anise
1 tsp. coriander
1/2 tsp. baking powder
1/2 tsp. cinnamon
1/2 tsp. ground cloves
Dash white pepper
2-1/2 cups flour

Place a medium-size pot over medium-high heat. Add water and sugar and stir. Bring to a boil and remove from stove (sugar should be dissolved). Add all other ingredients except flour in exact order. Water will froth up when baking powder is added. Stir for 30 to 40 seconds. Then add flour.

Allow to cool for at least 15 minutes and turn onto a floured pastry board. Dough should be heavy and sticky.

With floured knife cut dough into quarters. With floured hands roll each piece on pastry board into an inch-thick rope. Cut into 2-inch pieces with a floured knife (if you make the cookie smaller the baking time will be incorrect). Turn each cookie and flatten, leaving a thumb print. Continue until all dough is gone.

Heat oven to 350 degrees. Place cookies on a greased cookie sheet and bake for 25 minutes. Do not allow to brown. They will come out soft, but harden quickly.

Yield: 3 dozen.

Notes: This is a hard cookie. It can be frozen.

Ices and Frozen Desserts
Freddi e Semifreddi

Half Cold
Semifreddo

In 1956 Gigi and Quintina Pitti, Sandrina's brother and his wife, came from Italy to live with the Pelini family. Quintina brought this recipe with her.

Semifreddo is an elegant dessert with an exotic and wonderful taste. It can be made ahead and kept in the freezer.

2 eggs
1/2 pound butter
1-1/8 cups granulated sugar

1/2 cup strong coffee, divided
1/2 cup *Marsala*,* divided

24 ladyfingers
1 oz. grated chocolate
5 oz. slivered almonds

Separate eggs and beat whites until stiff. Set aside. Cream butter and sugar until creamy. Add yolks and continue beating.

Add 1/4 cup each of coffee and *Marsala*, a few drops at a time. When well mixed fold in egg whites.

Place remaining *Marsala* and coffee in shallow bowl. Lightly dip each ladyfinger, dampening the bottom.

Place 12 dampened ladyfingers on a flat oval platter to form a single layer (be sure you can freeze the platter). Cover with 1/2 of the egg mixture. Top with half of grated chocolate and almonds. Top with remaining dampened ladyfingers. Repeat toppings.

Set 10 minutes, cover with plastic wrap, and freeze overnight. Serve frozen.

Serves: 6-8.

Notes: *Marsala* is an Italian cooking wine found in supermarkets and liquor stores. The latter variety is better for this dish.

Coffee should be at room temperature.

Sponge cake can be substituted for ladyfingers. Cut cake into 5-by-1-by-1-inch pieces.

Pies
Crostate

Foolproof Pie Crust
Crostate per Torte

4 cups flour
1 T granulated sugar
2 tsp. salt

1 egg
1-3/4 cups shortening
1 T vinegar
1/2 cup water

In a medium-size mixing bowl combine flour, sugar, and salt. Mix with fork until well blended. In separate bowl beat egg, shortening, vinegar, and water. Combine, stirring with a fork until blended.

Divide into 6 even balls and chill at least 15 minutes. Roll out for pie or freeze for later. To freeze lay the balls on a cookie sheet and flatten like a hamburger. When frozen store in a baggie up to 6 months.

Yield: 3 double-crust shells or 6 single-crust shells.

Apple Pie
Torta di Mele

2 balls of foolproof pie crust
3 T flour, divided
6-8 Granny Smith apples
1/3 cup granulated sugar
2/3 cup brown sugar
Juice 1 lemon
1/4 pound butter

2 T milk
1 T granulated sugar

Place ball of dough (see preceding recipe) on pastry cloth, dust with flour, and roll to fit pie pan (we use a 9-1/2-inch pyrex). Once rolled, fold in half, and lift into pie pan. Sprinkle with tablespoon flour.

Peel apples. Cut into quarters, core, and slice each quarter into 5 to 6 pieces. Lay slices on dough. When half full sprinkle half the sugars and lemon juice over apples. Dot with half the butter and a little flour. Continue until apples rise over the top. Add remaining sugars, lemon juice, butter and flour.

Roll out second ball of dough. Fold in half and cut 6 short slits along folded end to allow steam to escape while cooking. Lift and lay over half of pie plate. Open fold to completely cover pie and press edges together with fingers. Trim excess dough from both top and bottom crusts. Once sealed, press edges with thumb to form ridges. Combine milk and a little sugar and sprinkle over top of pie to form a glaze while baking.

Heat the oven to 425 degrees. Bake pie for 15 minutes. Reduce heat to 350 degrees and bake an additional 45 minutes, or until crust is golden.

Serves: 6-8.

Cream Pie
Torta di Crema

This was Nonno's favorite pie. Along with *panforte, torrone,* and *amaretti,* it graced every holiday table (and half the Sundays in between). After Nonno died we never served it again. My mother just could not make it.

1 ball foolproof pie crust
1 T flour

filling:
1 quart and 1/2 cup cold milk
3 eggs
1/2 cup cornstarch
1 cup granulated sugar
1 tsp. salt

2 T butter
2 tsp. vanilla

meringue:
8 T granulated sugar, divided
1 T cornstarch
1/2 cup water
1/2 tsp. vanilla

3 egg whites
Very small pinch salt

Place dough ball (see recipe on page 94) on pastry cloth sprinkled with flour and roll out pie crust to fit your pie pan (we use a 9-1/2-inch pyrex). If pie pan is 9 1/2 inches roll dough to 12 1/2 inches to allow it to go up the sides of the pie pan. Once rolled, fold in half, and lift into pie pan. Trim off any excess dough and press down around the top of the pie pan to form a ridge. Pierce the pie dough 5 or 6 times with the prongs of a fork. Bake in 350-degree oven until slightly brown.* Remove and set aside.

Place a 4-quart saucepan over medium-high heat. Add milk. Separate the eggs, setting the whites aside. In a small mixing bowl add yolks, cornstarch, sugar, and salt and beat together slowly.

When milk on stove begins to scald (bubble around the edges) slowly add yolk mixture. Stirring constantly with a spoon, simmer for 10 to 15 minutes or until it thickens to a pudding consistency. Remove from burner and add butter and vanilla. Mix with a wooden spoon and pour into baked pie shell.

To make the meringue, combine 2 table-spoons sugar, cornstarch, and water in a small saucepan. Cook over medium-high heat, stirring constantly, until thick and glossy. Remove from stove, add the vanilla, and set aside to cool.

Place egg whites in a mixing bowl and add a few grains of salt. Beat at high speed for a few minutes or until peaks begin to form. Add remaining sugar 1 tablespoon at a time, alternating with cooled cornstarch mixture (also a spoonful at a time). Continue to beat until stiff.

Pile meringue high on pie and bake in 325-degree oven until browned to your taste.

Serves: 6-8.

Note: *Pie shell may shrink while baking. We place a smaller, empty pie plate over the shell while baking.

Puddings
Budini

Cream Pudding
Budino di Crema

This wonderful cream pudding filled with sponge cake and maraschino cherries is another of Nonno's favorite desserts. It is probably a version of *Zuppa Inglese*, recipe follows, for the dish has a number of variations. We never called it that, but it is always a hit when we serve it to guests.

4 egg yolks
9 T granulated sugar
4 T flour
4 T cornstarch
1 quart cold milk

1 tsp. vanilla
1 oz. butter

12 oz. pound or sponge cake
10 oz. maraschino cherries and juice

Beat egg yolks in small mixing bowl. Add sugar and continue beating. Meanwhile mix flour, cornstarch and milk together. Pass milk mixture through a strainer into yolks.

Place in medium-size saucepan and cook over medium-high heat stirring constantly until it boils (about 10 minutes). Lower heat and continue to simmer for 20 minutes or until it thickens. Stir constantly. Remove from heat, add vanilla and butter. Stir.

Slice cake into 1-inch slices. Line bottom of deep casserole with half of cake. Sprinkle each piece with a little cherry juice. Spoon in enough pudding to generously cover. Top with half of cherries. Lay in remaining slices of cake. Add cherry juice. Spoon on remaining cream. Top with cherries and remaining juice.

Eat hot or cold. Store in refrigerator.

Serves: 8.

Note: This recipe and the one for cream pie on page 95 are Nonna's recipes. The Pelini family made their cream as in the recipe on page 97. All recipes are interchangeable.

English Cream
Zuppa Inglese

Originally called *zuppa del Duca*, the Duke's soup, this rich dessert from Siena became *zuppa Inglese* because English residents in Tuscany enjoyed it so much.

Recently it has enjoyed a resurgence in Italy under the name *tiramisu*, "pick me up," a modern variant which includes *mascarpone* cheese.

4 egg yolks
9 T granulated sugar
4 T flour
4 T cornstarch
1 quart cold milk

1 tsp. vanilla or liqueur
of your choice
1 oz. butter

6-8 biscotti
or ladyfingers
Whisky or liqueur
to taste

Beat egg yolks in small mixing bowl. Add sugar and continue beating. Meanwhile mix flour, cornstarch, and milk together. Pass milk mixture through a strainer into yolks.

Place in medium-size saucepan and bring to a boil over medium-high heat stirring constantly until it boils (about 10 minutes). Lower the heat and continue to simmer for 20 minutes, or until it thickens. Stir constantly with a wooden spoon. Remove from heat, add vanilla or liqueur and butter. Stir.

Place *biscotti* or ladyfingers on a large platter. Sprinkle cookies with whisky or liqueurs. Slowly spoon cream over all and let cool.

Serve hot or cold. Store in refrigerator.

Serves 6.

Note: Some recipes for *zuppa Inglese* are reminiscent of English Trifle--layers of cream, cake, fruit, jello with whipped cream. We never made it that way.

Fresh Fruits, Nuts, and Cheeses
Frutta Fresca, Noci, e Formaggi

Fresh fruits, mixed nuts, and cheeses are a favorite way to end an Italian meal. Even when a rich dessert is served, this mixed medley follows. A glass bowl filled with an assortment of fruit, a wooden bowl with a variety of unshelled nuts, and a platter of assorted cheeses are placed on the table. The bread and the wine are already there. Today this is called a wine and cheese party.

2 apples
2 pears
Red & green grapes
1 wedge each of
Parmesan, Gorgonzola,
Gorgonzola con mascarpone, fontina
Assortment of Brazil nuts, walnuts, almonds, hazelnuts
1 loaf Italian bread
1 bottle dry red wine
1 bottle dry white wine or *vin santo*

Arrange apples, pears, and grapes in a fruit bowl. Arrange cheeses on a cheese board, each with its own small knife. Pile nuts into a wooden bowl, complete with nutcracker and picks. Place bread on bread board with knife. Place all on table along with bottles of wine. You will talk for hours while you pick and eat.

Serves: The various quantities depend on the number of guests. Prepare the cheese and nuts in equal proportions: pound for pound.

Note: This is good eating, especially when the tastes mingle in the mouth. As a child I would take one bite of an apple or pear, one bite of Parmesan cheese, and one bite of the bread, then chew.

Fresh Peaches with Red Wine
Pesca con Vino Rosso

When the peaches are ripe, the mouth waters in anticipation of this delicious concoction. Today, peaches tend to be hard, so we have a standing order at our local fruit store to buy the old, bruised, soft peaches.

1 very ripe peach
6 oz. dry red wine

Peel outer skin. Discard any dark or bruised parts. Cut peach in half. Remove stone. Cut into small wedges.

Place in a wine glass or deep crystal bowl. Add wine. Refrigerate for 1 to 2 hours or overnight. Serve cold.

Serves: 1.

Roasted Chestnuts
Castagne al Forno

Roasted chestnuts were a November favorite in our home, always accompanied by the first taste of the new red wine.

1-2 pounds chestnuts

Cut a crosswise slit on the flat side of each chestnut to vent. Place chestnuts on a cookie sheet and bake in the oven at 350 degrees.

Open the oven occasionally and, with a long-handled wooden spoon, rotate the chestnuts. Bake for 30 minutes (see note).

Remove chestnuts from oven. Place on a good-size clean cloth and fold the edges to cover the chestnuts. Press down on the cloth with your palm to crush the chestnuts. Allow to stand about 5 to 6 minutes. Remove. Skin and serve with dry red wine.

To microwave chestnuts prepare in the same manner. For 5 chestnuts zap for 60 seconds on High power. For 10 chestnuts zap for 2 minutes. Remove, cover, and let set for 3 minutes. Proceed as above.

Serves: 5-6.

Notes: To test, remove a chestnut from the oven and place it in a clean white cloth. Cover, and with the palm of your hand press down on the chestnut. If it crushes easily, it is done.

In every dozen chestnuts there is at least one that has mildewed, rotted, or gone bad. A good chestnut is firm, chewy, and pale yellow.

Notes

Fish and Game
Pesce e Cacciagione

When I would curl up on my Nonno's lap and beg for stories about Italy as ardently as I begged for a puff on his pipe, his stories always included the fish in the sea. The closer our imaginary boat got to Italy's golden shores, the bigger the fish. To my young mind they were all goldfish, each as big as a whale.

With seas on three sides of the Italian peninsula, Italy has an abundance of fresh fish, but our village of Quarata was inland and had a limited supply. In America we did not live near the sea, nor did our family have avid sportsmen, so fresh fish, when we could find it, was always a treat. But salted cod is as essential to our Christmas table as bread. We serve it in a variety of ways, all the delicious dishes prepared for the same meal.

Game, too, eluded us. Game dishes are a specialty of Tuscany where the hills and mountains hold wild boar, hare, pheasant, quail, and other game birds (once including peacocks). One of the most famous Florentine dishes of the Renaissance came from the kitchens of Catherine de Medici. It was rabbit prepared in a sweet and sour sauce flavored with rosemary and garlic to which candied lemon, lime, and orange peel had been added. Although we enjoy rabbit, we never prepared Catherine's exotic dish, so it is not represented in the recipes in this book.

But a dish equal to Catherine's rabbit is Pheasant with Black Olives. Whether prepared with pheasant or chicken, it is flavorful, delicious and worthy of your best china and your most important guest.

Braised Blue Pike
Luccio Blu in Umido

Pike is a freshwater fish that thrives in colder climates; thus it is abundant in northern streams and lakes. It is a fleshy and tender fish and can be prepared in a variety of ways. This is our favorite. Each fall Pino Guiducci would go to Canada to fish and always bring us a cooler full of Blue Pike.

2-pound blue pike
3-4 T flour
1 tsp. salt
2 tsp. pepper
2-3 cloves garlic
4-5 sprigs fresh sage
1 cup corn oil
1-1/2 cups canned whole or crushed tomatoes
1 cup broth or water

Be sure the pike is dressed. Wash thoroughly in running water. Pat dry with cloth. Place fish on a cutting board. Remove head and tip of tail and discard. Depending on the size, cut into 5 to 7 equal 3-inch pieces. First, cut the body into thirds and any large pieces in half. Set aside.

Clean cutting board and place flour in center. Add salt and pepper to flour, toss. Roll each piece of pike in flour until evenly coated. Peel and cut garlic into 3 or 4 pieces. Cut sage into small pieces. Do not use many stems.

Place medium-size iron skillet over medium-high heat and allow to heat. When hot, add oil. Heat to hot. Place floured fish into hot oil and sear. Turn once. Remove when golden brown and place on a paper towel to drain.

In the same oil (or if dirty from flour, discard, wipe skillet, reheat, and add new oil), saute garlic. When garlic is brown, crush with fork until mashed. Add sage and simmer a few minutes. Add tomatoes and crush with a fork; simmer 10 minutes. Rinse tomato can with 1/2 cup broth or water and add to mixture. Salt and pepper to taste, if necessary. Mix well. Lower heat and simmer uncovered for 15 minutes.

Remove from heat and run sauce through a sieve to remove pulp and sage. Return strained sauce to skillet, return heat to medium-high, simmer for 5 minutes; reduce heat, and simmer uncovered for 15 minutes or until sauce begins to lose bright red color. Add fish. Cover and simmer slowly for 30 minutes or until sauce is a brown-red and oil begins to separate and float on surface (skim if desired). Do not stir or turn. If sauce begins to dry, add remaining broth. Serve with fresh homemade bread.

Yield: 5-7 pieces.

Cod
Baccalà

Hard as nails, dried, salt-cured *baccalà* arrives in Italian food stores in late autumn, adding one more pungent aroma to an already saturated atmosphere. A week before Christmas the *baccalà* is set to soak in a pan of water to begin the process of removing the salt and softening the flesh. The water is drained daily and, if enough salt is not removed, the entire Christmas Eve feast is ruined.

Today *baccalà* is not as dry as in Nonna's day. It does not require as much soaking and can be bought without bones.

To prepare *baccalà*, soak in cold water for 8 hours, changing the water twice. Remove from cold water, rinse well in running water, and cut into serving pieces. A large fish yields 12-to-14, 3-by-3-inch pieces.

Boiled or Broiled Cod with Chickpeas
Baccalà Lesso o Arrostito con Ceci

Always, always, the second course of the Christmas Eve meal, boiled or broiled cod is refreshing, a good choice for a light meal.

1 salted and soaked
whole cod fish
2 quarts water
1/4 tsp. pepper
1-2 T olive oil

Soak and prepare cod as directed in the preceding introduction.

To boil: Cut cod into 3-inch pieces. Put water in a 6-to-8-quart pot and bring to a boil. Add the cod fish and boil until tender, about 8 to 10 minutes. Drain.

Place in a deep casserole, pepper to taste, and sprinkle with a good olive oil. Do not add salt.

To broil: Cut fish into 3-inch pieces. Place in broiler for 5 minutes, turn, and continue for 5 more minutes. Do the same over an open flame or on a grill. Arrange on a platter, sprinkle with pepper and oil. Do not add salt.

Serve boiled or broiled cod with chickpea salad (see recipe on page 223).

Serves: 5-8 depending on size of fish.

Cod in Sauce with Onions
Baccalà in Umido con Cipolle

Like boiled cod, cod in onion sauce or with sage and garlic (recipe follows) is part of our Christmas Eve tradition. Every time we eat it, we also serve up the story of the last time Nonna cooked this meal. She was 78 years old. It was a Friday in the late fall, and we came home expecting the aroma of simmering *baccalà* and onions. Instead when we opened the door there was no smell at all. When we took the lid off the iron skillet the *baccalà* smelled strange and when we tasted it, it was awful and fell to pieces. We had no choice but to throw it away and as we poured it down the disposal and turned on the water, mounds of bubbles filled the sink. Nonna had fried the cod in liquid detergent instead of oil. I could see the pain in her eyes. She never cooked again.

1 salted and soaked
whole cod fish
1/2 cup flour
1 tsp. pepper
1 cup corn oil

5-6 medium onions*
2 cups whole or crushed
canned tomatoes
1 cup broth or water

Soak and prepare cod fish as directed in the introduction to this section on page 103. Wash, drain and pat dry. Mix flour with pepper and place on a board (do not add salt).

Place a large-size iron skillet on medium-high heat. Heat to hot and add oil. Press fish into flour. Turn and press again. Coat well. When oil is hot, place fish in skillet. Cook until a golden brown, turning once to brown both sides. Remove from skillet and place on paper towel to drain.

If oil is dirty from flour, discard, wipe the skillet, reheat, and add new oil.

Peel, wash, and slice onions. Add to oil and saute for 10 minutes, or until transparent.

Add tomatoes and crush with a fork. Simmer 10 minutes. Rinse tomato can with 1/2 cup broth or water and add to mixture. Do not add salt. Mix well.

Lower heat and simmer uncovered for 15 to 20 minutes or until sauce begins to lose bright red color. Add fish. Cover and simmer slowly for 30 minutes or until sauce is a brown-red and oil begins to separate and float on surface (skim if desired). Do not stir or turn. If sauce begins to dry, add remaining broth.

Serves: 6-8, depending on size of fish.

Note: The amount of onions is a matter of taste: 1 to 2 onions add flavor, 3 to 5 make the onions, like potatoes, a component of the stew. We like lots of onions.

Cod in Sauce with Sage and Garlic
Baccalà in Umido con Salvia e Aglio

There is little difference in the preparation of cod with onions or cod with sage. The flavor, of course, is different. The choice is not an easy one and we always had to have a family council to decide which to prepare, keeping in mind that we would not taste the losing recipe for another year.

1 salted and soaked
whole cod fish
1/2 cup flour
2 tsp. pepper
1 cup corn oil

3-4 cloves garlic
6-7 sprigs sage
2 cups whole or crushed
canned tomatoes
1 cup broth or water

Soak and prepare cod fish as directed in the introduction to this section on page 103. Wash, drain and pat dry. Mix flour with pepper and place on a board. Do not add salt.

Place a large-size iron skillet on medium-high heat. Heat to hot and add oil. Press fish into flour. Turn and press again. Coat well. When oil is hot, add fish. Brown to a golden brown. Turn once and brown second side. Remove from skillet and place on a paper towel to drain.

If oil is dirty from flour, discard, wipe the skillet, reheat, and add new oil. Peel and cut garlic into medium-size pieces. Wash sage and cut into pieces. Do not use a lot of stems.

Add garlic to hot oil. When garlic is brown crush with fork until mashed. Add sage and simmer a few minutes. Add tomatoes and crush with a fork. Simmer 10 minutes. Rinse tomato can with 1/2 cup broth or water and add to mixture. Mix well. Lower heat and simmer uncovered for 15 minutes.

Remove from heat and run sauce through a sieve removing pulp and sage. Return sauce to skillet, return heat to medium-high, simmer for 5 minutes, reduce heat and simmer uncovered for 15 minutes or until sauce begins to lose bright red color. Add fish. Cover and simmer slowly for 30 minutes or until sauce is a brown-red and oil begins to separate and float on surface (skim if desired). Do not stir or turn. If sauce begins to dry, add remaining broth.

Serves: 6-8, depending on size of fish.

Cod with Sweet and Sour Sauce
Baccalà in Agro Dolce

This was not one of Nonna's favorites. It should have been. It was Tuscan. It was made by many of the fine cooks in our neighborhood, including our friend, Sophia Poletini, whose daughter Lena gave us this recipe. And it is absolutely delicious.

sweet and sour sauce:
1/4 cup olive oil
1 cup thinly sliced medium yellow onions
2-1/2 cups whole or crushed canned tomatoes
1/2 tsp. salt
1/2 tsp. pepper
2 T red wine vinegar
2 T sugar
2 T fresh mint; or 2 tsp. dried

1 salted and soaked whole cod fish
1/2 cup flour
1/4 tsp. pepper
1/2 cup corn oil

For sauce: Place a medium-size iron skillet over medium-high heat. Heat to hot and add oil. Heat to hot. Peel, clean and slice onions. Add to oil and reduce heat. Saute until soft and transparent (about 10 minutes) stirring regularly. Do not brown.

Add tomatoes, salt, pepper. Cook uncovered, stirring frequently until slightly thick, about 15 minutes, or until tomatoes begin to lose bright red color. Add vinegar, sugar, and mint (you can cut mint into small pieces if desired). Mix well and set aside.

Soak and prepare cod fish as directed in the introduction to this section on page 103. Wash, drain, and pat dry. Mix flour with pepper (do not add salt) and place on a board.

Place a large-size iron skillet on medium-high heat. Heat to hot and add oil. Press fish into flour. Turn and press again. Coat well. Fry until a golden brown, turning once to brown both sides. Remove from skillet and place on paper towel to drain.

Place *baccalà* in *agro dolce* sauce. Bring to a boil. Cover, reduce heat, and allow to simmer slowly for 20 to 30 minutes, or until the sauce is deep brown-red in color. Oil will float on surface when done (skim, if desired). Do not stir while simmering or *baccalà* will fall apart.

Serves: 6-8, depending on size of fish.

Notes: If sauce is too sour add a little more sugar, if too sweet, add more vinegar. If sauce becomes too thick, add a little broth and continue to simmer.

Other Fish
Altri Pesci

Fish Stew
Cacciucco o Zuppa di Pesce

The French call this dish *bouillabaisse*, but the origin is Italian. Folk legend maintains the fishermen of a small village near Livorno were lost in rough seas and the poor women sent the children begging for food. The children brought back bits and pieces. Out of the medley this wonderful stew, called *cacciucco* in the village, but *zuppa di pesci* in the rest of Italy, was created. Another myth relates that the men in lighthouses had an abundance of fish, but were forbidden to use oil needed to keep the lamps lit. They created the stew.

The choice of fish is really up to you, but in Italy, the belief is you should have five varieties of fish, one for each "C" in the dishes name.

1 pound lobster tail
1 pound cod, pike,
seabass, or roughy
1/2 pound shrimp
1/2 pound squid
12 clams or sea dates
1 pound scallops

2 T olive oil
1 cup sliced onions
1 cup chopped carrots
2 cloves minced garlic

4 cups fresh tomatoes
8 oz. clam juice
2 T parsley
3/4 tsp. thyme
1/8 tsp. salt
1/8 tsp. pepper
1/2 cup broth (optional)

Wash and clean all seafood. Cut lobster into 3 to 4 pieces, shell and all. Cut fish of choice into 3-inch pieces. Clean and de-vein shrimp and squid. Wash clams and scallops.

Place extra-large iron skillet over medium-high heat. Allow to heat and when hot, add oil. Wash and slice onions and carrots, add to oil. Peel garlic, add to oil. When garlic is brown, crush with a fork into small pieces. Saute until onions are transparent, about 10 minutes.

Add tomatoes, reduce heat, and simmer uncovered for 20 minutes, or until tomatoes begin to thicken and darken. Add clam juice, parsley, thyme, salt, and pepper. Bring to a boil, cover, lower heat and simmer for 15 to 20 minutes or until brown-red in color. Add lobster and fish. Simmer 5 minutes. Add shrimp, squid, clams, and scallops. Simmer 5 minutes or until clam shells begin to open. If sauce is too thick, add 1/2 cup broth and simmer for a few minutes. Serve in soup bowls with fresh Italian bread.

Serves: 6.

Notes: 5 pounds of fish feeds 6 people. You can add pasta to this fish stew by cooking it separately, laying down a bed of pasta on a plate, and covering with stew.

Grilled Fish
Pesce Arrostito

Sea bass, orange roughy, trout, halibut, and cod are good fish to grill. Fish is best when grilled whole rather than in fillets. The secret to grilling fish is to marinate the fish and oil the grill. Then the flesh does not stick.

1 whole, dressed fish
Salt and pepper, to taste
1 T lemon juice
1 clove crushed garlic
1 bay leaf
Dash olive oil

1 T corn oil
Lemon wedges

Wash and clean the fish. Salt and pepper the inside. Combine lemon juice, garlic, bay leaf, salt and pepper in a flat dish. Add fish and top with dash of olive oil. Allow to marinate for 20 minutes, turn, and marinate the second side for 20 minutes.

Place in broiler or on an oiled grill (to oil grill, place 1 tablespoon of corn oil on a paper towel, rub over grill, place fish on oiled area).

Grill for 4 to 5 minutes on one side, turn, and grill 4 to 5 minutes on second side. Serve with lemon wedges.

Serves: 1-4, depending on size of fish.

Halibut Steak with Anchovy Sauce
Passera di Mare con Acciugata

4 slices inch-thick halibut steaks
Pepper
Acciugata sauce*

Wash the fish. Place in broiler or on an oiled grill. Grill for 4 to 5 minutes on one side, turn, and grill 4 to 5 minutes on second side. Add pepper (no salt).

If you grill the fish be sure to oil the grill to stop the fish from sticking. Place oil on a paper towel, rub over grill, place fish on oiled area.

Remove fish from broiler or grill, place on a serving tray and cover with *acciugata* sauce.

Serves: 4.

Note: *Recipe for *acciugata* sauce is on page 230. It is good on any fresh fish--grilled, broiled, boiled, or baked--but especially good on halibut.

108

Smoked Herring or Shad on the Open Fire
Arringa o Salacca Arrostite al Fuoco

Smoked herring (*arringa*) and shad (*salacca*) are seasonal foods found in Italian food stores during Lent. Available in imported or domestic varieties, they once came crated in wooden boxes and the store would be saturated with the strong aroma, a smell Italians loved, but one that kept *stranieri* (foreigners) away.

Both fish are salty so additional salt need not be added. Nonno often cooked his afternoon lunch in the furnace. He simply stoked up the coal fire, opened the furnace door, and with specially made skewers held the meat or fish over the open fire. Gino cooked his smoked fish in the brick ovens of the cement factory where he worked.

1 smoked herring
or shad
3 T olive oil
1 T vinegar
Pepper to taste

Place whole fish in a wire rack over open coals for few minutes until hot (or broil in oven for 2 minutes on both sides). The fish has been smoked and therefore does not need to be cooked.

Remove from wire, peel off skin, split lengthwise, remove scales, trim fins and part of tail with scissors, and cut each side into thirds. Sprinkle with oil, vinegar, and pepper (no salt) to taste.

Serves: 1-2 depending on size of herring or shad.

Note: We always served smoked herring or shad with a side dish of boiled white beans (see bean salad recipe on page 222).

Tuna Fish in Oil with Radishes
Tonno all'olio con Ravanelli

When Nonno picked the first radish from the spring garden out came the tuna and this tasty entree was prepared.

6 oz. Italian tuna
12-14 fresh garden
radishes
Olive oil
Ground pepper
Vinegar

Drain tuna, break into chunks, and place in serving dish. Clean radishes and slice. Add to the tuna and mix well.

Top with olive oil, ground pepper, and vinegar to taste. Do not add salt.

Serves: 2-3.

Game
Cacciagione

We always treat game to eliminate the wild taste. After gutting and skinning, wash carefully in water and 1/2 teaspoon baking soda. Let stand 30 minutes. Drain and place in salt water. Let stand 2-1/2 hours. Drain, repeat salt bath overnight. Wash in clear water. This removes excess blood and eliminates the wild taste.

Pheasant
Fagiano

Pheasant was one of our favorite game birds, and because we did not have it often, we relished it whenever it came our way.

A freshly killed pheasant should be aged before cooking. To do this, hang it on a pole, gut it, and allow it to stand from 5 to 8 days. Do not remove the feathers. After it has aged, pluck the feathers, clean the bird, and soak as described above.

Pheasant with Black Olives and Sage
Fagiano con Olive Mature e Salvia

Early one Sunday morning the Pelini family arrived at our house picnic basket in hand. They had all the ingredients for this wonderful dish and the pots were soon simmering on the stove. We enjoyed it so much that, when we do not have pheasant, which is most of the time, we substitute chicken.

3-pound pheasant or
3-pound chicken
2-3 T butter

Salt and pepper
1/2 cup strips of
prosciutto (or *pancetta*)
1/3 cup sage leaves
1/4 cup broth or
dry white wine
12 oz. small black
pitted olives

De-game pheasant as described above. Place large-size dry iron skillet over medium-high heat. Do not add butter. Add pheasant. Cover. Simmer 5 minutes. Uncover and drain off any accumulated liquid. This rids the pheasant of gamy taste (if using chicken omit this step).

After removing all liquid add butter, salt, and pepper. Brown 15 minutes, turning at least once. Once brown, lower heat to medium and add prosciutto and sage. Simmer 10 minutes. Add wine or broth to keep moist. Simmer 10 minutes. Add black olives and a little of olive juice. Finish simmering on low burner for an additional 10 minutes or until done.

Serves: 4-6.

Note: Cook pheasant longer than chicken.

Quail
Quaglia

Nonno enjoyed sparrows served this way. When he did, he ate alone, for none of us enjoyed or approved. In fact, any small bird is good following this recipe.

4 quail
1 tsp. salt
1 tsp. pepper
8 sage leaves
4 tsp. butter
2 (1/4-inch-thick) slices *pancetta*
2 T corn oil

Wash quails inside and out, drain, and pat dry. Combine salt and pepper in a small bowl and mix well.

Rub inside cavity of each quail with a little salt and pepper mixture. Place 2 sage leaves in each cavity. Tie the legs of each quail together with a piece of string.

Rub salt and pepper mixture on the outside of each quail. Rub with unmelted butter and place half a strip of *pancetta* over the breast.

Heat oven to 400 degrees. Put oil in bottom of roasting pan. Place quails, breast side up, into the oil, moving each to coat bottom of bird.

Bake in oven for 15 minutes. Lower heat to 325 degrees and roast 45 minutes.

Serves: 4.

Note: You can add oven potatoes to the roasting quail. Peel and cut 3 large potatoes into 5 or 6 pieces, smaller ones in half (for crunchy potatoes cut into smaller pieces). Place the potatoes around the quail, making sure they are in the oil. Do not salt or pepper potatoes. Turn potatoes every 15 minutes, coating them with the oil in the pan.

Rabbit
Coniglio

A rabbit is a *lepre* when it is wild and a *coniglio* when it is domesticated. Either way, we prepare it in sauce and as a roast.

Rabbit Sauce
Salsa di Coniglio

1 dressed rabbit

4 onions
2 cloves garlic
1/4-inch-thick slice
pancetta
1 small carrot
1/2 cup celery
3-4 sprigs fresh parsley

1/4 cup corn oil
1 T pepper
1 T salt
1 pound ground chuck
1/2 pound pork sausage
4 oz. red table wine
(optional)

28 oz. whole canned
tomatoes
in puree
1 cup broth
12 oz. tomato paste
Salt
Pepper

De-game wild rabbit as described on page 110. Cut into serving-size pieces. Place medium-size skillet over medium-high heat. Do not add oil. Add rabbit. Cover. Cook a few minutes. Uncover, drain. Simmer. Drain. Repeat until no liquid is formed. Set aside. If using domesticated rabbit omit this step.

Peel onions, wash, cut into quarter wedges. Peel garlic, chop. Cut *pancetta* in half. Peel carrot and celery, wash, cut into pieces. Wash parsley. Combine and grind in a meat grinder or food processor (the grinder is better because it releases the juices).

Place large-size iron skillet over medium-high heat. Heat to hot. Add oil. Heat to hot. Add rabbit. Brown on both sides. Remove. Add chopped ingredients, pepper, salt, and saute until onions are transparent. The longer it cooks (at least 20 minutes), the better the sauce. When mixture begins to stick to skillet, add ground meat, shredding with fork into small pieces (you can add scraps of rabbit to this mixture). Simmer until meat is dark brown and turning crispy, stirring often so it does not stick to skillet. Add wine and continue to saute.

While meat mixture is simmering, heat tomatoes in 6-quart pot over low heat. Add paste.

Rinse both tomato and paste cans with broth or water and add to meat mixture. Let simmer 10 minutes, remove meat mixture from skillet and add to simmering tomatoes. Raise heat to high. When boiling reduce heat, cover, and simmer slowly.

Add rabbit to simmering sauce. Simmer very slowly for 3 to 4 hours. Stir often to avoid sticking. A good sauce will look dark, almost brown, not red, and oil will separate and float on top (skim if desired). Serve over wide pasta.
Serves: 10-12.

Rabbit in Tomato Sauce
Lepre in Salsa di Pomodoro

1 dressed wild rabbit

3 T corn oil
Salt and pepper
2-3 cloves garlic
Pinch allspice
5-6 sprigs of rosemary
1/4 cup red table wine

3-4 T whole or crushed
canned tomatoes
1 cup broth

De-game wild rabbit as described on page 110. Cut into serving-size pieces.

Place a dry iron skillet on medium-high heat. Do not add oil. Place rabbit into the dry skillet. Cover. Let simmer for a few minutes. Uncover and drain off any liquid that has accumulated. Simmer again. Drain again. Repeat until no more liquid is formed. This rids the rabbit of gamy taste. If using domesticated rabbit omit this step (see note).

Remove rabbit pieces from skillet. Heat skillet and add oil. Return rabbit to skillet. Add salt, pepper, garlic, allspice, and rosemary and allow to brown on all sides, turning once. Add wine and continue to brown for 5 minutes. Remove meat from the skillet.

Add tomatoes to the juices in the skillet, crushing with a fork into small pieces. Simmer 10 minutes. Rinse tomato can with 1/2 cup broth or water and add to mixture. Salt and pepper to taste, if necessary. Mix well. Reduce heat and simmer uncovered for 15 minutes or until sauce begins to lose bright red color.

Add rabbit. Cover and simmer slowly for 30 minutes or until sauce is a brown-red and oil begins to separate and float on surface (skim if desired). Do not stir or turn. If sauce begins to dry add remaining broth.

Serves: 4-6.

Note: If a domestic rabbit is used, once the rabbit has been cut, omit the dry skillet process. Instead, add a small amount of oil to the skillet, add the rabbit, and proceed as above.

Roast Rabbit with Rosemary or Fennel and Oven Potatoes
Lepre (Coniglio) al Forno con Rosmarino o Finocchio e Contorno di Patate

1 rabbit
Salt and pepper, to taste
3-4 slices prosciutto
4-5 cloves garlic
4-5 sausage links, optional
3-4 tsp. fennel seeds or 3 tsp. rosemary

Corn oil
4 large potatoes (red)

De-game wild rabbit as described on page 110. Rinse well and pat dry with a clean cloth.

Salt and pepper the inside of the cavity. Set aside. Lay in the prosciutto end to end covering the entire bottom of the cavity. Top with crushed garlic and fennel and fill remaining space with sausage (optional). Close the opening and sew it securely shut with a trussing needle and thick cord or wire.

Heat the oven to 350 degrees. Generously cover the bottom of a large roasting pan with oil. Place rabbit on its side in the roaster. Slide rabbit in pan and coat back with oil.

Roast for 20 minutes. Turn rabbit over on second side. Continue roasting.

Peel and cut large potatoes into 3 to 4 pieces, small ones in half (for crunchy potatoes cut into smaller pieces).

After the rabbit has been roasting for 30 minutes, add the potatoes. Do not salt or pepper potatoes. Turn all potatoes, coating them with the oil in the pan.

Roast for an additional 2-to-2-1/2 hours, basting the rabbit and turning the potatoes every 20 minutes. When almost done, salt and pepper the outside of the rabbit.

Serve with fresh garden salad and an additional vegetable.

Serves: 6-8.

Beef
Manzo

The beef used by many northern Italian chefs comes from the heavy *chianina* cattle from the valley of the Chiana River, just south of Arezzo. The name is often associated with Florentine dishes, but the Chiana River empties into the Arno near our small village of Quarata and the beef is enjoyed by peasant and noble alike in our area. The cattle are slaughtered at age 15 to 17 months when the meat is called *vitellone* (large veal), further enhancing its quality.

In the United States our immigrants did not live in an area that produced exceptionally fine beef, but Nonna always went to a neighborhood butcher to buy beef freshly cut and selected a specific type of beef for each dish prepared. The right cut of beef is as important to the Italian kitchen as the right brush is to a master artist, and years of experience have taught us which cut is the best for a particular dish.

One reason our meals are so delicious is that we never compromise on the quality of the meat. We never buy ground meat, we always use ground chuck. The shank, a tougher meat, is used mainly for soups and cubed stews. For roasts we used eye of round, prime rib, or rump, and for *umidi*, where the meat is not cubed, but kept intact and simmered in sauce, we use the top of the round or block rump.

As you can see from the variety of recipes in this chapter, beef is a major part of our diet. Ironically, it is never the main event at a holiday meal, but serves as a second course, boiled or in a sauce. The succulent sauce recipes speak for themselves, but a word is in order for the equally tasty boiled meats. Often the by-product of a good soup, boiled meat is never discarded, but carefully prepared in a number of ways.

To cut meat, whether roasted, boiled, or stewed, cut against the grain to keep the meat tender. If you cut with the grain the meat will be stringy, fall to pieces, and be tough.

Boiled Beef
Lesso

Whenever the soup pot is boiling, and that is once a week, one can be sure part of the meal of the day is a *bollito misto,* a mixed boil of beef or chicken.

1 pound boiled beef from
soup*
1 sweet onion
3-4 sprigs fresh parsley
1 T fresh basil
Salt and pepper
Olive oil
Wine vinegar

After removing the beef from the broth (see note), remove all fat from meat and discard fat. Cut meat into small pieces. Place on a platter. Slice onion and arrange around beef. Chop parsley and basil and sprinkle over top. Add salt and pepper. Top with olive oil and wine vinegar.

Serves: 2-3.
Note: *See soup recipes beginning on page 238.

Boiled Beef with Potatoes
Lesso Rifatto

1 pound boiled beef
from soup*
1 onion
1 tsp. parsley
1/2 tsp. basil
3 potatoes

2 T corn oil
Salt and pepper
1-1/2 cups crushed
tomatoes
1 cup water or broth

Remove beef from broth (see note), trim away fat from meat and discard fat. Cut meat into inch pieces. Peel and slice onion into thin slices. Chop parsley and basil. Cut raw potatoes into inch pieces.

Place a large iron skillet over medium-high heat. Heat to hot. Add oil. Heat to hot. Add boiled meat and stir. Meat is already cooked so it will break into smaller pieces. Cook for 4 minutes. Add onions and saute until transparent. Add parsley, basil, salt, and pepper. Allow to simmer a few minutes and add the tomatoes. Simmer for 15 minutes.

As sauce begins to dry, add a little broth or hot water. Add potatoes, cover, and let simmer for 20 to 25 minutes adding water if necessary. Turn potatoes carefully. Simmer until potatoes are cooked.

Serves: 3-4.

Notes: *See soup recipes beginning on page 238.
You can peel potatoes and add to simmering broth for last half hour, or until done. They will slightly alter taste of broth, but enhance the potatoes. Alternately, one can use left-over roast beef.
A variation is to dust the meat with flour before frying.

Boiled Meat Patties
Polpette

A true Italian hamburger which we always serve as a main course, *polpette* made in smaller portions, are excellent served as appetizers or on a buffet table.

2 small potatoes
Water or broth

1 tsp. fresh parsley
2 fresh leaves or 1/2 tsp. dry basil
1 clove garlic

1 pound boiled beef from soup*

2 eggs
1 tsp. salt
1/4 tsp. pepper
1/2 cup freshly grated Parmesan cheese

4-5 T corn oil
1 cup flour

Peel and dice potatoes, place in a small pot, add water or broth to cover, and boil until soft. Drain.

Chop parsley and basil. Peel garlic and chop into fine pieces or pass through a garlic press.

Remove meat from broth. Place meat in a medium-size bowl and add eggs. Mash potatoes, combine with meat. Add parsley, basil, garlic, salt, pepper and Parmesan cheese and mix well. Divide into 8 or 10 portions and form into patties.

Place a medium-size iron skillet over medium-high heat. Heat to hot. Add oil.

Place flour on a board, roll each patty in flour, coating well, and place in hot oil. Brown on one side. Turn. Brown on other side. Remove from skillet and place on paper towel. Serve hot or cold, as is, or in a delicious sandwich.

Yield: 8-10 patties.

Notes: *See soup recipes beginning on page 238.

You can peel 3 potatoes and add them to the simmering broth for the last half hour, or until they are done. They will slightly alter the taste of the broth, but enhance the taste of the potatoes (remember this dish was always prepared on soup day).

We always served *polpette* with Italian potato salad, see page 225.

Variation: Nonna always chopped the meat into pieces, and ground the meat and potatoes in a meat grinder or food processor. Then she would add eggs and continue as above.

Meatloaf Italian Style
Polpettone

3 hard-cooked eggs
2, 8-inch sausages

2 pounds ground chuck
1 cup bread crumbs
1/2 tsp. fresh parsley
1/2 tsp. basil
3 eggs
2/3 cup freshly grated
Romano cheese
1 tsp. salt
1 tsp. pepper

1 tsp. corn oil
2 fat slices provolone
cheese (1/2" thick)

sauce:
1 T corn oil
1 clove garlic
2 cups crushed canned
tomatoes
3 T tomato paste
1/4 tsp. salt
1/4 tsp. pepper
1 cup broth
or water

Place a small pot over high heat. Add water and bring to a boil. Add eggs and boil for 4 minutes (be sure eggs are at room temperature or they will crack). Allow to cool in water, and shell.

Place a medium-size iron skillet over medium-high heat. Do not add oil. Add sausage links and fry 10 minutes, turning once. Drain on paper towel, cool, and skin sausage. Set aside.

Combine chuck, bread crumbs, parsley, basil, eggs (unboiled), cheese, salt, and pepper. Mix. Oil pastry board. Turn meat onto board, keeping 1/2 cup aside. Roll with greased rolling pin until 10-by-14 inches in size. Place three boiled eggs in a row in center. Place a sausage on either side. Cover with provolone.

Fold sides up and over, placing extra meat on top. Once formed, patch with remaining meat. If not sealed properly the cheese will spill out. Slide onto an oiled cookie sheet and bake at 375 degrees for 1 hour and 10 minutes or until brown and firm.

Place medium-size iron skillet over medium-high heat. Heat to hot. Add oil. When oil is hot add clove of garlic. Allow to brown. When brown crush with a fork. Add tomatoes, crushing with a fork. Simmer 8 to 10 minutes. Add tomato paste, salt and pepper. Rinse both tomato and paste cans with 1/2 cup broth or sausage drippings and add. Simmer 30 minutes, or until sauce begins to thicken and deepen in color. If it drys, add remaining broth.

Check meatloaf. If cheese is spilling out, spoon onto top of loaf. Spoon 1/4 of sauce (about 1/2 cup) over top of meatloaf. Re-set oven to 300 degrees and bake for an additional 25 to 30 minutes.

Remove meatloaf from oven and place on cutting board. Slice meatloaf into equal slices. Lay each slice on serving tray. Cover with sauce. Each slice should have section of egg, 2 sections sausage, and piece of melted cheese (see illustration).

Yield: 12-14 slices.

Note: Make extra sauce and serve *polpettone* with spaghettini and sauce.

Roasts
Arrosti

Roast beef is served in a variety of ways in our home, all well-spiced and tasty.

Roasting Times for Beef

Roast	weight/pounds	temp.	rare	medium	well done
rib	2-3 rib	325	2 hrs.	3 hrs.	4 hrs.
rib eye	4-6	325	1-3/4 hrs.	2 hrs.	2 -1/4 hrs.
boneless rump	4-6	325	2 hrs.	2 -1/2 hrs.	3 hrs.
thermometer reading			140	160	170

Pot Roast
Arrosto Morto

2-3 sprigs fresh rosemary
4-5 large garlic cloves
1/4-inch-thick slice
pancetta
3 pounds rump roast
1-1/2 T salt
1 T pepper

Corn oil
2-3 T broth (optional)
4 potatoes (red)
3-4 carrots

Wash rosemary and set aside. Peel garlic and cut each clove in halves or thirds. Cut *pancetta* into strips. Make sure roast is at room temperature. With a sharp paring knife cut 1-inch-deep slits in the top of the meat, approximately 1-1/2 inches apart. Into each pocket place salt, pepper, a piece of garlic, a sprig of rosemary, and a piece of *pancetta* (in exact order). Salt and pepper entire outside of roast.

Place 4-quart pot on high heat. Add oil. Heat. Place meat into pot. Brown well on all outer edges to sear in the juices. Add broth. Lower heat to medium. Cover the pot with a lid and allow to cook for 30 minutes.

Wash and peel potatoes and cut in half or thirds. Wash and peel carrots and cut in 2-inch pieces. Add to pot roast and cook for 10 minutes on medium-high heat. Reduce heat to medium and cook an additional 1 to 1-1/2 hours.

When done remove meat and place on cutting board. Allow to set for 10 minutes. Slice against the grain to keep tender. Arrange on platter surrounded by vegetables and top with juice.

Serves: 6.

119

Roast Beef
Rosbif al Forno

3 pounds eye of round
or rump roast
2 cloves garlic
1/4-inch-thick slice
pancetta
1-1/2 T salt
1 T pepper

Place meat on pastry board and cut 3 or 4 half-inch slits in top. Peel garlic and cut in two. Cut *pancetta* into strips. Place a piece of garlic, slice of *pancetta*, and salt and pepper in each cut. Salt and pepper entire roast.

Place roast in shallow pan. Insert meat thermometer in center of thickest part of the roast. Do not hit fat pocket.

Roast in 325-degree oven 28 to 30 minutes for each pound or until the thermometer indicates the roast is done to your taste. Remove from oven and allow to set 20 minutes before cutting. To cut slice against the grain to keep it tender.

Serves: 6-8.

Note: Roast needs no oil or water.

Standing Beef Roast
Le Costole Ritte al Forno

3 rib standing rib roast
2 cloves garlic
1-1/2 T salt
1 T course pepper

Place meat on pastry board and cut 2 deep slits about 2 inches apart in the fleshy side of the ribs. Peel garlic and place one piece of garlic, salt and pepper in each cut. Salt and pepper the entire roast.

Place roast in shallow roasting pan with rib ends and fat side up. Insert a meat thermometer in the center of the thickest part of the roast. Be careful not to hit a fatty pocket or bone.

Roast in 325-degree oven 28 to 30 minutes for each pound or until the thermometer indicates the roast is done. Remove from oven and allow to set 20 minutes before cutting. To cut slice along the ribs and against the grain to keep it tender.

Serves: 8-10.

Note: Roast needs no oil or water.

Grilled Steak Florentine Style
Bistecca alla Fiorentina

Bistecca alla Fiorentina is an inch-thick T-bone steak grilled over a wood fire and seasoned with salt, pepper, and olive oil. Famous throughout the world, it is cooked *ble, quasi cruda* (raw), *al sangue* (rare), *cotta a puntino* (medium-rare), or *ben cotta* (well done).

For our recipe we have replaced the wood fire with a charcoal one, which diminishes the dish. A propane grill is a further insult. It would help to add a few chips of cherry wood to the fire. They are available in gourmet shops.

1 8-12-oz. T-Bone steak
Salt, pepper
Olive oil

Prepare the grill in your usual manner. Add enough charcoal to produce strong heat. Allow charcoal to reduce to red hot embers. Be sure the grate is hot and the steak is at room temperature.

Place the steak on the hot grill and allow to cook according to your taste (see chart below). Turn. Salt and pepper cooked side. Allow to cook as per your taste. Remove from fire and sprinkle with olive oil. Serve immediately.

With the grill 6 inches away from the coals:

rare, 3 minutes both sides
medium rare, 5 minutes both sides
well done, 7 minutes both sides

Serves: 1-2.

Note: Two sauces that are delicious with charcoal grilled steak are *acciugata* (anchovies and caper sauce), recipe on page 230, and mushroom with garlic and butter, recipe on page 270.

Stews
Umidi (Stufati)

The second course of the great Sunday feast is always an *umido*, a stew in deep red sauce. *Umido* means damp and the meat is usually accompanied by a specific vegetable, also in *umido*. The two dishes are even better reheated for a second meal.

Beef Rounds with Stuffing
Braciole Arrotolate con Ripieno

Once this specialty was served as a second course on Sundays, but today we serve it as a meal in itself. It can be made into one large roll or 3 to 4 equal pieces to make individual rolls.

stuffing:
1 small onion
1/4 cup celery leaves and tender ribs
1 small carrot
2 T fresh parsley

1/4 cup corn oil
1 T pepper
2 T salt
Pinch thyme

1/3 cup grated bread crumbs
1/4 cup freshly grated Parmesan cheese
2 eggs

1 slice round steak (3/4 inch thick)
2-3 thin slices prosciutto

Length of butcher cord or 5-6 small skewers

sauce:
1/4 cup corn oil
1-1/4 cups whole or crushed tomatoes
3 oz. tomato paste
1 cup broth

Peel onion and cut into quarter wedges. Peel celery and carrot, cut into 1-inch pieces. Combine with parsley and grind in meat grinder or chop in food processor into fine pieces (grinder is better because it grinds fine pieces and releases the juices).

Place medium-size iron skillet over medium-high heat. Heat to hot. Add oil. When oil is warm, add all chopped ingredients, pepper, salt, a pinch of thyme, and saute about 20 minutes until onions are transparent, stirring often. The longer this mixture simmers, the better the stuffing.

Remove from heat and place in a bowl. Add bread crumbs and cheese and mix well. Beat eggs in a separate bowl, then add to the mixture. Mix. Mixture must be moist enough to hold together. If dry, add water or broth.

Place steak flat on bread board with length running left to right. Lay prosciutto slices to cover steak. Spread mixture on top (see A). Beginning at the wide end nearest you form the steak into a roll (see B). Secure with skewers or tie with butcher cord. You may cut steak into several serving pieces, stuff and roll each one separately.

Sauce: Place medium-size iron skillet on medium-high heat. Heat to hot. Add oil. Heat. Place beef roll into oil and brown well, turning gently. When well browned remove from skillet and set aside.

To juices in skillet add tomatoes, crushing into small pieces. Simmer 8 to 10 minutes. Add tomato paste. Rinse tomato and paste cans in water or broth and add to mixture. Simmer 20 to 25 minutes.

122

Remove tomato mixture from heat, run through sieve, push pulp through with spoon. Throw excess pulp away.

Return to skillet, return heat to medium-high, simmer for 5 minutes; reduce heat and simmer uncovered for 15 minutes or until sauce begins to lose bright red color. Add rolled beef. Cover, simmer slowly for 30 minutes or until sauce is a brown-red and oil begins to separate and float on surface (skim if desired). If sauce begins to dry add broth.

To serve: Place beef on board. Cut and remove string. Slice into 1/2-inch-thick rounds. Place on a platter. Cover with sauce, serve with Italian bread.
Serves: 6-8.

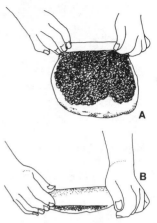

Beef Rounds Without Stuffing
Braciole Arrotolate Senza Ripieno

Rind of 1/3 lemon
1/3 cup parsley
4 fresh basil leaves
or 1 tsp. dry basil
1 clove garlic

1 pound thinly sliced
round steak

3/4 tsp. salt
1/8 tsp. pepper
1/4 cup freshly grated
Romano cheese

10 to 12 small skewers

2 T corn oil
8 oz. crushed canned
tomatoes
1/4 cup broth

Wash and chop lemon rind with parsley and basil into fine pieces. Peel garlic and mince. Combine.

Place steak flat on bread board. Cut into 8 to 10 pieces. Top each piece with mixture, then salt, pepper, and cheese. Roll, secure with skewer.

Place medium-size iron skillet on medium-high heat. Heat to hot. Add oil. Heat. Place rolls in oil, brown well, turning gently. When browned remove from skillet and set aside.

To the juices in the skillet add tomatoes, crushing into small pieces. Simmer 8 to 10 minutes. Rinse tomato can with broth or water and add to mixture. Simmer 20 minutes. Remove from heat, run through sieve, push pulp through with spoon. Throw excess pulp away.

Return to skillet, return heat to medium-high, simmer for 5 minutes; reduce heat and simmer uncovered for 15 minutes or until sauce begins to lose bright red color. Add rolled beef. Cover and simmer slowly for 30 minutes or until sauce is a brown-red and oil begins to separate and float on surface (skim if desired). If sauce begins to dry, add broth.

To serve: Remove skewers. Place on a platter. Cover with sauce and serve.

Serves: 6-8.

123

Beef Rump in Red Sauce with Celery
Manzo in Umido con Sedano

2-3 sprigs fresh rosemary
4-5 large garlic cloves
1/4-inch-thick slice
pancetta

3-pound beef rump
2 tsp. salt
1 tsp. pepper

2 T corn oil

1-1/4 cups whole or
crushed canned
tomatoes
3 oz. tomato paste
1 cup broth

Wash rosemary. Set aside. Peel and cut each clove of garlic into 2 to 3 pieces. Set aside. Dice *pancetta* into strips. Make sure roast is at room temperature.

With a sharp paring knife cut 1-inch-deep slits in the top of the meat approximately 1-1/2 inches apart. Into each pocket place salt, pepper, a piece of garlic, a sprig of rosemary, and a piece of *pancetta* (in exact order). Salt and pepper entire outside of roast.

Place 4-quart pot on burner. Heat to hot. Add oil. Heat. Place meat into pot. Brown well on all outer edges to sear in juices. Lower the heat. Cover the pot with a lid and allow to simmer about 40 to 45 minutes. Turn occasionally. Remove meat from pot.

To the juices in the pot, add tomatoes and crush with a fork. Simmer 10 minutes. Add tomato paste. Rinse tomato and paste cans with 1/2 cup broth or water and add. Simmer 20 minutes. Salt and pepper to taste. Mix well.

Lower heat and simmer uncovered for 15 minutes or until sauce begins to lose bright red color. Add beef. Turn occasionally and simmer for an additional hour, or to taste (use a meat thermometer).

If the sauce begins to dry, add remaining broth. When done, remove meat and place on cutting board. Slice against the grain to keep it tender.

Arrange on platter and cover with 8 to 10 tablespoons of the tomato mixture.

Serve with fried celery in thin sauce, recipe on page 257.

Serves: 6-8.

Note: For a thinner sauce, eliminate the tomato paste and add 2 or 3 tablespoons of canned unflavored tomato sauce.

Beef Rump in Red Sauce with Spinach
Manzo in Umido con Spinaci

Working in the mill carried responsibilities outside the mill gate, including entertaining the boss. Nonno's boss was a friend, never a duty, but the boss's boss was. The first time Nonno invited his family, Nonna prepared a usual Sunday feast: homemade pasta, an *umido*, a roast, and dessert. The guests only saw the pasta. When Nonna served this *umido*, everyone laughed. They did not expect more food and vowed they could not eat another bite. But as the *umido* was piled on their plates, they ate and laughed and became lifelong friends.

5 pounds fresh spinach
1 cup water
1 T salt

Wash spinach. Place water in 6-quart pot. Boil, add salt, spinach; boil again, turn, cover, remove from stove. Cool, drain, squeeze well, chop, set aside.

2-3 sprigs fresh rosemary
4-5 large garlic cloves
1/4-inch-thick slice
pancetta
3-pound beef rump
2 tsp. salt
1 tsp. pepper

Wash and cut rosemary. Peel and cut garlic into 2 to 3 pieces. Cut *pancetta* into strips. With roast at room temperature cut inch-deep slits in top 1-1/2 inches apart. Into each pocket place salt, pepper, garlic, rosemary, and piece of *pancetta* (in exact order). Salt and pepper outside.

1/4 cup corn oil

Place 4-quart pot on burner. Heat to hot. Add oil. Add meat and sear all sides. Cover, lower heat, roast 40 to 45 minutes. Remove roast from pot.

1 cup canned tomatoes
3 oz. tomato paste
1/2 cup broth

2-3 T butter
1/3 cup freshly grated
Parmesan cheese

To juices in pot add tomatoes, crushing with fork into small pieces. Simmer 8 to 10 minutes. Add tomato paste. Rinse cans with 1/2 cup broth or water and add to mixture. Simmer 20 minutes or until tomatoes lose bright red color. Remove from heat and run through a sieve pushing pulp through with a spoon. Throw away remaining pulp. Return to pot. Simmer 10 minutes. Add meat, salt and pepper to taste. Turn occasionally. If sauce begins to dry, add more broth. When done oil should rise to top. Remove meat, slice, arrange on platter, cover with 8 tablespoons of tomato mixture.

Melt butter in medium-size iron skillet. Add spinach turning to coat. Spoon 1/4 of tomato sauce over spinach and simmer, adding sauce to moisten.

To serve: Place meat, spinach, and sauce in separate dishes. Then lay bed of spinach on dinner plate, add 2 to 3 slices of meat and tomato sauce. Top with Parmesan cheese. Serve with Italian bread.

Serves: 8-10.

Notes: Spinach will absorb sauce, so always serve it separately. Makes a good sandwich.

Beef Rump in Red Sauce with String Beans
Manzo in Umido con Fagiolini

3-4 pounds fresh green beans

2 cloves garlic
1/4-inch-thick slice *pancetta*
2 T rosemary
3-pound beef rump
2 tsp. salt
1 tsp. pepper

1/4 cup corn oil
1-1/4 cups whole or crushed canned tomatoes
3 oz. tomato paste
1/4 cup broth

Snap both ends off green beans, wash and break into 2-inch pieces.

Peel each clove of garlic and cut in halves or thirds. Cut *pancetta* into strips. Wash rosemary and cut. Make sure roast is at room temperature and cut 1-inch-deep slits in top of meat. Into each pocket place salt, pepper, a piece of garlic, a sprig of rosemary, and a piece of *pancetta* (in exact order). Salt and pepper entire outside of roast.

Place medium-size iron skillet over medium-high heat. Heat to hot. Add oil. Add meat and brown well to sear in juices. Cover, lower heat, and allow to cook 40 to 45 minutes. Remove meat.

To the juices in the skillet add tomatoes, crushing with a fork into small pieces. Simmer 8 to 10 minutes. Add tomato paste. Rinse both tomato and paste can with broth or water and add to mixture. Simmer 20 minutes, or until tomatoes begin to lose their bright red color. Remove from heat and run through a sieve, pushing pulp through with a spoon or fork. Throw away any pulp remaining in the sieve.

Place tomato mixture in 6-quart pot. Simmer. Add green beans. Allow to simmer 15 to 20 minutes. Place meat in tomato and bean mixture and continue until done to your taste. Add salt and pepper to taste. Turn occasionally. If the sauce begins to dry, add a small amount of broth.

When done sauce should be a deep brown-red. Test, add salt and pepper if necessary. Remove meat and place on cutting board. Slice against the grain to keep it tender. Place in serving dish and spoon on sauce to cover. Remove beans and sauce from pot and place is deep tureen. Serve with good bread.

Serves: 6-8.

Note: This meal is even better served the next day when the juices and spices have had a chance to blend well.

Beef Organs
Frattaglie di Manzo

Calf's Liver and Onions
Fegato di Vitello con Cipolle

1/2 cup flour
1 tsp. salt
1/2 tsp. pepper
1-1/2 pounds sliced
calf's liver
8-9 T corn oil, divided

4-5 large onions
1 tsp. salt
1/2 tsp. pepper
1/2 to 3/4 cups broth

Place flour on pastry board. Add salt and pepper and toss. Place liver slices on flour and coat both sides.

Place large-size iron skillet over high heat. Heat to hot. Add half of oil to cover the bottom of the skillet. Heat to hot. Add liver and quickly sear until brown, about 2 minutes. Turn, sear second side, about 2 minutes. When done, remove from skillet.

Remove skillet from burner. Drain oil and clean skillet with paper towel. Add remaining oil. Heat to hot. Add finely sliced onions, salt and pepper.

Saute onions over medium-high heat until transparent, about 10 minutes. Add broth, lower heat, simmer for 5 minutes; add liver, cover, simmer 20 minutes.

If the liquid begins to dry, add additional broth a little at a time.

Serves: 4-6.

Tripe in Sauce
Trippa nel Sugo

Tripe is the stomach the cow uses to store its cud before chewing. It is not a meal enjoyed by everyone, but those who like it are fanatical.

Tripe is very Tuscan and in Florence it is sold by street vendors. It can be served a variety of ways, including simply boiled and garnished with olive oil. You must have a good meat sauce for this recipe.

Nonno and my father loved tripe. I never enjoyed it, but loved to dip fresh Italian bread in the sauce once the tripe was made. The sauce is absolutely delicious.

6-8 pounds tripe
1 carrot
1 onion
1 rib celery
1 tsp. salt
1 tsp. pepper
2 quarts meat sauce*
1/3 pound butter
1/2 cup freshly grated Parmesan cheese
Red hot pepper (optional)

Wash and clean tripe in running water. Place a large pot over medium-high heat, add water, and bring to a boil. Add carrot, onion, celery, salt and pepper. Add tripe and simmer 15 minutes. Drain.

Place in large bowl, cover with cold water (tripe can be stored in the refrigerator overnight) and let stand until ready to use.

Remove tripe from water, cut into 1/2-inch-wide, 3-to-4-inch-long strips. Fill a large pot with a good meat sauce (see note). Add butter and heat. Add tripe, turn, coat and simmer for 2 to 3 hours. Serve hot with grated cheese and red hot pepper.

Serves: 6-8.

Note: *We always made our traditional meat sauce for tripe. The recipe is on page 234.

Lamb and Veal
Agnello e Vitello

Lamb is the heart and soul of the Easter feast, and each spring in preparation for Easter Nonna and Nonno made an excursion into the countryside to select the baby lamb, the *abbacchio*, or *agnello da latte*. As in all things Italian, there is strict criteria for the selection. The *abbacchio* must be between 30 and 60 days old and weigh 15 to 20 pounds. Younger, it is too fatty, older, too tough. Some families follow the same tradition, but, instead of an *abbacchio*, prepare a *capretto*, which is a baby kid (goat).

Many people do not like to eat lamb, some perhaps because of the reminder of the gentle animal, others because their first taste of lamb was really not the young lambs of spring, but an older sheep or mutton. Mutton has a stronger taste and is unpleasant if cooked in the variety of ways described in the *Immigrant's Kitchen*. New Zealand lamb also is not recommended for these dishes for it, too, has a strong taste.

Like lamb, veal plays an important part in our kitchen. Although it was never a tradition that carried a symbolic meaning, and therefore was seldom served on holidays, it is considered a specialty and is always served with our best china and linens.

Veal is a young calf. It has a delicate pink meat and is very tender; therefore, veal must be carefully prepared. Roasts are best cooked well done, but the less you cook slices or medallions of veal, the more tender and delicate the taste.

All of the lamb and veal dishes in this chapter are elegant enough to serve your most important guests.

Stewed Lamb in Thin Sauce with Spinach
Agnelletto in Umido con Spinaci

The second course of the Easter meal, this succulent lamb stew is a favorite all year round. It is delicious as a leftover, alone or in a sandwich.

5 pounds fresh spinach
1 cup water
1 T salt

2 lamb shanks or
3 slices lamb shoulder
4-5 large cloves garlic

2 T corn oil
2-3 sprigs fresh rosemary
2 tsp. salt
1 tsp. pepper

1 cup whole or crushed
canned tomatoes
3 oz. tomato paste
1 cup broth

2-3 T butter
1/2 cup freshly grated
Parmesan cheese

Wash and clean spinach. Place water in a 6-quart pot. Bring to boil. Add spinach and salt. Stir, remove from heat, cover, set aside to cool. Once cool, drain and squeeze out water. Before using squeeze again. Chop fine with a knife. Set aside.

Have the butcher cut each lamb shank into 3 or 4 (2-inch) pieces. If pieces are too large cut again. They should be 2 inches square (lamb shanks shrink considerably when cooked). Crush garlic by hitting it with a kitchen mallet or blunt object (do not peel).

Place a medium-size iron skillet over medium-high heat. Heat to hot. Add oil. Heat oil until warm, add lamb, garlic, rosemary, salt and pepper. Turn frequently. When browned (15 minutes) remove meat and set aside.

To same oil add tomatoes, crushing with a fork. Allow to simmer 20 minutes and add tomato paste that has been softened with 1/2 cup broth (may use water). Stir and simmer slowly for 30 to 40 minutes or until tomatoes lose bright red color.

Press tomato mixture through a sieve. Throw away pulp. Return sauce to skillet, simmer 10 minutes. Add lamb. Simmer for 1 to 1-1/2 hours. It is done when sauce is thick and oil rises to top (skim if desired). Taste, add salt and pepper if necessary.

Place medium-size iron skillet over medium-high heat. Add butter and melt but do not brown. Add spinach, turn to coat well. Spoon 1/4 of tomato sauce over the spinach and simmer for 15 minutes. You may have to add more sauce as the spinach simmers. If it begins to dry, add remaining broth.

To serve: Bring lamb, spinach and sauce to table in separate containers. For individual servings, lay bed of spinach on dish, top with 2 to 3 pieces of meat, 2 tablespoons of tomato sauce, and 1 tablespoon Parmesan cheese. Do not place spinach and meat in same platter as spinach absorbs too much sauce. Serve with homemade Italian bread.
Serves: 4-6.

Stuffed Crown Lamb Roast
Costolette di Agnellino Ripiene e Arrostite

2 lamb rib rack
of 6-8 chops
2 cloves garlic
2 tsp. salt
1-1/2 tsp. pepper
1 T fresh rosemary

2 onions
1/4-inch-thick slice
pancetta
3 celery ribs
1 carrot
1 tsp. fresh parsley
1 clove garlic

1/2 cup corn oil, divided
1/2 tsp. pepper
1 tsp. salt

3 cups bread crumbs
or cubes
1/2 cup freshly grated
Parmesan cheese
1/4 pound butter
3 eggs

Have the butcher crack the bone between the ribs. Lay meat on a pastry board. Cut 3 to 4 (1-inch) slits in meaty part of each rib. Peel garlic and cut each piece in half. Stuff slits with salt, pepper, rosemary and 1/2 clove of garlic (in exact order).

Peel onions, wash and cut into quarter wedges. Cut *pancetta* into 1/2-inch pieces. Peel celery and carrot, wash, and cut into 1-inch pieces. Chop parsley. Peel garlic and cut in half. Combine all and grind in meat grinder or food processor (the grinder is better because it releases the juices).

Place a medium-size iron skillet over medium-high heat. Heat to hot. Add 1/4 cup oil. When oil is hot add chopped ingredients, pepper, and salt. Saute until onions are browned, stirring often. The longer this mixture simmers, the better it tastes. It is done when onions are transparent and begin to stick to the skillet, about 20 minutes.

In a large bowl combine bread crumbs and grated cheese. Melt the butter, pour over crumbs. Beat the eggs and add to crumbs. Add onion mixture. Mix well. Mixture must be moist enough to hold together. If dry, add water or broth.

Select a deep-sided, large roasting pan. Cover bottom with remaining oil and stand rib rack up to form a circle. Tie ends together with strong butcher cord. Place some foil in center of roast. Fill center with stuffing and cover with additional foil to keep stuffing moist. Put meat thermometer into fleshy part of roast, taking care to avoid the bones.

Roast in oven at 375 degrees for 1-1/2 to 2 hours or until meat thermometer reaches desired temperature. Remove from oven, remove foil from top of stuffing, and place on a serving dish.

Serves: 6.

Note: To add potatoes, peel and cut 4 potatoes into 3 or 4 pieces (for crunchy potatoes cut smaller). After lamb has been roasting for 30 minutes, add potatoes, turning to coat with oil. Turn every 20 minutes. Do not salt potatoes.

Leg of Lamb Roast with Rosemary and Oven Potatoes
Coscia di Agnellino con Rosmarino e Contorno di Patate

The final meat course of the Easter meal is always roast leg of lamb with oven potatoes. We never serve a sauce or gravy with any of our roasts; they are so well seasoned they do not need additional flavoring.

5-6 large cloves garlic
8-10 sprigs fresh rosemary
1/4-inch-thick slice *pancetta*
1 leg of baby lamb (5 pounds)
2 tsp. salt
1-1/2 tsp. pepper
1/4 cup corn oil

4-5 potatoes (red)

Juice of 2 lemons

Peel garlic and cut in halves or thirds depending on size. Set aside. Wash rosemary and cut into small pieces. Cut *pancetta* into 8 or 9 strips. Set aside.

Make sure roast is at room temperature. With a sharp paring knife cut 1-inch deep slits on all sides of the leg of lamb approximately 1-1/2 inches apart. Into each pocket place salt, pepper, a piece of garlic, a pinch of rosemary, and a strip of *pancetta* (in exact order). Salt and pepper entire outside of roast. Allow to set 1/2 hour before putting in oven.

Preheat the oven to 450 degrees. Cover bottom of roaster with oil. Place leg of lamb in roaster and put into oven. Sear the lamb in the hot oven for 10 minutes. Reduce the temperature to 350 degrees.

Peel and cut large potatoes into 3 or 4 pieces, small ones in half (for crunchy potatoes cut into smaller pieces). After the lamb has been roasting for 30 minutes, add the potatoes. Turn all potatoes coating them with the oil in the pan. Do not salt potatoes.

Roast an additional 2 hours, basting the roast and turning the potatoes every 20 minutes. Insert a meat thermometer halfway through the roasting time, making sure to avoid fat pockets or bones. Roasting time depends of the size of the leg of lamb, but usually averages 2 to 2-1/2 hours.

Just before serving pour lemon juice over the lamb. Serve with fresh garden salad and an additional vegetable.

Serves: 8-10.

Snack Idea: Cold lamb is an excellent snack. Make a sandwich with mayonnaise and lettuce.

Veal
Vitello

Veal Roast with Oven Potatoes
Vitello al Forno e Contorno di Patate

3-4 garlic cloves
1/4-inch-thick slice
pancetta
6-7 sprigs fresh
rosemary or 1 T dry

4 to 4-1/2 pounds veal
loin
2-1/2 tsp. salt
1-1/2 tsp. pepper
1/4 cup corn oil

5-6 potatoes (red)

Peel each clove of garlic and cut in halves or thirds depending on size. Set aside. Cut *pancetta* into 1/2-inch pieces. Set aside. Wash rosemary and cut into 1-inch strips. Set aside.

Make sure roast is at room temperature. With a sharp knife cut 1-inch slits in the top of the veal loin approximately 1-1/2 inches apart. Into each pocket place salt, pepper, a sliver of garlic, a pinch of rosemary, and *pancetta* (in exact order). Salt and pepper entire outside of loin.

Heat the oven to 350 degrees. Cover the bottom of a large roasting pan with oil. Place roast, slit side up, in the roaster. Roast for 30 minutes.

Peel and cut large potatoes into 3 or 4 pieces (for crunchy potatoes cut into smaller pieces). After the veal has been roasting for 30 minutes, add the potatoes. Turn all potatoes, coating them with the oil. Do not salt potatoes.

Roast for an additional 2 hours, basting the veal and turning the potatoes every 20 minutes. Use a meat thermometer.

Serve with fresh garden salad, and an additional vegetable.

Serves: 8-10.

Note: We often ordered a veal roast with kidney attached because my father enjoyed the kidney so much.

Snack Idea: Left-over veal roast makes an excellent sandwich served with mayonnaise and lettuce on good Italian bread.

133

Pocket Veal Roast with Stuffing
Vitello Ripieno

4 pounds veal breast
with pocket

2 onions
1/4-inch-thick slice
pancetta
3 celery ribs
1 carrot
1 tsp. parsley
1 clove garlic

2 T corn oil
1/2 tsp. pepper
1 tsp. salt

3 cups bread crumbs or
cubes
1/2 cup freshly grated
Parmesan cheese
1/4 pound butter
3 eggs

1/2 T salt
1/4 tsp. pepper
1/4 tsp. thyme
1/4 cup corn oil*

When buying veal breast have the butcher cut a pocket by cutting the meat away from, but not completely off, the bone.

Peel onions, wash and cut into quarter wedges. Cut *pancetta* into 1/2-inch pieces. Peel celery and carrot, wash, and cut into 1-inch pieces. Chop parsley. Peel garlic and cut in half. Combine all and grind in meat grinder or food processor (the grinder is better because it releases the juices).

Place a medium-size iron skillet over medium-high heat. Heat to hot. Add oil. When oil is hot add chopped ingredients, pepper, and salt. Saute until onions are browned, stirring often. The longer this mixture simmers, the better it tastes. It is done when onions are transparent and it begins to stick to the skillet, about 20 minutes.

In a large bowl combine bread crumbs and cheese. Melt butter, pour over bread. Beat the eggs and add. Add onion mixture. Mix well. Do not add salt and pepper. Mixture must be moist enough to hold together. If dry, add water or broth.

Place veal pocket on a work space. Spread the pocket away from the bone and fill with stuffing. Skewer the opening of the pocket with sticks or cooking pins. Rub outside of roast with salt, pepper and thyme.

Place oil (see note) in roasting pan. Add veal. Bake in 350-degree oven for 1-1/2 to 2 hours. Serve with green salad.

Serves: 4-6.

To serve with oven potatoes: Peel and cut 4 or 5 potatoes (red) into 3 or 4 pieces (for crunchy potatoes cut into smaller pieces). After veal has been roasting for 30 minutes, add potatoes. Turn all potatoes, coating them with oil in pan. Do not salt potatoes.

Note: *This roast can be roasted without oil, but in that event you cannot make oven potatoes. Simply lightly grease the bottom of the roasting pan and continue as above.

In Sauces
Nella Salsa

With veal as expensive as it is today, we often substitute chicken for some of the following recipes.

Veal Birds
Uccellini di Vitello

2 slices veal steak
1/4 pound
fontina cheese

1 cup bread crumbs
2 T freshly grated
Parmesan cheese
2 T olive oil
1 egg
2 T celery leaves
2 tsp. fresh parsley
2 small onions, diced

2 T butter
1/4 tsp. salt
1/8 tsp. pepper

1/2 pound prosciutto
or ham
10-12 cooking pins

1-1/2 cups bread crumbs
2 T freshly grated
Parmesan cheese
Dash salt
2 eggs
3/4 cup corn oil

2 cans cream of
mushroom soup*
1 cup broth

Both veal and fontina cheese should be thinly sliced. Place veal on a pastry board and pound with a mallet or the heavy side of a knife until it is 1/4-inch thick. Remove excess fat; cut into 3-by-5-inch pieces.

In a small bowl, combine bread crumbs, grated cheese, olive oil, egg, celery leaves, and parsley (cut with scissors). Dice onions.

Place small iron skillet over medium-high heat. Heat to hot. Add butter, melt. Add onions, salt and pepper and saute until transparent (5 to 7 minutes). Remove from heat, add to bread crumb mixture and mix well.

Cover piece of veal with slice of prosciutto. Add 1-1/2 tablespoons of bread mixture and top with slice of cheese. Roll and fasten with a cooking pin. Repeat until all pieces are filled and rolled.

Mix second batch of bread crumbs, cheese, and dash of salt together, lay on flat dish. Beat eggs in a wide bowl. Place a medium-size iron skillet over medium-high heat. Heat to hot. Add oil. Heat to hot.

Roll birds in beaten egg and immediately into bread crumbs, pressing firmly. Place in hot oil and fry until golden brown, rolling to fry all sides (about 7 minutes). Remove from skillet one at a time and place on a paper towel to absorb extra oil. Continue until all are fried. Place in a baking dish.

Place a medium-size saucepan over medium-high heat. Add soup. Rinse cans with broth, add to saucepan, and stir. Heat to simmer and pour over birds. Bake in 350-degree oven for 1 to 1-1/2 hours or until tender. Serve with mashed potatoes and a good green salad.

Serves: 6-8.

Note: *This recipe was originally made with no sauce. Over the years we began to use cream of mushroom soup. Nonna liked it, too!

135

Veal Jump in Your Mouth
Saltimbocca

4 thinly sliced veal steaks
Salt, to taste
Pepper, to taste

16 fresh sage leaves or
1 T dried sage
8-10 thin slices of
prosciutto (or ham)

2 T butter, divided
1-2 T olive oil

1 cup dry white wine

Lay veal on pastry board and pound with kitchen mallet or heavy side of a knife until 1/4-inch thick. Cut each slice into 2 pieces. Season with salt and pepper to taste.

Place 2 to 3 fresh sage leaves on each piece of veal. Cover with a slice of prosciutto.

Place a medium-size iron skillet over medium-high heat. Heat to hot. Melt 1 tablespoon butter and when melted add oil. Be sure butter does not burn. When hot add veal, prosciutto side up, one piece at a time. Saute quickly for 1 to 2 minutes until lightly browned. Do not turn. Remove and place in an oven-proof dish. Do not stack. Heat oven to 350 degrees and bake for 5 minutes.

To the juices of the skillet add wine and bring to a boil over high heat. Scrape up juices from bottom of skillet until all are dissolved. Reduce to half. Whisk in the remaining butter, season with salt and pepper to taste. Remove veal from oven. Pour sauce over all and serve at once.

Serves: 6-8.

Variations:
With cheese and nuts. Prepare veal as above. When ready to assemble, place sage and prosciutto on veal. Top each serving with a slice of fontina or mozzarella cheese and 1 tablespoon pine nuts or walnuts. Roll each piece of veal and secure with cooking pins or tie with butcher cord. Brown as directed, but turn to brown all sides, and bake in 350-degree oven for 20 minutes. Add the juice of 1 lemon to the wine sauce. Serve hot.

With Mushrooms. Prepare veal as above. To the juices in the skillet add wine and bring to a boil over high heat. Scrape bottom of skillet until juices are dissolved. Reduce to half. Add 16 sliced mushrooms. Simmer for 5 minutes. Whisk in the remaining butter, season with salt and pepper to taste. Remove veal from oven. Pour sauce over all and serve at once.

Veal Parmesan
Vitello alla Parmigiana

3/4 cup corn oil, divided
2 cloves garlic

1-1/2 cups whole or
crushed canned
tomatoes
4 oz. tomato paste
3/4 cup broth
Salt, to taste
Pepper, to taste

1-1/2 pounds veal steak*

1 cup bread crumbs
3/4 cup freshly grated
Parmesan cheese
2 eggs

1/2 tsp. salt
1/4 tsp. pepper

4 (1/2-inch-thick) slices
mozzarella cheese

Peel each clove of garlic and cut in halves or thirds depending on size.

Place medium-size iron skillet over medium-high heat. Heat to hot. Add 1/4 cup oil. Heat to hot. Add garlic to skillet. When brown, mash into small pieces. Add tomatoes crushing with a fork into small pieces. Simmer 15 to 20 minutes. Add tomato paste. Rinse both tomato and paste cans with broth or water and add to mixture. Simmer 25 to 30 minutes, or until tomatoes reduce and begin to lose their bright red color.

Remove from heat and run through a sieve pushing pulp through sieve with a spoon or fork. Throw away any pulp remaining in the sieve. Taste and add salt and pepper to taste.

While sauce is simmering, place veal (see note) on a pastry board. Pound with a kitchen mallet or the handle of a knife to tenderize. Cut away any excess fat. Cut each slice in half.

Mix bread crumbs and 1/2 cup freshly grated Parmesan cheese and place on a flat dish. Beat eggs in a shallow dish, and add salt and pepper.

Place a large-size iron skillet over medium-high heat. Heat to hot. Add remaining oil. Heat to hot. Dip lightly and quickly into egg, then press into bread crumbs coating both sides, and place in hot oil. Fry on one side, then the other (8 to 10 minutes total). Remove from skillet one at a time and place on a paper towel to absorb extra oil. Continue until all is fried.

Place veal in a baking dish. Cover with tomato mixture and mozzarella. Place in 350-degree oven for 30 minutes. Remove from oven and sprinkle with remaining Parmesan cheese. Serve immediately.

Serves: 4.

Note: *Can substitute chicken for veal.

Classic Veal Scaloppine
Scaloppini di Vitello

7-8 mushrooms

1 pound veal steak

Salt, to taste
Pepper, to taste
2 T flour

2 T butter
1/2 cup broth
1/3 cup white wine or
*Marsala**

Take one mushroom at a time and cut off the tip of the stem and remove any blemishes on the crown. Slice lengthwise into 1/4-inch-thick slices.

Lay veal steak on a pastry board and beat with a kitchen mallet (or the handle of a knife) to tenderize. Cut into 2-to-3-inch cubes. Salt and pepper to taste. Place flour on a board. Roll each scaloppine in flour.

Place a medium-size iron skillet over medium-high heat. Heat to hot. Add butter. When melted add veal pieces and cook quickly, turning once. After 10 minutes add broth and wine. Simmer 5 minutes.

Add mushrooms to veal. Cover and simmer for 20 minutes. If mixture begins to dry, add a little more broth. Serve at once.

Serves: 4.

Variation: A variation is to add slices of green pepper when you add the mushrooms.

Note: *Marsala* is an Italian cooking wine found in supermarkets and liquor stores. The latter variety is better for this dish.

Veal Scaloppine with Prosciutto
Scaloppini di Vitello con Prosciutto

1 pound veal scaloppine
(or veal steak)
1 T corn oil
1 T butter

1/2 cup flour
1/2 tsp. salt
1/4 tsp. pepper

3/4 cup crushed canned
tomatoes
3 T fresh parsley

1/4 pound thinly sliced
prosciutto
3/4-1 cup white wine

2/3 cup shredded
mozzarella cheese

Be sure veal is thin and scaloppine cut into mouth-size pieces. Place a medium-size iron skillet over medium-high heat. Heat to hot. Add oil and butter. Heat.

Place flour, salt and pepper on pastry board. Dust each scaloppine in flour and add to oil. Saute 5 minutes, turning occasionally. Remove, set aside.

Place small saucepan over medium heat. Add tomatoes. Dice parsley and add. Allow to simmer for 10 minutes.

Place scaloppine in baking dish. Top with prosciutto. Add tomato mixture. Pour wine around meat. Bake in 350-degree oven for 45 minutes.

Remove from oven, top with mozzarella cheese and return to oven until cheese is melted (about 5 minutes).

Serves: 4.

Veal in White Wine
Vitello con Vin Bianco

2 veal steaks
2 eggs
1 T flour
1 T milk
3/4 tsp. salt
1/4 tsp. pepper

1/4 cup corn oil

1/4 pound butter
1 cup white wine,
sauterne or Chablis

2 T chopped fresh
parsley
1 lemon

Veal should be thinly sliced, then cut into serving pieces. Beat eggs in a medium-size bowl. Add flour, milk, salt, and pepper. Beat into a batter.

Place a medium-size iron skillet over medium-high heat. Heat to hot. Add oil. Heat to hot. Dip veal pieces in batter and one at a time place in hot oil. Brown until golden, turn, brown second side. Place in a shallow casserole dish.

In a second skillet melt butter until hot, but not brown. Add wine and simmer on high heat for 2 to 3 minutes. Pour mixture over veal. Bake at 325 degrees for 45 minutes to an hour. If liquid is soupy, raise oven to 350 degrees and bake an additional 5 to 10 minutes, or until liquid drys a bit.

Remove from oven. Place on serving tray. Sprinkle with freshly chopped parsley and serve with lemon wedges.

Serves: 6.

139

Stews
Stufati

Veal Stew with Potatoes and Peppers
Stufato di Vitello con Patate e Peperoni

1-1/2 pounds cubed
veal shank
1 clove garlic
6 potatoes (red)
4 green peppers

1/4 cup corn oil
1/4 tsp. salt
Dash pepper

1 cup dry white wine
1 cup crushed canned
tomatoes*
1/2 cup broth

Remove extra fat from veal and, if not cubed, cut into 2-inch pieces. Peel garlic. Peel and dice potatoes into quarters or eighths (depending on size). Slice green peppers into strips.

Place a medium-size iron skillet over medium-high heat. Heat to hot. Add oil. When oil is hot, add the garlic; fry until brown, and remove from skillet.

Place cubed veal in the skillet and salt and pepper to taste. Turn the meat often until all is lightly browned. Remove meat from skillet.

Add wine and tomatoes (see note) to oil in skillet. Crush tomatoes with a fork into small pieces. Rinse can with broth and add to skillet. Simmer 8 to 10 minutes or until they reduce slightly.

Remove from heat and run through a sieve pushing pulp through with a spoon or fork. Throw remaining pulp away and return sauce to skillet. Simmer an additional 10 minutes, or until sauce begins to lose its bright red color.

Add meat and simmer slowly for 20 minutes. Add potatoes and continue to simmer for 20 minutes. When meat is tender, add peppers and simmer an additional 10 minutes or until tomato sauce is thick, dark in color, and oil rises to the top (skim if desired).

Turn into a serving dish and serve with good Italian bread.

Serves: 6.

Note: *You can eliminate the tomatoes from this dish if you desire.

Veal Stew with Peas
Stufato di Vitello con Piselli

One of my favorite dishes, veal stew with peas is excellent, excellent, excellent served with fresh Italian bread. It is even better the second day and I am always careful that there is enough left over for my lunch.

1-1/2 pounds cubed
veal shank
1/4 cup corn oil
1/4 tsp. salt
Dash pepper
2 tsp. fresh thyme leaves

3 cups peas*

1/2 cup broth (optional)

Veal cubes should be 2 inches square. Cut fat or gristle from the cubed veal.

Place a large-size iron skillet over medium-high heat. Heat to hot. Add oil. When oil is hot, add veal cubes. Salt and pepper to taste. Add thyme and quickly saute the veal until it is browned on all sides (about 7 minutes).

Pour the peas, liquid and all, into the skillet. Stir. Cover and simmer about 1-1/2 hours, stirring every 15 minutes.

When veal is tender the stew is done. If it begins to dry add 1/2 cup broth.

Serve with good Italian bread.

Serves: 4.

Note: *Over the years we found we prefer the softer canned peas to fresh peas for this dish. In fact, I often mash some of the peas while they are cooking to make a thicker sauce.

Notes

Pork
Maiale

Pork, offered as a sacrifice to the gods in ancient Rome, is eaten often in an Italian home. In our home we eat both fresh and cured pork, and some of the best and most exotic recipes in this book are found in this chapter. *Arista* is a dish fit for a king, and so tasty it is certain to bring accolades to the cook time and time again. Not to be outdone, pork chops on a spit and suckling pig in *porchetta* are the culinary art brought to perfection. You will find these pork dishes, often wedded to garlic, rosemary, sage, or fennel, are the centerpieces of good Italian eating, the reason why Italian cooking is rated the best in the world (I am a bit prejudice, but not wrong).

In most Italian immigrant families a meal of pork began with dressing the pig, a process called the *maialatura*. For one week every winter the whole family was involved in the process. The *maialatura* could be done anytime from November to February. Many families saved the labor for after the Christmas holidays, but we did not. As soon as the October wine was stored, the cellar was cleaned and the *maialatura* began.

In Italy, the *norcino*, a pork butcher, would often come to the family to kill and bleed the pig. But the immigrants either had to do it themselves, or call on a friend for help. Not all people raised their own hogs, so a trip to the farm was in order. Buying a pig was a major event and one often selected the pig just after it was born and it was raised expressly for the family.

Our Nonnos and Nonnas are gone and Nonno had no sons to carry on the traditions of making wine and cured pork. We relied heavily on Bob Pelini and Maria Albertini for the special dishes of the *maialatura*. It was a struggle. All of us remember, but what we remember is not exactly the same. For example, we agree Gino and Nonno rubbed the leg of the ham with a garlic paste when making prosciutto, but we have different recollections as to when this process was done. Despite the obstacles, these recipes had to be included in this book for they are so important to our lives and represent the men's contribution to our heritage. It took a lot of searching to find all the answers.

Suckling Pig in Porchetta
Maialino da Latte in Porchetta

Italians say, *"Non è festa se non c'e la porchetta"* (It is not a festival if there isn't a *porchetta*), and they buy *porchetta* from vendors and eat it while strolling through the streets.

Suckling pig in *porchetta* was a specialty of my Nonno. When my mother was a young girl, Nonno was responsible for the barbecue at the October Saturday night dances at the NIPA (Northern Italian Political Association) in our town. He would prepare the pig early in the day and take it to a local bakery where it was baked in the ovens for 6 to 10 hours and delivered to the club around 9 p.m.

Traditionally the pig used for *porchetta* was milk-fed. Our version of *porchetta* is Tuscan, filled with garlic and sometimes sausage, but there are as many variations in Italy as there are provinces including stuffings of bread and fruit. Through the years we devised a method of making *porchetta* without using a whole pig. That recipe is also presented following our more traditional version.

2-3 buds garlic
1 pound prosciutto
or *pancetta*
7 T fresh fennel seeds
1/8 cup peppercorns
1/8 cup salt

1 (20-pound) suckling
pig
3 pounds sausage
(optional)

1 cup olive oil
1 potato
1 apple
Aluminum foil

Lemons for garnish

1 trussing needle
and thin wire or thread

Break garlic buds into individual cloves. Crush each with a mallet and set in a small dish (do not peel). Slice prosciutto or *pancetta* into thin slices and place in a dish. Crush fennel seeds and place in a dish. Grind pepper, mix with salt, and place in yet another dish.

Place dressed pig (see note) on a large pastry board. Be sure it has been cleaned inside and out. Turn pig on its back. Rub inside of pig with a damp cloth and then the salt and pepper mixture. Lay in the prosciutto end to end covering the entire bottom of the cavity. Top with crushed garlic and fennel and fill remaining space with sausage (optional). Close the opening and sew it securely shut with a trussing needle and thick cord or wire. Rub entire pig with oil.

Rub a large roasting pan with oil. Place the pig in the pan. Tuck the legs under the body. Insert whole potato in the snout. Wrap snout, ears, and tail with aluminum foil to avoid burning. Insert a meat thermometer (do not hit a bone).

Bake at 350 degrees for at least 6 hours (could take considerable longer) or until meat thermometer reaches 170 degrees and skin is brown. Baste often with drippings. When cooked raise oven temperature to 450 degrees and roast 15 minutes to crisp the skin. The crisp skin is a delicacy and a portion should be included with each serving.

144

Remove pig from oven. Slide onto a large platter or board. Remove foil. Replace potato with apple. Garnish with lemons. Set for 15 minutes.

To cut: Remove a leg and slice chunks of meat away from bone. Then do remaining legs. Split the body exposing the steamed sausage. Cut one half at a time, not in slices, but in chunks.

Note: You can use half a pig and place stuffing under the carcass.

Serves: 30-35.

Pork Pocket in Porchetta
Maiale Ripieno in Porchetta

If you never intend to roast a suckling pig, you can still enjoy the wonderful taste of pig in *porchetta*.

3 pound pork loin
with pocket
1/2 T pepper
1 tsp. salt
3 large cloves garlic,
crushed
2 thick slices prosciutto
1/2 T fennel seeds
3-4 sausage links
(optional)

Corn oil as needed
3-4 kitchen skewers

When buying the loin, ask the butcher to cut a pocket close to the bone. It would be wonderful if you could find a loin with the rind on it, but that is highly unlikely.

Prepare the loin following the instructions in the preceding recipe, but with the quantities in this recipe. Use half the salt and pepper to rub the inside and half to rub on the outside.

Lay the prosciutto in the pocket topped by garlic, fennel, and sausage (optional). Close pocket with skewers.

Rub bottom of roaster with a little oil, add roast, place in oven and roast for 3 to 3-1/2 hours. Remove from oven and slice along bone.

Serves: 4-6.

Note: Despite the lack of oil, you can add potatoes to this roast. Peel and cut 5 large potatoes (red) into 4 or 5 pieces (for crunchy potatoes cut smaller pieces). After pork has been roasting for 30 minutes, add potatoes. Turn potatoes, coating them with the juice in the pan. Baste every 20 minutes. Do not salt potatoes.

Fresh Pork Belly in Porchetta
Pancetta Fresca in Porchetta

This recipe calls for fresh pork belly, not one that has been cured. And it should still have the rind on it. Pork Belly is usually used as a savory, added to roasts and *soffritto*. This is the only recipe we have where it is a meal in itself.

2 pounds fresh
pork belly with rind
3-4 cloves garlic

1 tsp. salt
1 tsp. freshly ground
pepper
3 thick slices prosciutto
1/2 tsp. fresh fennel
seeds

Lay the fresh pork belly *(pancetta)* on a pastry board, rind side down. Crush garlic cloves (do not peel) by hitting each one with a kitchen mallet or the handle of a large knife.

Salt and pepper the *pancetta* to taste. Scatter the crushed garlic over the *pancetta* and lay on slices of prosciutto to completely cover it. Next scatter the fennel seeds.

Beginning at one end roll the pork belly into a roll. Tightly secure the roll with butcher cord (the rind should be on the outside).

Place in a low baking pan. Do not add oil for it has plenty of fat for basting.

Roast in a 325-degree oven for 2-1/2 to 3 hours or until the rind becomes crisp.

Remove from oven and eat immediately. Rind is delicious hot, but not very appetizing when cold.

Serves: 4-6.

Note: Despite the lack of oil, you can add potatoes to this roast. Peel and cut 5 large potatoes (red) into 4 or 5 pieces (for crunchy potatoes cut smaller pieces). After pork has been roasting for 30 minutes, add potatoes. Turn potatoes, coating them with the juice in the pan. Baste every 20 minutes. Do not salt potatoes.

Pork Chops with Sage on a Spit
Costolette di Maiale con Salvia allo Spiedo

Pork chops with sage on a spit is a must for *Martedi Grasso*, the last feast of carnival before the Lenten season. My aunt in Italy prepares this wonderful dish over an open grate, and has a special machine to turn the spit. We are not as fortunate and do not have an open fireplace in our kitchen, so my mother bought a broiler with rotisserie, which we used exclusively for this dish. Vivian and Tom had a fireplace built in their kitchen and bought a machine in Italy to turn the spit.

8 (3/4-inch-thick)
pork loin chops
Salt and pepper, to taste
3-4 T olive oil
12 sprigs fresh sage

Place chops on a large platter. Sprinkle with salt and pepper to taste. Pour olive oil over chops turning each until well-coated. Place a sprig of sage on each chop and let stand for 20 minutes.

Pick up a chop and hold it in the palm of your hand.

Fold the loin (fillet) side toward the bone (see A) to tuck in the flap. This is a short fold. Make sure the sage sprig is not tucked into this fold. Fold again bringing the flap side to the bone and enclosing a sprig of sage (see B).

Place the skewer through the center of the chop, the sage within. Do this for each chop. Be sure to skewer both folds and alternate them on the skewer so that the first chop has the bone side up, the second chop the closed side up (see C), etc. This balances the chops and helps them stay firm on the skewer. Secure firmly.

Place skewer 6 to 7 inches from heat. Skewer must rotate. Take the final 4 sprigs of sage, tie them together with a cord to use as a brush. Dip the sage brush into the remaining oil mixture on the platter and brush the chops every 10 to 15 minutes. Let cook for 3 to 3-1/2 hours. If using an electric spit, lower the spit to 3-to-4 inches for the last 45 minutes.

Yield: 4 servings.

Note: A variation is to add chicken wings. Salt and pepper wings. Fold tip of wing under the back and fill the hole with a sprig of sage. Place on the spit, alternating with the pork chops.

147

Pork Roast with Oven Potatoes
Arista con Patate al Forno

The king of all pork dishes in Italy and in our home is *arista*, named in Florence at a meeting of the Ecumenical Council of the Catholic Church. The time was around 1440 and Constantinople was being threatened by the Ottoman Turks. The emperor of the Eastern Roman Empire came to Italy for help (the moment is immortalized in Benozzo Gozzoli's painting, *Journey of the Magi*). Many of the meetings of this lengthy council were held in Florence and at one feast this dish was prepared. When it was served one of the visiting orthodox bishops exclaimed in Greek, *arista*, "the best." And it is.

3 large cloves garlic
6-7 sprigs fresh rosemary
3 pounds center cut pork rib roast*
1 T salt
3/4 T pepper

1/4 cup corn oil

5 large potatoes (red)

Peel each clove of garlic and cut in halves or thirds, depending on size. Set aside. Wash rosemary and cut into 1-inch strips. Set aside.

Make sure roast is at room temperature. With a sharp paring knife cut 1-inch-deep slits in the top of the pork center cut, approximately 1-1/2 inches apart. Into each pocket place a sprig of rosemary, salt, pepper, and a piece of garlic (in exact order). Salt and pepper entire outside of roast.

Heat the oven to 325 degrees. Add enough oil to cover the bottom of a roasting pan. Place roast in roaster bone side down. Slide in pan to coat bottom with oil. Insert oven thermometer. Be sure not to touch a bone. Place in oven.

Peel and cut potatoes into 4 or 5 pieces (for crunchy potatoes cut smaller pieces). After the pork has been roasting for 30 minutes, add the potatoes. Turn all potatoes, coating them with the oil in the pan. Cook for an additional 2 to 2-1/2 hours, basting the roast and turning the potatoes every 20 minutes. Do not salt potatoes.

Serve with garden salad and a vegetable (fried savoy cabbage in garlic is an excellent choice, see page 258).

Serves: 6-8.

Note: *In order to slice the roast easily, ask the butcher to crack the bone in 2 or 3 places.

Snack Idea: Cold pork roast makes an excellent sandwich.

Stews
Umidi

Pork Chops with Cauliflower in Sauce
Costolette di Maiale con Cavolfiore nella Salsa

1 cauliflower

1 cup flour
Salt and pepper, to taste

3 eggs
3/4 cup corn oil, divided

4-5 loin pork chops
2-3 cloves garlic
2-3 tsp. fresh rosemary

2 cups whole or crushed
canned tomatoes
1/2 cup broth or water

Place 4-quart pot on medium-high heat. Fill 1/2 full with water, add salt. Cut cauliflower in half. Add to boiling water, cover, and boil 3 minutes. Turn off burner (if overcooked it will fall apart in final preparation). When cool, remove and drain.

Break into florets. Place flour on pastry board. Add dash salt and pepper, stir. Gently roll each floret in flour, coating generously. Stack on flat dish. Beat eggs with a dash of salt. Set near stove.

Place medium-size iron skillet over medium-high heat. Heat to hot. Add 1/2 cup oil. When hot, dip a floret in beaten egg, coating generously. Drop into oil. Repeat until skillet is full. Fry golden brown, turning as necessary. Remove, place on paper towel to absorb oil. Continue until all are fried. Set aside.

Place large-size iron skillet over medium-high heat. Heat to hot. Add remaining oil. Salt and pepper pork chops. Place in skillet. Crush garlic with mallet or side of knife (do not peel), place in skillet. Add rosemary. Sear chops quickly, about 3 minutes each side. Remove chops from skillet and set aside.

To juices in skillet, add tomatoes and crush with a fork. Simmer 10 minutes. Rinse tomato can with broth or water and add to mixture. Taste, salt and pepper if necessary. Mix. Lower heat, simmer uncovered 15 minutes.

Remove from heat and run sauce through a sieve removing pulp. Return sauce to skillet, return heat to medium-high, simmer for 5 minutes; reduce heat and simmer uncovered for 15 to 20 minutes or until sauce begins to darken. Add cauliflower. Cover and simmer slowly for 10 minutes. Add chops. Simmer an additional 20 minutes or until chops are tender, sauce is brown-red, and oil begins to separate and float on surface (skim if desired). Do not stir or turn. If sauce begins to dry, add additional broth.

Serves: 3-4.

Pork Chops with White Beans
Costolette di Maiale con Cannellini

1-1/2 pounds dried or 1 (2 pound 8 oz.) can Great Northern White beans*

2 T corn oil
6 thick pork loin chops
2 tsp. salt
2 tsp. pepper
2 tsp. dry rosemary

4 large cloves garlic
1-1/2 cups whole or crushed canned tomatoes
3 oz. tomato paste
1 cup broth

If using dry beans (see note), place the beans in a 4-quart pot. Fill pot with water. Allow to soak overnight, drain, add fresh water, cover, and boil for 4 to 5 hours or until tender. If using canned beans (softer than dry), simply open the can and pour the contents into a 4-quart pot and heat. Rinse can with a little broth and add to pot.

Place a large-size iron skillet over high heat. Heat to hot. Add oil. Add pork chops, but do not stack. Sprinkle with salt, pepper, and rosemary and sear on both sides. Lower heat. Remove chops, set aside.

Peel garlic and add to oil in skillet. When garlic browns, crush with fork until broken into small pieces. To juices in skillet add tomatoes, crushing with a fork into small pieces. Simmer 8 to 10 minutes. Add tomato paste Rinse both tomato and paste cans with 1/2 cup broth or water and add to mixture. Taste, salt and pepper if necessary. Mix well. Lower heat and simmer uncovered for 30 minutes, or until tomatoes begin to lose bright red color.

Place boiled beans in a 4-quart saucepan or a deep Dutch oven over medium-high heat. Add 1 cup sauce and simmer (about 10 minutes). Add remaining sauce and the chops and allow to simmer about 15 minutes. Reduce heat, cover, and simmer for 1 to 1-1/2 hours. If sauce begins to dry, add more soup stock or water. Serve with good Italian bread.

Dish is done when chops are tender.

Serves: 4-6.

Notes: This meal is even better the second day. You can also chop the meat into small pieces or use pork steak.

*Nonna never used canned beans, and although they are softer, dried beans are better for this dish.

Pork Steak with Potatoes in Sauce
Braciole di Maiale con Patate e Salsa di Pomodoro

1/4 cup corn oil
2 cloves garlic
2-3 pork steaks
1 tsp. salt
1 tsp. pepper
1 T rosemary

1-1/2 cups whole or
crushed canned tomatoes
3 oz. tomato paste
1/2 cup broth
Salt and pepper, to taste

4-5 potatoes (red)
4 T corn oil

Place a large-size iron skillet over high heat. Heat to hot. Add oil. Peel garlic and add to oil. When browned, crush with a fork into small pieces. Cut pork steaks in half and add to skillet. Sprinkle with salt, pepper, and rosemary and sear on both sides. Lower heat. Remove steaks and set aside.

To the juices in the skillet add tomatoes, crushing with a fork into small pieces. Simmer 8 to 10 minutes. Add tomato paste. Rinse both tomato and paste cans with broth or water and add to mixture. Simmer 20 minutes, or until tomatoes reduce and begin to lose their bright red color.

Remove from heat and run through a sieve, pushing pulp through sieve with a spoon or fork. Throw remaining pulp away. Return sauce to skillet and continue to simmer. Taste, add salt and pepper if necessary.

While tomatoes are simmering, peel and dice potatoes into 1-1/4-inch cubes. Place a smaller iron skillet over medium-high heat. Heat to hot. Add oil. Add potatoes to oil and cook until golden brown.

Add pork steaks and potatoes to tomato mixture. Simmer for 1/2 hour or until tomatoes are dark brown-red and oil floats on top (skim if desired). Pork should be tender.

Serves: 4-6.

Note: For a lighter sauce, eliminate the tomato paste.

151

Sausage
Salsiccia

Most Americans have eaten sausage at least once in their lives, and my guess is the majority enjoy it. Almost every ethnic group has its own version of sausage: The Polish have kielbasa, the Germans have at least a dozen variations including knockwurst and bratwurst.

Italian sausage is prepared in a variety of ways. Hot and savory sausage with garlic and red pepper is often found in southern Italian homes. A sweet sausage using cinnamon or cloves is a breakfast sausage in northern Italian homes.

Just as it was for most immigrants, sausage is a staple in our Italian kitchen. We prefer it spiced with garlic and nutmeg. The Pelini family prefers it with garlic and fennel. Both Tuscan recipes are found on pages 160-61.

Aging is a factor in sausage. Fresh is the most well-known and the most popular way Americans eat it. But we also have a dry sausage, *salsiccia secca*. Once the sausage is made, it is hung in a cool, dry place. Nonno always hung it in his wine cellar. One line of sausage was set aside and as we used the fresh links it was not touched. As time passed the untouched sausage began to cure. After it hardened it was sometimes cooked, but more often sliced like a salami, and eaten raw.

There are dozens of recipes in this book that use sausage as an ingredient. Sausage is the flavor that makes the Stuffed Mushrooms appetizer on page 46 so tasty. Sausage as a sandwich appears as Sausage in a Blanket on page 73 and Sausage with Onion and Green Pepper Sandwich on page 228. Sausage works well with eggs and is found in the Sausage Omelet on page 169 and the Easter Pie on page 171. Accompanying pasta it is found in the Grand Lasagna with Sausage, Ricotta, and Bechamel on page 193 and Polenta with Sausage on page 195. As a stuffing sausage is used in the Meatloaf Italian Style on page 118, the Suckling Pig in *Porchetta* on page 144, the Pork Pocket in *Porchetta* on page 145, and Roast Capon with Fennel and Oven Potatoes on page 205.

The recipes that offer sausage as a main ingredient in a stew are featured on the following pages. To fry a sausage see below.

Sausage
Salsiccia

1 sausage link

Place a small-size iron skillet over medium-high heat. Heat to hot. Add sausage and cover. Do not add oil. Allow to fry for 5 minutes. Turn. If sausage sticks (the more sausages you fry at one time the less likely they will stick), add a little water to the skillet. Cover, lower heat to medium, and continue to fry for 10 minutes.
Serves: 1.

Sausage and Potatoes in Sauce
Salsiccia con Patate in Umido

6 sausage links

3-4 large potatoes (red)
4 T corn oil

2 cups whole or crushed canned tomatoes
3 oz. tomato paste
1 cup broth
Dash of salt, pepper

Place a medium-size skillet over medium-high heat. Add sausage and brown (do not add oil as sausage will produce its own grease).

While sausages are frying, peel potatoes and cut into 1-inch cubes. Place a second medium-size iron skillet over medium-high heat. Heat to hot. Add oil. Heat to hot. Add potatoes and fry until browned.

Remove sausage from first skillet. To the juices in the skillet add tomatoes crushing with a fork into small pieces. Simmer 8 to 10 minutes. Add tomato paste. Rinse both tomato and paste cans with broth or water and add to mixture. Simmer 20 minutes or until tomatoes reduce and begin to lose their bright red color.

Remove tomatoes from heat and run through a sieve pushing pulp through sieve with a spoon or fork. Throw away any pulp remaining in the sieve.

Return tomato mixture to skillet. Taste and add salt and pepper if necessary. Simmer 10 minutes.

Place sausage and potatoes in tomato mixture and continue simmering for an additional 10 minutes or until potatoes are cooked and sauce is dark brown red. Oil should rise to the top (skim if desired). Turn occasionally. If the sauce begins to dry, add a small amount of broth. Serve with good Italian bread.

Serves: 3-4.

Note: This is a good recipe for dry sausage.

153

Sausage Roll with Lentils
Cotechino con Lenticchie

This is a New Year's Day dish said to bring prosperity and good fortune all year long.

1 *cotechino* sausage*
(1 pound)

1 pound lentils
6 cups water
1/8 tsp. salt

4 cups broth

2 medium onions
1 celery rib
1 carrot
2 cloves garlic
1/4-inch-thick slice
pancetta

4 T corn oil
8 fresh sage leaves
1/2 tsp. salt
1/2 tsp. pepper

1 cup whole or crushed
canned tomatoes

1/4 cup freshly grated
Parmesan cheese

If *cotechino* is dry and hard like a salami, soak it overnight. Remove from water and set aside. If wrapped in plastic seal you do not need to soak.

Rinse lentils in running water. Place a medium-size pot over medium-high heat. Add fresh water, salt, and lentils. Boil for about 30 minutes or until tender to taste.

Place a large-size pot over medium-high heat. Add broth and *cotechino*. Boil. Cover and lower the heat. Simmer 45 minutes. Remove and cool. Broth need not cover *cotechino*, but turn it at least once.

Wash, peel, and chop onions, celery, and carrot. Set aside. Peel garlic and cut into 2 to 3 pieces. Dice *pancetta* into 1/2-inch pieces. Combine all and grind in a meat grinder or food processor (the grinder is better because it releases the juices).

Place medium-size skillet over medium-high heat. Heat to hot. Add oil. Add onions, celery, carrots, *pancetta*, and garlic. Stir, saute 5 minutes. Dice and add sage, salt and pepper. Saute until onions are transparent, about 15 to 20 minutes. The longer it simmers, the better it tastes.

Add tomatoes, crushing with fork into small pieces. Rinse tomato can with broth from *cotechino* and add. Simmer 40 minutes or until tomatoes reduce and lose bright red color. If sauce drys, add broth. Taste, add salt and pepper if necessary.

Drain lentils, combine with tomato sauce. Stir well. Simmer 15 minutes. Remove from stove, lay on large platter and sprinkle with Parmesan cheese.

Remove bladder or plastic (may have broken while boiling) from *cotechino* and slice; lay on top of lentils.

Serves: 3-4.

Variation: Add pasta. Use a short, heavy pasta like *diti*. Par cook for 5 minutes in water and pinch of salt. Add to tomatoes with lentils last 15 minutes.
Note: *Cotechino* is available in Italian meat markets.

Sausage Roll with Savoy Cabbage
Cotechino con Verza

1 *cotechino* sausage*
4 cups broth

1 head savoy cabbage
2 tsp. salt

2-3 T pan drippings or
olive oil
2-3 cloves garlic
Salt, pepper

If *cotechino* is dry and hard like a salami, soak it overnight. Remove from water and set aside. If wrapped in plastic seal you do not need to soak.

Place a large-size pot over medium-high heat. Add broth and *cotechino*. Broth need not cover *cotechino*, but turn it at least once. Bring to a boil, cover, and lower the heat. Simmer 45 minutes. Remove and cool.

In the meantime wash the cabbage and cut in half. If extra large cut again. Place in a large pot over medium-high heat. Fill to half with water and add salt. Boil for 8 to 10 minutes until soft. Test with a fork. Remove and drain (may be placed in the refrigerator for up to 4 days).

When ready to fry, take 1 to 2 pieces of boiled savoy. Squeeze out as much liquid as possible. On a pastry board chop savoy into small pieces.

Place a medium-size iron skillet over medium-high heat. Add oil or pan drippings from a good roast. Peel garlic, add to oil in skillet, brown, and crush with a fork until no large pieces remain.

Place savoy in oil and salt and pepper to taste. Allow to brown about 15 minutes, turning often. If it begins to dry, add 2 to 3 tablespoons of broth from the *cotechino*.

When ready to serve, remove *cotechino* from the broth and cut into 1/2-inch-thick slices. Arrange the savoy cabbage on a large serving tray and place the *cotechino* slices on top. Cover and allow to set 5 minutes. Serve with good Italian bread.

Serves: 4-6.

Note: **Cotechino* is available in Italian meat markets.

Cured and Dressed Pork
Maiale Salato e Condito

The preparation of the meal was woman's work in the immigrant's kitchen, but the preparation of the food before the meal belonged to everyone in the family, especially the men. The garden, the wine cellar, and the curing of pork products was definitely the work of my Nonno. He brought his bounty to the kitchen where Nonna turned it into food fit for the gods. One of the most important steps in this process was dressing the pig, the *maialatura*.

Once the pig was killed it was never refrigerated. Boiling water was poured over the carcass and the skin was scraped to remove dirt and hair. Then the pig was hung by its hind legs, scrubbed, and gutted. The organs--liver, kidneys, lungs, heart, intestines, and caul--were set aside to be used in the various recipes which follow. Then the carcass was cut to make prosciutto, salami, sausage, roasts, chops, blood pudding, headcheese, lard, pork rinds, etc. Nothing was wasted.

Lard and Pork Rinds
Strutto di Maiale e Ciccioli

All the fat on the pig was rendered into lard, which was one of the most important products the pig gave the immigrants, for before refrigeration lard was not only used for cooking but, more importantly, to preserve foods.

Lard has impurities, or pork rinds, and as it renders they do not melt. They were stored and used in breads and pizzas, or eaten by themselves.

Lard

Remove all fat from pork with a sharp knife. Dice or grind fat into very small pieces and place in a large pot (preferably an iron kettle). Place pot over medium-high heat and cook the fat until it melts into a liquid. This could be an all-day affair depending on the amount of fat.

Once the fat is rendered into lard, strain, drain into a large crock, and allow to set.

Pork Rinds

Once lard has liquefied and solid impurities are visible and become golden brown, run through a sieve to catch impurities and place lard in a crock.

The small hard pieces that remain are rinds. Place rinds in a cloth. Roll up and squeeze tightly to remove excess lard. Place cloth on a board, sprinkle rinds lightly with salt, and eat. To store, place rinds in crock and cover with liquid lard. Stir and store.

Headcheese
Soprassata (Coppa)

Some Italians call this dish *coppa*, but we call it *soprassata*. In some Italian homes a *soprassata* is more like a salami, and that is how it is sold in Italian food stores. Headcheese, our *soprassata*, is the boiled head of the freshly slaughtered pig: chopped, spiced, stuffed into a casing, and eaten as a cold cut. The only difference between *soprassata* and *cotechino* (page 162) is the first is chopped and cooked and the second is ground and raw.

1 pig's head or
4 pounds pork butt and
1 pound pork rind*

1-1/2 T salt
3/4 T pepper
1 T peppercorns
1/4 tsp. nutmeg

Canvas or sturdy cloth
or large pan

A

B

Clean head, sear off all hair by holding head over burner, remove eyes and discard. Remove brains and set aside.

Place an 8- to-10-quart pot over medium-high heat. Fill half full with water and bring to a rolling boil. Cut pig's head in half and add to boiling water (if using butt and rind, slice into large chunks). Cook until meat falls from bone (for head several hours, for butt and rind 1 hour). Skim off impurities as needed.

Remove from water, drain, place on large work space. Remove tender, cooked meat of tongue, cheeks, and jaw. Cut into 1-inch pieces, including fat and rind. Discard bones. Add salt, pepper, peppercorns, and nutmeg to meat. Mix 15 minutes and taste. Add additional seasonings if necessary (including àccent).

Lay cloth on board (or sew 3 sides together). Fill cloth with mixture and fold over to form a cylinder (if using a sack, fill sack, and tie tightly at top). Wrap outside with sturdy cord (see illustrations on page 166). Squeeze hard to release excess fluids.

Alternately, press mixture into large, deep (4-5 inch) pan (see A) and place a weight on top.

Place a heavy (5-pound) weight on mixture and let set overnight, press occasionally. This will press out excess moisture and make firm. Grease will rise to top or sides and gel. It can be taken off. Hang wrapped *soprassata* in a cool place for a day or two.

Once meat has set, remove cloth and slice like lunch meat (it will have a marbled pattern, see B). Can be stored in a cool place, preferable a wine cellar.

Yield: 1 roll.

Note: *Pork rind, or skin, can be ordered at most supermarkets.

Blood Pudding
Migliaccio

Sounds awful, but blood pudding is delicious and Italians enjoyed it long before Boccaccio made it famous in the *Decameron*. Called by a variety of names throughout Italy and *sanguinaccio* as well as *migliaccio* in some parts of Tuscany, *migliaccio* is served in a variety of ways with a host of different ingredients including fennel, milk, onions, raisins, brains, chocolate, and pistachio nuts. It can also be made into a sausage called, of course, blood sausage. Ours is a savory pudding, with Parmesan cheese.

The secret in preparing blood pudding is that once the blood is drained from the pig's throat a handful of salt must be added to keep it from clotting.

2-1/4 pounds fresh pig blood
3 T corn oil
1/4-inch-thick slice *pancetta*

2 eggs, beaten
Salt and pepper, to taste
1/2 cup freshly grated Parmesan cheese

Run the blood through a sieve to remove any small clots.

Place a medium-size iron skillet over medium-high heat. Heat to hot. Add oil. Allow to heat. Dice *pancetta* and allow to render, mashing with a fork. Simmer 10 minutes.

In a medium-size bowl beat eggs and add salt and pepper. Combine blood with beaten eggs and add cheese.

Pour into skillet mixing with a fork until it begins to thicken and solidify.

Turn onto board (like an omelet). To serve, cut into wedges like a pie.

Serves: 4-8.

Brain Fritters
Frittelle di Cervello

1 pig brain
Salt, to taste

2 cups rice
1/4 cup flour
1 T lemon rind
1 tsp. lemon juice
1/2 cup sugar
1/2 cup corn oil

Remove brain from pig and wash. Place a medium-size pot over high heat. Add water, brain, and a pinch of salt. Bring to a boil and boil for 2 minutes. Remove and cool. When cool remove membrane from around brain and discard. Mash brains like potatoes.

Place medium-size pot over high heat. Cook rice as directed. Drain. Combine brains, rice, flour, lemon rind and juice, and sugar. Mix well. Place a medium-size iron skillet over medium-high heat. Heat to hot. Add oil. Place heaping tablespoonfuls of mixture into skillet and fry golden. Serve at once.
Serves: 4-8.

Pork Liver Wrapped in Web
Fegatelli Avvolti con Rete di Maiale

One of the first meals Nonna prepared from the dressed pork was delicious tasting *fegatelli*. The entire pork liver was cubed and prepared. Leftovers were placed in a deep crock, covered with rendered lard, and stored for future use.

The web (caul) is the fatty, net-like membrane which covers the intestines of the pig. It is essential for this dish for it bastes the liver and keeps it tender. While cooking, it nearly disappears.

Traditionally, *fegatelli con rete di maiale* is fried, or roasted over a wooden fire. The stems of fresh bay leaves are used as skewers, adding additional flavor. The recipe below is the fried version.

1 pork web (caul)*
1 whole pork liver
1/4-inch-thick slice
pancetta
1/2 T salt
1/2 T pepper
1/3 cup fennel seeds

15-20 bay leaves

1/4 cup corn oil
5-8 wooden skewers

Soak the pork web in water for about 10 minutes, then lay it on a clean cloth. Top with a second cloth and gently roll the cloth into a roll. Let set until needed. Cut *pancetta* into 5-8 pieces.

Wash the pork liver and pat dry with a clean cloth. Cut into 2-inch squares. Cut away any fat or gristle. Allow to dry. Unwrap the web and cut into as many pieces as you have chunks of liver. Set aside.

In a flat dish combine salt and pepper. Mix. Place fennel seeds on another plate. Roll the individual pieces of pork liver in the salt and pepper mixture, then in the fennel seeds. Wrap the liver in a piece of the web. Take a wooden stick and skewer one bay leaf, wrapped liver, *pancetta*, bay leaf, second wrapped liver, and a final bay leaf. Pick up next skewer, continue until all the liver is skewered.

Place a medium-size iron skillet over medium-high heat. Heat to hot. Add oil. Heat to hot. Add liver and sear quickly on all sides. Lower the heat, cover, and cook 20 to 30 minutes.

Serve hot with good bread and endive salad (see page 224).

Serves: 4-6.

Note: *Caul, like blood and other specialty items from the pig, is only available from a farmer.

Pork Sausage
Salsiccia di Maiale

Sausage is easy to make, especially if one is satisfied with making patties instead of links. Links require a little more work for they need casings. A sausage casing is the thin intestine of the pig. Casings can be purchased from any supermarket and are usually packed in salt. Once the package of casings is opened it should be stored in the refrigerator and can be kept for over a year as long as casings are covered with salt. Some markets are willing to sell a few casings at a time.

Sausage Patties

4-1/2 pounds ground pork butt
2 large cloves garlic
1 T salt
1 T ground pepper
2 tsp. nutmeg

Ask your butcher to **fine** grind the pork butt. Place ground pork on a pastry board or in a large low pan. Peel garlic and press through a garlic press releasing the juices over the ground pork until very little pulp remains. Discard extra pulp. Sprinkle the meat with salt, pepper, and grated nutmeg.

Using your hands, mix the ground pork for at least 15 minutes to be sure that all the seasonings are evenly distributed. Allow to stand for 10 minutes and taste for seasonings (if you do not want to taste raw pork, fry a little and then taste).

Form into patties. You can freeze sausage patties for more than a month.

Sausage Links

3-4 lengths pork casings
Butcher cord

Ask your butcher to **course** grind the pork butt (if too fine it will be harder to stuff into the casings).

If you prefer to grind your own meat, ask the butcher to remove the bone from the pork butt. Cut pork butt into 1-inch cubes and run the cubes through a meat chopper with a coarse blade. Then follow the recipe for sausage patties (above). When the pork has been mixed it is time to stuff the casings.

Select 4 to 5 casings and soak them in cold water for a few minutes. Squeeze, wrap in a clean cloth, pat dry, and set aside.

Select a casing, find an end and blow into it with your mouth. It will blow up like a balloon. If it does not inflate, discard it, for there is a hole somewhere in the casing.

Gently place the end of the casing over the funnel (see A) of a meat grinder and slide it until all the casing is on the funnel (if casing resists, run a little meat through the funnel and then push the casing on--the meat greases the inside of the casing). Tie the opposite end in a knot.

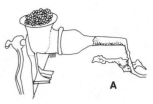

Stuffing the Sausage
Slowly stuff meat into grinder and run through. It will begin to enter the casing (see B). These links should be 1-1/4-inches in diameter. Make sure stuffing is not packed too tight or casing will break (it might not break right away, but will when cooking). When you reach the end of the casing, remove it, place another casing on the funnel, and begin again. Continue until all meat is gone.

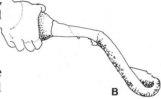

Making Links
Once all casings have been stuffed, tie sausage into 4-to-5-inch links (see C). Begin at end with cord. Measure (or judge) desired length, pinch sausage with your thumb and forefinger, wrap cord around dent forming a knot. Continue to the end.

Prick sausage with pin or needle 2 to 3 times in each link to release air that may be trapped in casings. Hang sausage over pole and allow to dry overnight. Place in cool cellar, refrigerator, or freezer.

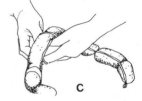

Yield: 25-30 (4-inch) links, or 25 patties.

Variations
Breakfast Sausage *(Salsiccia per Prima Colazione)*. Eliminate garlic, add 2 tsp. cinnamon or 2 tsp. cloves.

Fennel Sausage *(Salsiccia con Finocchio)*. Boil 2 cloves garlic in 1/4 cup dry red wine. Discard garlic. Add wine and 1 T fennel to mixture.

Hot Sausage *(Salsiccia Coppa)*. Keep garlic, add 2 T hot pepper.

Dried Sausage *(Salsiccia Secca, stagionata)*. As sausages age they take on different textures and Nonno would hang them in the cellar. Dried sausage wrinkles up and is very good sliced and eaten like salami, uncooked. Age at least 40 days.

161

Sausage Roll
Cotechino

Cotechino is a sausage made from left-over and second grade pork meat. It looks like a salami, but is 3 inches in diameter and 8-to-9-inches long. When stuffed into a pig's foot, as they do in Moderna, it is called *zampone*, but when stuffed into a casing like a sausage, it is *cotechino*.

The filling begins with ground pork, but the other ingredients vary from district to district in Italy. For us, *cotechino* is the same as headcheese (*soprassata*), except it is ground and raw whereas headcheese is diced and cooked. You cook the *cotechino* just before eating.

4 pounds pork butt
or 1 pig's head
1 pound pork skin (rind)
1-1/2 T salt
3/4 T pepper
1/4 tsp. nutmeg
3-4 casings*

Ask the butcher to **fine** grind the pork butt. If you prefer to grind your own meat, ask the butcher to remove the bone from the pork butt. Cut pork butt into 1-inch cubes, and run the cubes through a meat chopper with a fine blade. If using a pig's head follow instructions on page 157.

Select 3 to 4 casings and soak them in cold water for a few minutes. Squeeze, wrap in a clean cloth, pat dry, and set aside.

Combine pork, rind, salt, pepper, and nutmeg and mix for 15 minutes or until well blended. Let set for 10 minutes and taste (if you do not want to taste raw pork, fry it in a skillet).

Wash the casings one more time and dry with a clean cloth. Select one, find an end and blow into it with your mouth. It will blow up like a balloon (if not, discard). Tie one end in a knot. Slowly stuff the meat into the casing using your hands or a large spoon. Be gentle or the casing will break.

When casing is full, tie remaining end. Pierce casing in several places with a toothpick to allow trapped air to escape. Attach a string to one end and hang it in a cool place. Continue until all casings are stuffed.

Store in a cool place. Allow to age for 2 to 3 weeks. *Cotechino* is not aged like salami and should be eaten before 3 months.

Yield: 3-4 sausages.

Note: *You need a wider casing for *cotechino* than the casing used for sausage.

Salt Belly
Pancetta

Pancetta is the Italian answer to bacon. It is used so often in our cooking that no stew, stuffing, pasta sauce, or roast would be complete without the rich flavor *pancetta* provides.

Called by various names including pork belly and salt belly, *pancetta* is available in supermarkets. It is usually next to the bacon.

Making *pancetta* is like making prosciutto. The difference is the time it ages and the cut of meat.

1 side fresh
bacon with rind
2 cups salt, divided
1/2 cup pepper

6-8 cloves garlic
(optional)

large wooden box

The cut of meat for *pancetta* is from the side of the hog, next to the ribs. When buying meat ask for an uncured piece of bacon with rind. If the meat has been refrigerated, it can still be cured, but do not make this recipe with frozen meat. Fresh meat is available from a slaughterhouse or a farmer.

Lay meat on a clean work space. Combine 1 cup salt and pepper in a large bowl. Rub salt mixture generously over both sides of the meat. Be sure to coat well.

Place 1 cup salt in wooden box (box should be slightly larger than piece of meat). Be sure bottom of box is covered (use more salt if necessary).

Place pork in salt-lined box rind side down, and cover with remaining salt and pepper. Age 10 days, massage the salt into the meat daily, and add more salt as needed (see prosciutto illustrations that follow).

After 10 days, remove from salt. Wash in warm water. Soak for half hour. Pat dry. Rub more pepper into meat.

Garlic is optional. To add garlic place *pancetta*, rind side down, on a flat surface. Make 1/2-inch slits in a diagonal pattern across the surface. Peel garlic and place half a clove in each slit (see A).

Begin at one end and roll the *pancetta* like a jelly roll (see B). Tie securely and hang in cool, dry place for 90 days.

If meat smells rancid or pungent it is spoiled and must be thrown away.

Yield: 1.

A

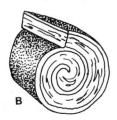

B

Prosciutto

A hundred men will have 100 secrets for homemade prosciutto, but only five men will talk about them. All will agree that the pig must be 10 to 11 months old and weight about 400 pounds, and prosciutto must be made in winter, begun before February in a cool, dry place. In addition to the secrets, salting is the most important process in making prosciutto. If salted too little, the prosciutto will go bad. If salted too much, it will be cured, but inedible.

1 hind leg of pig
5-10 pounds salt, or
more as needed
1-2 cups pepper

5-6 cloves garlic
1 cup dry red wine

Large wooden or
plastic box

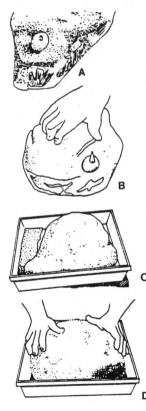

Be sure the leg is cleaned of dirt and hair and still has its skin. Be sure meat is dry before beginning the process.

Lay leg on a clean work space. Clean, and be sure two bones are visible: the round leg socket and a rectangular bone slightly below and to the side of the socket bone (see A). The round bone is the gauge that tells you when to stop salting the meat.

You must remove excess blood from the vein that runs the length of the leg between the two bones. Begin at the bottom and with your thumb press and move firmly to the top (see B). A little blood will come out. Pat dry. Do this at least twice a day for two days.

Now you are ready to salt. The rule is 1 day of salt bath for every pound of meat, or 7 days for every inch of thickness measured at the thickest part of the fresh leg. Begin by rubbing the entire leg with salt. Cover the bottom of the box with 1/2-inch layer of salt. Lay leg on top. Spread salt over leg to 1 inch thickness, adding more in the middle of the leg. Keep one end of the box elevated (see C) to allow the juice to settle away from the meat.

Allow to sit a few days. You will notice a little moisture in the bottom of the box. This must be drained daily.

After the second day the leg must be massaged each day (see D) to break the salt crust. Massage for about 5 minutes. Never turn the leg. Add additional salt as it is depleted.

164

This process will continue for at least a month. Our family maintains the meat must be left in the salt for 40 days, others say 25 to 30 days. The gauge is the socket bone (see E). In the center of the bone is a little bit of flesh. It will be pure white and malleable when the process begins. As the days pass it will begin to turn color, and when the meat is cured it will have formed a black spot in the center of the bone. When the center is black, the meat is cured.

Once the prosciutto is cured it must be cleaned. Soak it in warm water for 10 to 15 minutes to remove excess salt. Pat dry.

Rub the entire prosciutto generously with black pepper kneading it into fleshy parts.

The prosciutto must now be sealed to hold in the flavor. In our family we crush 2 heads of garlic and boil in wine. Mash it into a paste and rub into the cured prosciutto. Rub with the palm of the hand, pressing with great care for at least 30 minutes. Be sure pepper remains on the prosciutto.

Cut a slit in the skin near the end of the leg and run a piece of cord through the hole. Hang the prosciutto from the rafters in a cool, dry place for 6 months before cutting (see F).

When cutting prosciutto (see G) begin at round end and slice down. Remove an inch of rind (good as a flavoring in cooking). Cut each slice paper thin.

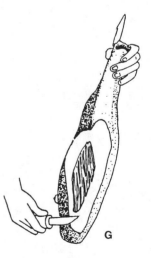

If meat smells rancid or pungent it is spoiled and must be thrown away. In Italy they test the prosciutto with a long needle made of horse bone. They insert the needle into the fleshy part of the meat and withdraw it. The odor left on the needle attests to the success of the curing process.

Once cut the prosciutto can remain hanging in a cool place. Wrap it in a cotton cloth to keep it fresh. Never wrap in plastic or freeze any cured ham.

165

Salami
Salame

There are an endless variety of salamis. Almost every Italian village had their own method of making this excellent pork cold cut. This recipe is our standard, but true Tuscan salami is *finocchino,* salami with fennel.

8 pounds pork butt
1-1/2 T salt
1 T pepper
1/3 cup whole
peppercorns
1 cup red wine
4-5 large cloves garlic

1 T corn oil
Casing
Cord

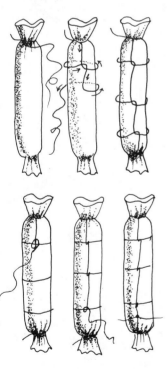

Pork butt must be unchilled. Ask your butcher to **course** grind the pork butt (if too fine it will be hard to stuff into casings). If you prefer to grind your own meat, ask the butcher to remove the bone from the pork butt. Cut pork butt into 1-inch cubes and run the cubes through a meat chopper with a course blade.

Place pork on large work space. Combine salt, pepper, and whole peppercorns with pork. Mix for 10 minutes and allow to set.

Place a medium-size pan over medium-high heat. Add wine. Bring to a boil. Crush garlic cloves (do not peel) and add to wine. Simmer for half hour. Remove garlic from wine and pour wine over ground pork. Mix pork for at least 15 minutes. Let stand for a few hours to allow flavors to blend.

Place a medium-size iron skillet over medium-high heat. Heat to hot. Add 1 tablespoon oil. Take a handful of pork mixture and add to skillet. Allow to fry until cooked. This is a tester. Taste the meat to see if it needs additional flavoring. Add as necessary.

Wash the casing and pat dry. Put the remaining pork in casings, one handful at a time pressing down to firm and eliminate air pockets. Tie the casing. Allow to set in casing overnight.

The next day tie the salami with cord (see illustration) by beginning at the top of the salami and circling it twice so the salami is in quarters. Tie very tightly. Now circle the salami with the cord every inch or so.

Hang salami in a cool dry place and pierce the casing with a needle in 5 or 6 places to let out any air. Allow to cure for 3 months.

Note: Salami casings are not the same as sausage casings: they are larger and thicker.

Omelets, Eggs, and Egg Tortes
Frittate, Uova, e Torte di Uova

Eggs appear in almost every course of an Italian meal from appetizers, soups, stuffings, and sauces to salads and desserts. Italians do not use eggs sparingly, but abundantly.

The Italian omelet is not puffy and fluffy, but flat and filled with vegetables and cheeses. The choice of vegetables will be considered exotic to some palates, for in addition to the traditional peppers, onions, and mushrooms Italian omelets feature artichokes, asparagus and tomatoes. As usual, the dish is well-spiced and tasty.

Egg tortes are another Italian specialty enjoyed for years in our family. Popularly called quiches in America and offered in upbeat restaurants, the egg pie is stuffed with vegetables and meats and dressed with a pastry shell. Our versions are prepared not only for daily fare, but on special occasions and include Italian cured meats.

Americans have embraced many Italian dishes from pastas and pizzas to scaloppine and Parmesan, but yet to be discovered by the majority of Americans is the marriage of eggs to tomatoes. Three recipes are listed here, each one a favorite. Seldom served for breakfast, the tomato recipes are good for any daily meal. They will also delight guests served on a buffet. Our favorite is poached eggs in tomato sauce laced with garlic.

Eggs have not fared well in the modern day battle against high cholesterol. We have tried all the egg recipes in this chapter with low cholesterol egg substitutes which are available on the market. Elizabeth will not concede, but, except for the poached egg recipe, the substitutes can be used.

Basic Omelet
Frittata Classica

3 T corn oil
3 eggs
Salt and pepper

Place a medium-size iron skillet over medium-high heat. Heat to hot. Add oil. Heat. Add ingredients as listed in following variations. Beat eggs in a bowl and add salt and pepper to taste. Pour over simmering ingredients. Cover and allow to cook for 2 to 3 minutes or until firm. Serve immediately.

Serves: 2-3.

Variations
Variazioni

Artichoke Omelet (*Frittata di Carciofi*): 2 fresh artichokes, 1 tsp. lemon juice, 3 T corn oil, 1/4 cup water, 3 eggs, salt, pepper. Wash artichokes. Clean by removing outer hard leaves (see page 260 for illustrations). Spread to expose center of artichoke. Remove pointed and hairy parts in center of artichoke. Cut away the tips of all hard leaves with kitchen shears. To loosen the leaves hit each artichoke on a drain board three or four times. Wash by placing in fresh water to which a teaspoon of lemon juice has been added. Drain upsidedown on drain board. Cut each artichoke in half lengthwise. From each half cut 5 to 6 wedges Check each edge for prickly centers and if any remain remove them. Place a medium-size iron skillet over medium-high heat. Add oil. Place the artichoke pieces in the oil and add 1/4 cup water. Allow to boil and lower the heat. Simmer until tender. Add eggs, salt, and pepper, and continue as for Basic Omelet.

Asparagus Omelet (*Frittata di Asparagi*): 1 bunch fresh asparagus, 3 T corn oil, 1/4 cup water, 3 eggs, salt, pepper. Wash asparagus. Discard the hard white bottom and drain asparagus on a paper towel. Place a medium-size iron skillet over medium-high heat. Heat to hot. Add oil. Cut the asparagus into 2-inch pieces and place in oil. Add water. Allow to boil and lower the heat. Simmer for 5 minutes. When water is gone, add beaten eggs, salt and pepper, and continue as for Basic Omelet.

Cheese Omelet (*Frittata di Formaggio*): 1-1/2 cups shredded fontina or Cheddar cheese, 3 eggs, salt, pepper, 3 T corn oil. Prepare Basic Omelet and just before eggs are done add cheese, salt, and pepper. Cover and allow the cheese to melt. Serve immediately.

168

Green Pepper and Onion Omelet *(Frittata di Peperoni e Cipolle)***:** 2 green peppers, 2 onions, 3 T corn oil, 3 eggs, salt, pepper. Wash peppers and onions. Clean and cut peppers in strips, onions in slices. Place a medium-size iron skillet over medium-high heat. Heat to hot. Add oil. Place peppers and onions in oil and fry until tender. Add eggs, salt and pepper, and continue as for Basic Omelet.

Mushroom Omelet *(Frittata di Fungi)***:** 1/4 pound fresh mushrooms, 2 T butter, 2 cloves garlic, salt, pepper, 3 eggs, corn oil. Take one mushroom at a time, clean and cut off the very tip of the stem and remove any blemishes on the crown. Slice mushrooms. Place a medium-size iron skillet over medium-high heat. Heat to hot. Melt butter in skillet. Add garlic. When garlic is brown mash with fork into small pieces. Add mushrooms, salt, and pepper to taste. Lower heat and saute for 5 minutes. Add eggs and continue as for Basic Omelet.

Green Onion Omelet *(Frittata di Cipolle)***:** 6 fresh green onions (scallions) or 1 onion, 3 T corn oil, 3 eggs, salt, pepper. Wash onions. Clean and dice. Place a medium-size iron skillet over medium heat. Heat to hot. Add oil. Place onion pieces in oil and allow to fry until transparent. Add eggs, salt and pepper and continue as for Basic Omelet.

Salami or Dried Sausage Omelet *(Frittata di Salame o Salsiccia Secca o Stagionata)***:** 3-4 thick slices of salami or 2 dry sausages (see page 161), 2-3 eggs, salt and pepper, 2 T butter. Cut meat into pieces, skin sausage and cut in half lengthwise. Place in a medium-size iron skillet over medium-high heat and saute quickly. Do not add oil. Beat eggs until frothy, add salt and pepper. Add butter to skillet. Melt. Add meat. Add eggs and continue as for Basic Omelet.

Omelet with Tomatoes
Frittata con Pomodori

1 large very ripe tomato
Sprig fresh parsley
3 eggs
3 T corn oil
Salt and pepper
3 T freshly grated
Parmesan cheese

Place a medium-size iron skillet over medium-high heat. Heat to hot. Dice tomato and parsley, add to warm skillet. Cook 10 minutes, or until juices evaporate.

While tomatoes are reducing, place a medium-size iron skillet over medium-high heat. Add oil. Heat to hot. Beat eggs, add salt and pepper to taste. Add eggs to warm oil, cover, and allow to cook for 2 to 3 minutes or until firm. Turn if desired.

Remove omelet from skillet. Lay on platter (you can fold the omelet over and stuff it with cheese if you like). Pour tomatoes over omelet and sprinkle with cheese.
Serves: 2-3.

Omelets in Tomato Sauce
Frittate con Sugo di Pomodoro

2 T corn oil
6 eggs
2 T freshly grated
Parmesan Cheese
Salt and pepper, to taste

2 T butter
2 cloves garlic
1 cup whole or crushed
canned tomatoes
or 2 very ripe fresh
tomatoes

Place a small-size iron skillet over medium-high heat. Heat to hot. Add oil. Beat 1 egg in bowl, add pinch of cheese, salt and pepper to taste. Pour into oil. Cover, allow to cook for a few minutes. Remove, place on a board, begin at one end and roll. Repeat for remaining eggs.

Place a medium-size iron skillet over medium-high heat. Heat to hot. Add butter, allow to melt. Peel and dice garlic. Add to butter and saute until brown. Add tomatoes, crushing with a fork into small pieces. Simmer 15 to 20 minutes, or until tomatoes begin to solidify. Remove from heat, run through a sieve pushing pulp through sieve. Throw remaining pulp away. Return tomato mixture to skillet. Add salt and pepper if necessary, but should be savory enough. Continue to simmer until tomatoes begin to lose their red color and turn brown-red, about 20 minutes. If tomatoes begin to dry, add 1/4 to 1/2 cup broth. Add omelets, simmer 10 minutes.

Serves: 3-4.

Note: Stuff omelets with salami, sausage, or cheese.

Poached Eggs in Tomato Sauce
Uova Affogate in Sugo di Pomodoro

5-6 very ripe fresh
tomatoes
3 T corn oil
2 cloves garlic
1/4 tsp. salt
1/4 tsp. pepper
6 eggs

Wash tomatoes and blanch in boiling water for a few minutes. Peel, quarter, and set aside.

Place a medium-size iron skillet over medium-high heat. Heat to hot. Add oil (or pan drippings) and heat. Peel and dice garlic. Add and saute until brown, then crush with fork into small pieces. Add tomatoes crushing with a fork into small pieces. Add salt and pepper. Simmer 10 to 15 minutes or until tomatoes begin to lose their liquid.

Break and add eggs one at a time. Salt and pepper to taste. Do not allow to touch. Occasionally spoon tomatoes over eggs. Simmer 5 to 10 minutes or until poached to taste. Serve at once with good Italian bread.
Serves: 3.

170

Egg Pies
Torte di Uova

Egg pies are a specialty at Easter. Some immigrant families made such big pies that they were steamed in buckets over the open hearth.

Easter Pie
Torta di Pasqua

dough:
3 cups flour
1/4 oz. dry yeast
2 tsp. granulated sugar
1 tsp. salt
2 T corn oil
1 cup warm water

filling:
6 oz. sausage
6 oz. ham
6 oz. basket cheese
12 eggs*
1/4 tsp. salt
1/4 tsp. pepper

Place flour in a bowl. Add yeast, sugar, and salt. Mix together. Make a well in flour mixture. Add oil and water. Mix together until it forms a stiff dough. Knead until all flour is absorbed, about 15 to 20 minutes.

Cover dough and let rise for 1 hour. Punch down and let rise again for 1/2 an hour.

Place a medium-size pot over high heat. Add enough water to cover meats. Bring to a boil. Add sausage and ham. Boil for 15 minutes, drain, cool; remove skin from sausage and cut meats into bite-size pieces. Cube basket cheese.

Place eggs in a large bowl and beat. Add sausage, ham, cheese, salt and pepper. Stir. Set aside.

Place dough on floured pastry board. Divide in half, setting one half under a bowl to rest. Using a rolling pin, roll dough until 12-to-13 inches in circumference (at least 4 inches wider that pie plate).

Grease 2 deep-sided (9-inch) pie plates (see note) with a little oil. Lift dough and place in one pie plate allowing to spill over the sides. Press down. Do the second dough in the same manner.

Divide egg mixture into two equal amounts and pour egg mixture into dough-lined pie plates. Lift remaining dough up over the eggs to form a large 2-to 3-inch-wide crust.

Place both pies in oven and bake at 350 degrees for 1 hour or until eggs are set and top is slightly brown.

Yield: 2 pies, each serving 6 to 8 persons.

Notes: Pie plates must be deep to keep eggs from spilling in oven. Placing the crust over the edges of the torte helps prevent spillage.
    *If using extra large eggs use only 10.

171

Savory Prosciutto and Ricotta Pie
Torta di Prosciutto e Ricotta Gustosa

This tangy and savory egg pie with cheese and meat is a meal in itself and stunning on a buffet.

crust:
1 cup flour
Pinch salt
2 T granulated sugar
3 oz. shortening
1/2 tsp. vanilla
3-4 large eggs

filling:
6 slices prosciutto
or cured ham
6 slices salami
3-4 oz. fontina cheese
1/2 cup freshly grated
Parmesan cheese
1-1/3 pounds ricotta
1 egg

In a mixing bowl combine flour, salt, sugar. Mix. Cut in shortening with a pastry cutter. Add vanilla and eggs (save the yolk of 1 egg in a separate bowl). Slowly combine ingredients. Knead until firm. Add additional flour as needed to keep from sticking.

Turn out onto pastry board. Using a rolling pin, roll out to 12-to-13 inches in circumference. Line the bottom of an 9-inch pie plate, allowing to spill over at least 4 inches.

Dice all meats and hard cheese into 1-inch pieces. Mix together in a large mixing bowl. Add Parmesan cheese, ricotta cheese, and egg. Mix again.

Fill the pie shell. Bring the edges of the pie crust up and over the filling leaving a 2-to-3-inch hole in the middle of the pie.

Beat the remaining egg yolk and brush the top of the pie crust.

Bake in a 325-degree oven for 50 to 60 minutes, or until the top browns.

Yield: 1 (9-inch) pie.

Note: You can create your own filling for this ricotta pie, adding sausage or other meats.

Pasta

Pasta

Pasta is Italy's gift to the world, and is at the heart of Italian cooking. Despite the popular misconception that Marco Polo brought pasta to Italy from China, Italians have been enjoying pasta since the Etruscan civilization of the fifth and fourth centuries B.C. It did not become the popular dish it is today until 150 years ago, and it was not wedded to tomatoes until they arrived from the Americas and the Neopolitans discovered the blending in the last century. Since then, the number of sauces and cuts of pasta has grown into what seems to be an endless variety (see "Shopping all'Italiana" for list). Every region in Italy has unique pasta dishes, not all well-known in America.

Traditionally, pasta was intended as a first course, but for many immigrants (and peasants in Italy) it often became the meal, an inexpensive way to feed a large family. Nonna had only one child and Nonno was lucky enough to work during the Depression, so in our family we were able to follow the tradition of pasta as a first course. We ate some type of pasta everyday—either in soup or in sauce—and it was always homemade.

To help you make the different pasta specialties in various quantities we have created a variety of choices. There are three different pasta recipes in this chapter, each for a different quantity: homemade pastas on pages 174-77 and 186; and crepes on page 181; and another on page 186. The two pastas are interchangeable (the crepe is not). There is one meat stuffing, but two cheese stuffings in various quantities. All pastas and stuffings can be cut in half or in fourths successfully.

Quantity is an issue. When we make the dish we get the yield. If you make your cappelletti, ravioli, or cannelloni smaller than we do, you will get more, and if you make them larger, you will get less.

Specialty sauces appear with the pasta dishes, but our basic pasta sauce and sauces that can be used in a number of ways are in the sauce chapter. In that chapter we have also created a chart for various quantities of sauce.

Homemade Pasta
Pasta della Casalinga

Pasta is at the heart of Italian cooking and the immigrant women took great pride in the delicacy of their noodles and the thinness of their cuts.

Pasta making was a day-long affair, especially if the pasta was to be stuffed for ravioli or cappelletti. The whole kitchen was turned into a pasta factory. When I think of Nonna, the moment I remember most is the image of her in the kitchen bending over an old yellow crank pasta machine, her hair in a net, her apron covered with flour, and surrounded by a variety of cut pastas.

Nonna used this pasta recipe for everything from ravioli and lasagna to fine noodles for soup: only the quantity and cut varied. When she made pasta, she called it *pasta asciutta* when it was drained after cooking and topped with a sauce, and *pastina* when it was cooked in a broth.

Nonna never made less than double the following recipe, that is why she worked all day. Sandrina's recipe for homemade pasta is found on pages 186-87.

Making the Sponge

4 eggs
1/8 cup water
1 tsp. salt
2 T butter
2 T olive oil
3 cups flour

In mixer: Break eggs and place in large mixing bowl. Add water, salt, butter, and olive oil. Beat with heavy dough-beater. Gradually add 2-to-2-1/2 cups flour to mixture until all is firm. Remove from bowl and place on pastry board (*spianatoia*) that has been slightly coated with fresh flour. Knead.

Mix by hand: Sift flour onto a pastry board. Make a well in center of flour by scooping out a hole (see A). Crack each egg and place in small bowl or the center of the flour (see A). Add water, salt, butter, olive oil and beat till fluffy with whisk or fork. If using a bowl, pour egg mixture into flour well. Slowly begin to pick up flour from inner ring of well, blending it into egg mixture (see B).

Continue to pick up flour until dough becomes firm and manageable. Use your hands. Knead until dough is firm and no longer sticky (could be 5 minutes, could be 20). Set aside. Clean lumps on board with dull side of knife, clean board. Dust board with flour.

174

Once dough is firm and board is cleaned and dusted, place dough on board and knead for 30 minutes (see C). While kneading, dough may become sticky. Keep adding small quantities of flour and continue kneading. Once no longer sticky, form into a ball. Sprinkle a small quantity of oil on a corner of the board. Place ball on top. Brush top of ball with oil to keep from getting crusty, cover with a bowl, and allow to rest 1 to 1-1/2 hours.

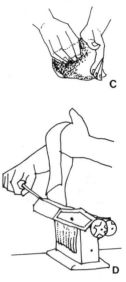

Rolling Out the Dough

Rolling out dough is a very important step in the process of making pasta. If rolled dough is allowed to sit too long, it will dry out and be unmanageable, so work at a good pace. Send the family to the movies, and put telephone answering machine on.

To roll out with pasta machine: Cut prepared dough into 6 pieces. Dust hands with flour and take 1 piece at a time. Flatten into an oblong shape. Set pasta machine to highest (thickest, usually an 8) setting. Place short end of dough into rollers and roll 3 times (see D). Each time the dough will become longer and wider. Set machine to thinner setting (6) and roll 2 to 3 times. Change position to number 4 setting and roll 2 to 3 times. By this time the dough is thin and nearly a yard long (for soup noodles roll one more time at the No. 2 setting). Place on drying rack (a clean broom handle covered with a cloth and stretched between 2 chairs will do--see E). Repeat process for each piece of dough.

To roll out by hand: Good hand rolling depends on a good rolling pin (*matterello*). Cut dough into 3 pieces. Roll first piece with the *matterello* into a round shape allowing to get larger and larger (see F) until the desired thickness is reached. For *tagliatelli* dough should be 1/4-inch thick. Once dough is rolled out, lay on a clean sheet to dry a little before cutting.

175

Cutting the Dough

It is important to cut the dough at the right time, especially for soup noodles. If allowed to dry too long the dough becomes stiff and breaks apart as you cut. As far as we know there is no way to save the dough once this happens. There is no set time for drying as each batch of dough has its own life, but the dough should have some elasticity in it.

Cutting with the pasta machine: Today one does not have to bother with rolling out and cutting by hand, the pasta machine does it all.

All you have to do is prepare the dough for the machine, allow to dry, cut 14-to-18-inch lengths, (see G), select the proper cutter, and run the dough through the machine (see H) one time.

Cutting by hand: The pride of the cook was bound up in the way she cut her noodles. Sandrina was a master at cutting pasta. She worked so fast her knife would sing. Her noodles were thin and wonderful.

Dry the noodles as directed.

Then fold the dough over on itself twice (see I, J) and perhaps again, until it is 3 inches wide.

Begin at one end and cut to desired thickness (see K).

Drying the Pasta

Once pasta is cut it must be dried again. Either lay on a clean sheet, turning to dry all sides, or hang over a pole or cardboard-lined coat hanger (see L). They are dry when they break when pressed. After the noodles have dried they can be stored in a plastic bag until ready to use. We put our soup noodles in a long wicker bread basket and cover basket and all with plastic.

L

Cooking

For sauce: If you are preparing 4 cups pasta you will need 8 cups water. Fill a pan with water and boil. As water bubbles, add 2 teaspoons salt. Bring to rolling boil. Add pasta and turn immediately to keep from sticking. Boil for 6 to 8 minutes for *al dente*, or 8 to 9 minutes for well done. Test by taste. Drain. Place on serving dish and cover with sauce. Sprinkle with freshly grated Parmesan cheese (some prefer to cover the pasta and let stand for 15 minutes before serving for the pasta to absorb the sauce. In this case store in warm oven).

For soup: Replace water with soup stock. Use 1 quart broth to 3 handfuls of homemade pasta. Boil soup, add pasta, and turn to keep from sticking. Lower the heat and allow to soft boil for 6 to 8 minutes or until done to taste.

Yields: A full pasta recipe will yield approximately 35 cannelloni, 70 ravioli, and 300 cappelletti or copious amounts of fettuccine and smaller pasta cuts.

Stuffed Pastas
Paste Imbottite

Some form of stuffed pasta exists in most cultures. In Italy, the varieties of stuffings are astounding--everything from the traditional meat or cheese found in this chapter to more exotic blends of fish, spinach, and even squash. Tuscan cuisine includes *nicchi*, also called *cappelli del prete* (priest's hats) but we never made them. The sauces also vary from a little butter and herbs to a hearty deep-red meat sauce.

Meat Stuffing
Ripieno di Carne

4 oz. chopped Swiss chard or spinach
1/2 cup water
1/2 tsp. salt

10 oz. boneless veal (steak preferred)
10 oz. chicken breast
2 T butter
Pinch salt
Pinch pepper
Pinch thyme
1/4 cup broth

1 medium onion
1/4-inch-thick slice *pancetta*
1 small carrot
2 small celery rib with leaves
1 tsp. fresh parsley

3 T corn oil
1/4 cup freshly grated Romano cheese
1/3 cup freshly grated Parmesan cheese
1/4 cup fine bread crumbs
1 grate nutmeg
2 eggs, beaten

Clean and wash Swiss chard (or spinach). Remove stalks and save. Place medium-size pot over medium-high heat and add water. Allow to boil, add salt and leaves of chard. Cover and boil for 1 to 2 minutes, remove from stove, steep until cool. Drain, squeeze dry, and set aside.

Cut veal and chicken breasts into 1-to-2-inch pieces. Discard fat, chicken skin, and bones. Place a large-size iron skillet over medium-high heat. Heat to hot. Add butter and melt, but do not brown. Add meat mixture, salt, pepper, and thyme. Cook until browned, 25 minutes, stirring often. Remove from skillet. Run through a meat grinder, adding chard as you grind. Add 1/4 cup broth to the skillet, return to burner and stir. Add to mixture and mix well.

While meat is browning, peel onion, wash, cut into 1/4 wedges. Dice *pancetta*. Peel carrot and celery. Wash, and cut into 2-inch pieces. Wash parsley. Combine and grind in a meat grinder or chop in a food processor (the grinder is better because it releases the juices).

Place medium-size iron skillet over medium-high heat. Heat to hot. Add oil. When oil is hot add chopped ingredients and saute until onions are transparent (20 minutes), stirring often. The longer you cook this mixture the better the taste.

While both mixtures are cooking, combine cheeses, bread crumbs, and nutmeg in a bowl and mix. When onions are well cooked, remove from skillet and add to the cheese mixture. Add meat mixture. Mix well. Add beaten eggs and mix again (see note).* If dry, add another egg. Set aside until ready for use. Can be stored in refrigerator overnight. Be sure to bring to room temperature before using.

Yields: This stuffing is enough for 70 cannelloni, 140 ravioli, or 600 cappelletti, depending on how big you make them. It can be divided in half, a fourth, or an eighth (and probably more) for smaller yields.

Note: *We add eggs and refrigerate stuffing, but with the current concern about contamination of poultry products, one can refrigerate the stuffing and add eggs just before using.

Stuffed Canes
Cannelloni (Manicotti)

Of all stuffed pastas, *cannelloni* (canes) are the largest and easiest to prepare. Ravioli are small by comparison, and cappelletti tiny. Cannelloni take big portions of stuffing and serve well for hearty appetites. Topped with bechamel sauce they are delicious. You can buy large *manicotti* in the pasta department of any supermarket, but we always preferred to make our own crepes.

1/2 stuffing recipe
1/2 pasta recipe
1 T corn oil
3-1/2 cups sauce recipe

2 cups broth
2-1/3 cups bechamel
sauce

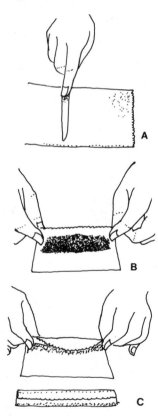

A

B

C

Prepare half recipe stuffing found on pages 178-79 and set aside. Prepare half of the pasta dough recipe found on pages 174-77. Roll the dough to 1/16-inch. Cut into 4-to 5-inch squares (see A).

Place a large pot over medium-high heat. Add water and oil and bring to a boil. Parboil the squares for 5 to 10 seconds.* Remove squares one at a time from boiling water and place in cold water. Place a square of pasta on a pastry board. Pat dry. Add 2 tablespoons stuffing at the very edge of the pasta (see B). Beginning at the edge with the stuffing, roll the pasta into a tubular shape (see C).

Prepare meat sauce recipe (found on page 234). Heat 3-1/2 cups of sauce to boiling. Add broth to thin sauce (see note).**

Place half the sauce in a long baking dish. Place the cannelloni on top of the sauce to form a row, or, if individual servings are preferred, place cannelloni in a small casserole (3 to 4 cannelloni per serving). Pour remaining sauce over cannelloni.

Prepare a double recipe of bechamel sauce (recipe on page 231). Spoon the bechamel sauce carefully over the cannelloni, covering entirely.

Place in a 350-degree oven and bake for 45 minutes. Remove, cover with aluminum foil, and allow to stand for 10 to 15 minutes. Serve carefully.

Yield: 20-25 cannelloni, depending on size.

Notes: *If you plan to freeze cannelloni, do not parboil. Place stuffed pasta on wax paper-lined cookie sheet, freeze, remove from freezer, place in plastic container, and refreeze. Now you can take out as many as you want.

**Cannelloni absorb most of the sauce. If you like a lot of liquid, add more sauce and broth.

180

Mrs. Amico's Cheese Stuffed Canes
Manicotti al Formaggio della Signora Amico

Mrs. Amico, Bob Pelini's mother-in-law, is the master chef when it comes to fried *manicotti,* so we Tuscans bow to her Sicilian culinary expertise. She also creates another type of basic pasta in the recipe below. This recipe has become a tradition of the Pelini family in America.

sauce:
3 T olive oil
1 clove garlic
29 oz. canned tomatoes
6 oz. tomato paste
1 cup water
3 sprigs fresh parsley
1 fresh basil leaf
1 tsp. salt
1 tsp. pepper

crepes:
4 eggs
1/4 cup corn oil
2 cups flour
1/2 T salt
2 cups cold water
1 T corn oil

stuffing:
2 pounds ricotta
3/4 cup freshly grated
Parmesan cheese
4 T chopped parsley
2 eggs
1/2 T salt
1/4 T pepper

Place a 6-quart pot over medium-high heat. Heat to warm and add olive oil. Peel garlic and add to hot oil. Brown garlic and remove from oil. Blend tomatoes into a puree. When garlic has been removed from oil pour tomatoes quickly into the hot oil (there should be a whoush sound) and simmer for 45 minutes. Dissolve tomato paste in water and add to simmering tomatoes. Chop parsley and basil. Add parsley, basil, salt and pepper to tomatoes. Simmer for an hour. If you want to add meatballs or sausage do it at this time. Simmer for another hour. If too thick, add a little water. This sauce can be used on any pasta.

In a large bowl combine eggs, 1/4 cup oil, flour, salt, and water. Beat to consistence of a thin pancake batter. Place a small iron skillet over medium-high heat. Heat to hot. Grease slightly with remaining oil. Pour 1/4 cup batter into skillet. Fry one side until dry; turn, fry second side (should not be browned). Continue until you have 20 pancakes.

Mix together ricotta, Parmesan, parsley, eggs, salt, and pepper. Place a crepe on a pastry board. Pat dry. Add 3 tablespoons stuffing at the very edge of the crepe. Beginning at the edge with the stuffing, roll the crepe into a tubular shape (see illustrations on page 180).

Prepare a large baking dish. Cover bottom of dish with sauce. Add the crepes (if individual servings are preferred, place into a small casserole, 3 to 4 *manicotti* per serving). Cover with sauce.

Bake in 350-degree oven for 30 to 45 minutes, or until bubbly.

Yield: 20.

Little Hats
Cappelletti (Tortellini)

The shape determines the name of these stuffed pastas. Cappelletti means "little hats" and, true to the name, each looks like a hat, while *tortellini* means "look like little bellybuttons" and by wrapping the stuffed dough around the finger, a bellybutton is made. Both can be filled with any stuffing.

In our home we make cappelletti in copious quantities, and prefer a meat filling. We always serve cappelletti in good broth with either freshly grated Parmesan or Romano cheese.

1 full stuffing recipe
(either meat or cheese)
2 full pasta recipes

Prepare stuffing recipe on pages 178-79 (or cheese recipe on page 186). It is important to prepare your work space for comfort and convenience. Line a cookie sheet with wax paper. If you have made the stuffing ahead, take stuffing mixture from refrigerator and bring to room temperature.

When you are ready to make the cappelletti prepare two full recipes of pasta from pages 174-77. Do not allow pasta to dry. Instead keep the dough covered and work with small quantities--roll one pasta line at a time, make the cappelletti, roll another pasta line, and continue until all is done.

Run dough through the pasta machine until desired thickness and length, or roll with a rolling pin until 1/16-inch in thickness. Place long dough in front of you. Cut into 1-1/2-inch squares, placing the excess in a pile that can be rerolled.

A

Fill square with a small pinch of stuffing (see A).

B

Bring one edge diagonally over the stuffing to opposite edge. Pinch down to seal on all sides (see B).

C

Take two edges of rectangle and bring behind the mound of stuffing and seal again, forming into a small hat (see C).

Place on wax paper-lined cookie sheet. Continue until strip of dough is gone. Knead remnants. Repeat making squares and stuffing.

Take another piece of dough. Run through the pasta machine until desired thickness and length, or roll with a rolling pin until 1/16-inch in thickness. Proceed as with the first long dough.

When cookie sheet is filled place in freezer. Prepare another cookie sheet with wax paper. Continue until finished.

When finished remove one cookie sheet at a time from freezer, remove from cookie sheet, and place cappelletti in plastic storage containers. Be sure all have frozen for at least 1 hour. Cappelletti are now individually frozen and will not stick together.

Yield: 600 cappelletti. For 300 use 1/2 the stuffing recipe and 1 pasta recipe. For 150, 1/4 stuffing, 1/2 pasta, etc.

Note: It is best to prepare the cappelletti ahead of time, but if you wish to prepare and serve it immediately you must allow the freshly made cappelletti to age 10 minutes before putting them into broth, or they will fall apart.

To cook: Place 2 quarts of broth in a 4-quart pot. Heat over high heat until boiling.

When broth is at a boil remove 60-70 cappelletti from freezer and slowly add to broth. Stir. Return broth to boil. Reduce heat. Cover and simmer for 15 minutes or until done to taste.

Serve with freshly grated Romano or Parmesan cheese.

Serves: Two quarts of broth serves 8 generously.

Ravioli

Ravioli is a Renaissance dish. It is now ubiquitous and some version of stuffed pasta appears in every region of Italy, albeit under different names, shapes, and with a variance in ingredients: from brains and fish, to cheese, cured meats, pumpkin and the meat stuffing on page 178.

For us, ravioli are the same as cappelletti--only larger. In our home ravioli are always served with a sauce while cappelletti are exclusively for broth --that is until the great pasta salad revolution of the 80s. Now, it is anything goes, although we have trouble convincing my mother that cappelletti in salad is not a sacrilege.

Ravioli with Meat Stuffing
Ravioli Ripieni di Carne

1/2 stuffing recipe, plus double quantity of Swiss chard
1 full pasta recipe

It is important to prepare your work space for comfort and convenience. Stuffing the ravioli is a long process, so you may prefer to sit down. Line a cookie sheet with wax paper and place on the table or work space. Take stuffing mixture from refrigerator and set on table (see stuffing recipe on pages 178 and 179).

When you are ready to make the ravioli prepare pasta as described on page 174. Do not allow pasta mixture to dry. Instead keep the dough covered by a bowl and work with small quantities--roll one pasta line at a time, make the ravioli, roll another pasta line, and continue until all is done.

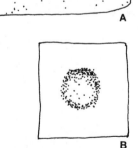

Run through the pasta machine until desired thickness (1/8-to-1/4-inch) and length. Place long dough in front of you (see A). Cut into 2-1/2-inch squares, placing the excess in a pile that can be rerolled.

Fill one square with 1 tablespoon of stuffing (see B).

Bring one edge diagonally over the stuffing to opposite edge (see C).

Pinch down to seal on all sides (see D).

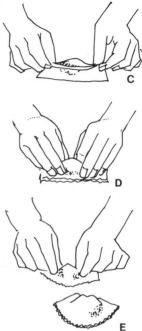

Turn slightly to alter shape (see E).

Place ravioli on wax paper-lined cookie sheet. Continue until strip of dough is gone. Knead remnants. Make squares and stuff. Take another piece of dough. Run through the pasta machine until desired thickness (1/8-to-1/4-inch) and length. Proceed as with the first long dough (there are forms available to make 10 ravioli at a time).

When cookie sheet is filled place in freezer. Prepare another cookie sheet with wax paper. Continue until finished.

When finished remove one cookie sheet at a time from freezer. Be sure last cookie sheet has been in the freezer for at least 1 hour. The ravioli are now individually frozen and will not stick together. Remove from cookie sheet and store in plastic container in freezer until ready to use.

Ravioli can be served in tomato sauce, meat sauce, cream, butter, vegetable sauce, or in a salad.

Yield: 60-70.

To cook: Place 2 quarts of water in a 4-quart pot. Heat over high heat. Just as bubbles begin to appear at the bottom of pot, add a little salt. When at rolling boil remove 25 ravioli from freezer and slowly add to boiling water. Stir. Return to boil. Reduce heat. Cover and simmer for 15 minutes or until done to taste.

Drain ravioli and keep in colander for 10 minutes until all water is drained. This is very important for water can enter the ravioli and make even the thickest sauce runny.

Heat 3 to 4 cups meat sauce (see recipe on page 234). Place ravioli on a dish, top with sauce and serve with freshly grated Romano or Parmesan cheese.

Serves: 4-6.

Ravioli with Cheese Stuffing
Ravioli Ripieni di Formaggio

This is the Pelini's favorite cheese ravioli recipe and it includes a different pasta dough from the one on pages 174 and 181 and a new filling. The pasta recipe is the Pelini standard and is used to make everything from ravioli and cannelloni to pasta for soup.

filling:
1 pound ricotta
1 egg
1/2 cup freshly grated Romano cheese
1 tsp. salt
1/2 tsp. pepper
2 tsp. fresh parsley
1/2 tsp. basil

pasta:
2 to 2-1/2 cups flour
3 eggs
1 tsp. salt
2 T corn oil

In a large bowl combine ricotta, egg, cheese, salt, pepper, parsley, and basil. Mix well and allow to stand for 30 minutes or more to allow the ingredients to blend.

Prepare a large work space, preferably a pastry board. Place flour on board and make a well. Add eggs, salt, and oil to the well. Beat eggs and work flour into them until dough is firm (see illustrations on pages 174-75).

Knead dough for 10 to 20 minutes. Form into a ball and cover with a bowl. Let stand for 30 minutes.

Do not allow pasta mixture to dry. Instead keep the dough covered by a bowl. Roll one pasta line at a time, make the ravioli, roll another pasta line and continue until all is done.

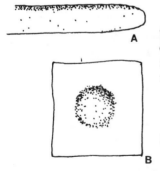

Run through the pasta machine until desired thickness (1/8-to-1/4-inch) and length. Place long dough in front of you (see A). Cut into 2-1/2 inch squares, placing the excess in a pile that can be rerolled.

Fill one square with 1 tablespoon filling (see B).

Bring one edge diagonally over the stuffing to opposite edge (see C).

Pinch down to seal on all sides (see D).

Turn slightly to alter shape (see E).

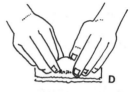

Place ravioli on wax paper-lined cookie sheet. Continue until strip of dough is gone. Knead remnants. Make squares and stuff. Take another piece of dough. Run through the pasta machine until desired thickness (1/8-to-1/4-inch) and length. Proceed as with the first long dough (there are forms available to make 10 ravioli at a time).

When cookie sheet is filled place in freezer. Prepare another cookie sheet with wax paper. Continue until finished.

When finished remove one cookie sheet at a time from freezer. Be sure last cookie sheet has been in the freezer for at least 1 hour. The ravioli are now individually frozen and will not stick together. Remove from cookie sheet and store in plastic container in freezer until ready to use.

Ravioli can be served in tomato sauce, meat sauce, cream, butter, vegetable sauce, or in a salad.

Yield: 32-36.

To cook: Place 2 quarts of water in a 4-quart pot. Heat over high heat. Just as bubbles begin to appear at the bottom of pot, add a little salt. When at rolling boil remove 25 ravioli from freezer and slowly add to boiling water. Stir. Return to boil. Reduce heat. Cover and simmer for 15 minutes or until done to taste.

Drain ravioli and keep in colander for 10 minutes until all water is drained. This is very important for water can enter the ravioli and make even the thickest sauce runny.

Heat 3 to 4 cups meat sauce (see recipe on page 234). Place ravioli on dish. Spoon on sauce and let stand 10 minutes. Serve with freshly grated Romano or Parmesan cheese.

Serves: 6-8.

Fettuccine or Tagliatelle

Thick and called *fettuccine* in Bologna, or thinner, with more eggs and called *tagliatelle* in Florence (and Arezzo and Quarata), this long, flat, 1/4-inch wide pasta is used for a variety of specialty dishes. You can buy fettuccine in any supermarket, or you can make your own (see recipe on page 174).

Fettuccine Alfredo

2-3 quarts water
1 T salt
1 pound fettuccine
2 T butter
1/4 pound butter
1 cup heavy cream
1 cup freshly grated
Parmesan cheese
Freshly ground pepper

Place a 4-quart pot on the burner. Fill 3/4-full with water. Bring to a boil. Just as bubbles begin to appear at the bottom of the pot, add salt. When at a rolling boil add fettuccine. Stir with a wooden spoon a few times. Water will stop boiling. Return to boil, then reduce heat and simmer for 10 minutes or until done to your taste. Drain. Return to pot, add 2 tablespoons butter, and toss.

Place a second 4-quart pot over medium-high heat. Melt remaining butter. Add cooked noodles. Mix well. Add half the cream and half the cheese. Mix again until cheese is melted. Add remaining cream and cheese. Mix. Place on serving dish. Top with freshly ground pepper. Serve.

Serves: 4-6.

Note: This sauce can be used with any pasta.

Fettuccine Carbonara
Fettuccine alla Carbonara

The name of this dish is not a tribute to bacon or cream, but to black pepper that should appear in abundance, like black coal dust.

2-3 quarts water
1 T salt
1 pound fettuccine
(or spaghetti)
1/4-inch-thick slice
pancetta or bacon
1/2 cup heavy cream
2 eggs plus 2 egg yolks
1/2 cup freshly grated
Parmesan cheese
4 T butter
Coarse black pepper

Place a 4-quart pot on burner. Fill 3/4 full with water. Just as bubbles begin to appear at the bottom of the pot add salt. Slowly add fettuccine and cook until tender or to taste (about 10 minutes). While fettuccine are cooking, prepare sauce.

In a medium-size skillet fry the bacon. Do not add oil. When crisp remove from skillet and place on paper towel to drain. Throw away half the drippings. Add cream to remaining drippings and allow to simmer. Crumble bacon and add to cream. Beat eggs and extra yolks in a small bowl. Add cheese to eggs and beat again.

Drain fettuccine in a colander. Place in large bowl. Add butter and toss until well blended. Add cream and bacon and toss. Add egg mixture and toss again. The heat from the pasta will cook them. Now sprinkle with an abundance of black pepper, the coarser the better. Serve at once.

Note: Carbonara can be made with any pasta.

Serves: 4-6.

Fettuccine with White Clam Sauce
Fettuccine con Vongole e Salsa Bianca

2-3 quarts water
1 T salt
1 pound fettuccine

1/2 cup green onions
4 cloves garlic
24 oz. minced clams

4 T butter
4 T flour
1-1/2 cups milk
4 T chopped fresh parsley
Dash salt
Freshly ground pepper

Place a 4-quart pot on burner. Fill 3/4-full with water. Bring to a boil. Just as bubbles begin to appear at the bottom of the pot add salt. When at a rolling boil, add fettuccine. Cook until tender or to taste (about 10 minutes). While fettuccine is boiling prepare sauce.

Peel and dice onions and garlic; open and drain clams, keep half the juice.

Place a medium-size iron skillet over medium-high heat. Heat to hot. Add butter and melt. Do not allow to brown. Add onions and garlic and saute until onions are transparent (about 5 to 7 minutes). Stir in flour until all liquid is absorbed. Slowly add milk, stirring constantly to keep from forming lumps. Add clams and juice, parsley, salt, and freshly ground pepper.

Simmer on medium-high heat for 3 to 4 minutes until sauce thickens. Keep stirring. When done remove from heat and allow to stand for 10 minutes for flavors to blend.

Drain fettuccine. Return to pot. Add sauce and stir until well blended. Turn into serving platter. Serve at once.

Serves: 4-6.

Notes: If sauce dries out, add a little broth or milk and stir.

This sauce can be used with any pasta.

189

Dumplings
Gnocchi

All hail the mighty gnocchi that had its birth centuries ago as a ravioli with no filling. Throughout Italy it is made in a variety of ways, either with semolina, cornmeal, potatoes, or ricotta. In Verona, where the potato variety was invented, gnocchi are celebrated on the last Friday of carnival.

Two varieties of gnocchi are presented here: potato and ricotta. Like most Italian pastas, there is a traditional sauce in each region where it is served, but any chef can create a new, exciting sauce for the gnocchi lends itself to creams, vegetables, meats, and casseroles. We always serve gnocchi steeped in our traditional meat sauce (recipe on page 234) and topped with plenty of freshly grated Parmesan cheese.

Potato Dumplings
Gnocchi di Patate

3 cups riced potatoes (red)
2 beaten egg yolks
1-1/2 cups flour, divided
2 T freshly grated Parmesan cheese
1/2 tsp. salt

2 cups meat sauce
Freshly grated Parmesan cheese

Peel potatoes and boil until soft. Drain, set aside to cool. When cool, pass through a ricer. Turn out into a large pan and add egg yolks, 1-1/4 cups flour, cheese, and salt. Mix slightly with hands.

Place remaining flour on large bread board. Turn out potatoes onto floured board. Knead lightly together until firm (about 5 minutes). The longer you knead, the tougher the dough. Divide dough into 3 to 4 pieces.

Roll each piece by hand into a long cylinder about 1-inch in circumference (see A). Keep floured so it does not stick to the board.

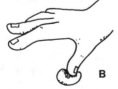

A

B

Begin at one end and cut small 1-inch pieces until the dough is gone (see A). As each piece is cut, flick it with the thumb (see B) to slightly flatten and place on cookie sheet that has been lined with wax paper. Do not stack the individual gnocchi or they will stick together. Repeat until all the dough is gone.

Cook (see note), add sauce and cheese. Serve.

Serves: 2-3.

Note: Cooking instructions follow on page 191.

Ricotta Dumplings
Gnocchi di Ricotta

We prefer the delicate texture of ricotta to potato in gnocchi; therefore, this is our favorite gnocchi recipe.

1-1/2 pounds ricotta
3 egg yolks
3 T freshly grated
Parmesan cheese
1 tsp. salt
3-4 cups flour

3 cups meat sauce
Freshly grated Parmesan
cheese

Turn ricotta onto floured pastry board. Combine egg yolks, cheese, and salt. Stir. Add flour and combine mixture with ricotta. Knead lightly together until firm (about 5 minutes). The longer you knead, the tougher the gnocchi.

Divide dough into 3 to 4 pieces. Roll each piece by hand into a long cylinder about 1-inch in circumference (see illustrations on page 190). Keep floured so it does not stick to the board.

Begin at one end and cut into 1-inch pieces until the dough cylinder is gone. As each piece is cut flick it with the thumb to slightly flatten and place on wax paper-lined cookie sheet or other flat surface. Do not stack the individual gnocchi or they will stick together. Repeat until all the dough is gone.

Yields for potato and ricotta gnocchi:

	1/2 recipe	full recipe	doubled recipe
servings:	2-3	4-5	8-10

To freeze potato or ricotta gnocchi:

After preparing the gnocchi as described above, put entire cookie sheet into freezer. Allow to freeze for an hour. Remove from freezer and place gnocchi in a storage container. If frozen in this manner, gnocchi freeze separately and not in one lump.

To cook potato or ricotta gnocchi:

To serve in meat sauce: Fill an 8-quart pot 3/4 full of water and place over high heat. As bubbles begin to appear at the bottom of the pot, add 1 teaspoon salt. Bring to a rolling boil. Slowly add gnocchi a few at a time and turn immediately or they will stick. Boil until they all rise to the surface and float (8 to 10 minutes). Drain well. Rinse out the 8-quart pot. Put 3 cups of good meat sauce (see recipe on page 234). Add gnocchi. Stir well over very low heat for 2 to 3 minutes. Add more sauce if desired and 3/4 cup freshly grated Parmesan or Romano cheese. Remove from heat. Cover with lid and allow to steep for 5 to 10 minutes. Serve hot.

Note: Gnocchi require less sauce than pastas.

Lasagna

Lasagna was born in ancient Rome when it was called *Laganum*. It was a favorite of Cicero who liked it with cheese, saffron, and cinnamon. Not to be outdone, Horace wrote about it in his satires. In modern times, blended with the tomato, it re-emerged in Naples and was made exclusively for carnival before Lent. Since then it has spread throughout Italy where each region has developed its own variation.

Lasagna in the Oven
Lasagna al Forno

2 T salt
2 T corn oil
1 pound lasagna noodles

1 pound mozzarella cheese
1/2 cup freshly grated Romano cheese
1/2 cup freshly grated Parmesan cheese
1-1/2 quarts meat sauce
2 cups broth

Half fill a wide 8-quart pot with water and place on burner over high heat. When bubbles begin to appear at the bottom of the pot, add salt and oil. Place noodles one at a time into boiling water. Turn with long-handled spoon to keep from sticking and boil for 3 to 4 minutes. Do not cook noodles until done. Drain noodles, rinse in cold water, and leave in water while assembling lasagna.

Cut mozzarella into 1-inch squares. Grate cheeses. Make piles of each on a pastry board. Empty sauce into a large bowl (see recipe on page 234). Add broth and stir until blended (thick sauce must be diluted for lasagna).

Select a large, 9-by-9-by-2-1/2-inch pan. Place 2 soup ladles full of diluted sauce in bottom of pan coating every corner. Place a layer of lasagna noodles one beside the other (see A) along bottom of pan. Do not overlap. Cover with enough sauce (see B) to coat well. Scatter 9 squares of mozzarella over noodles. Sprinkle 1 tablespoon each Romano and Parmesan cheese over the noodles.

Arrange next row of noodles in the pan running perpendicular to the first layer (see C) of noodles (forming a checkerboard). Add sauce, mozzarella, Romano, and Parmesan. Continue alternating until noodles are gone. Top with extra sauce and cheeses. Cover with aluminum foil.

Heat oven to 350 degrees and bake for 30 to 45 minutes. Remove from oven. Let set 10 minutes and uncover. Cut the lasagna into 9 square pieces: three cuts lengthwise and three cuts widthwise. Serve with a steel spatula.

Serves: 6-9.

Grand Lasagna with Sausage, Ricotta, and Bechamel
Gran Lasagna con Salsiccia, Ricotta, e Besciamella

bechamel sauce:
8 cups milk
16 T butter
12 T flour
3/4 tsp. salt

8 T salt
8 T corn oil
4 pounds lasagna noodles
12 (3-inch) sausage links
4 pounds mozzarella cheese
2 cups freshly grated Romano cheese
2 cups freshly grated Parmesan cheese
3 pounds ricotta
6 quarts meat sauce
2 quarts broth

Prepare bechamel sauce first. Place a small pot over medium-high heat and heat milk to near boiling. Do not boil or it will curdle. Place a medium-size pot over medium-high heat and melt butter. Do not allow to brown. When butter is melted, add all the flour to the butter, stirring constantly. If the flour discolors you have overcooked it.

Remove flour mixture from heat and slowly add the hot milk a tablespoon or two at a time, stirring constantly. When more than half the milk has been added you may add in larger portions. If thickening slows, return to heat. When all is mixed, add salt. Sauce should be the consistency of thick cream. Set aside until ready to use.

Place an 8-quart pot filled with water over high heat. Add salt and oil. Add 1 pound of noodles one at a time. Turn to keep from sticking. Boil 3 minutes. Drain, rinse, and leave in water while assembling lasagna. Repeat as necessary.

Select 1 extra-large (18-by-13-by-4-inch) or 2 large pans. Place 4 soup ladles of sauce in bottom of pan, coating every corner. Lay in lasagna noodles one beside the other along the bottom of the pan. Do not overlap. Cover with enough sauce to coat well. Sprinkle 18 squares of mozzarella over the pasta. Do the same with the sausage and ricotta, laying them beside the other ingredients. Sprinkle 4 teaspoons each of Romano and Parmesan. Continue alternating noodles and dressings ending with sauce and cheese.

Pour bechamel sauce over the top layer and spread with a spatula. Be sure it completely covers the noodles. Cover with aluminum foil to keep moist.

Heat the oven to 350 degrees and bake for 45 minutes. Remove from oven, but allow to set 10 minutes before uncovering. You may wish to place it under the broiler for 5 minutes to brown the bechamel sauce. Before serving cut the lasagna into 2-1/2-by-2-1/2-inch squares. Serve with a steel spatula.

Serves: 25-30. To serve 40 to 50 people use 6 pounds lasagna noodles, 3 pounds mozzarella, 2 pounds Parmesan, 1 pound Romano, 2-1/2 gallons meat sauce, 1 gallon broth.

193

Cornmeal and Semolina Mush
Polenta e Farina

Polenta, made with maize, was a staple of the Roman legions as they went out to conquer the world. Corn came from the Americas and was introduced to Italy by Christopher Columbus in the 1400s.

Ancient recipes call for polenta to be cooked over a wood fire in a *paiolo*, a copper pot with a round bottom, and stirred with a wooden spoon. When it was done it would come away from the sides of the pot and be poured onto a wooden board and cut with a thread.

Although we did not have a fireplace and thus no wood fire or *paiolo*, Nonna used a wooden spoon and poured the polenta onto a wood board and cut it with a thread. We never ate the polenta directly from the board. It was always placed on plates after cutting. Today the only portion of the ancient traditions we still maintain is the use of a wooden spoon.

Polenta is good with any sauce, but especially flavorful with *baccalà* or sausage, and extra, extra special with butter, the way true polenta aficionados enjoy it.

Basic Polenta
Polenta

Over the years we have used our good stock (broth) to replace the water in making polenta. It definitely adds flavor.

4 cups broth
(water may be used)
2 cups yellow cornmeal
1-1/2 cups cold water
1-1/2 tsp. salt

Place broth in a 4-quart pot on high heat. Place cornmeal in a large bowl and pour the cold water and salt over meal. Stir well. When broth is at hard boil stir in cornmeal and keep stirring until well mixed or lumps will form.

When mixture comes to a boil again, turn burner to low. Stir often, but be sure meal continues to soft boil. Cover with a lid and allow the contents to slow boil for 25 to 30 minutes. Remove from heat.

Serves: 3-5 (6 cups).
Note: Polenta sticks to the pot. To clean pot, fill with water and soak until polenta lifts off easily.

Polenta with Tomato Sauce
Polenta col Sugo

Polenta, recipe above
3 cups meat sauce, recipe on page 234.
1/4 cup Parmesan cheese

Prepare polenta as above. Pour onto a large platter. Cover with your favorite tomato sauce and freshly grated Parmesan cheese.
Serves: 3-5.

Polenta with Mushroom Sauce
Polenta con Funghi

6 cups cooked polenta
1/2 pound fresh
mushrooms

4 T butter
2 cloves garlic
Salt, pepper

Prepare polenta according to the basic recipe on page 194. Wash or brush dirt from mushrooms. Take one mushroom at a time and cut off the tip of the stem and remove any blemishes on the crown. Slice mushrooms.

Place a medium-size iron skillet over medium-high heat. Heat to hot. Melt butter in skillet. Peel and add garlic. When garlic is brown, mash with fork into small pieces. Add mushrooms, salt, and pepper to taste. Lower heat and saute for 5 minutes. Pour polenta onto a large platter. Top with mushrooms and juice.

Serves: 3-5.

Variation: Try adding 1 porcini mushroom to the white mushrooms for added flavor.

Polenta with Sausage
Polenta con Salsiccia

6 cups cooked polenta
3 cups meat sauce*
6 sausages
1/2 cup freshly grated
Parmesan cheese

Prepare polenta according to the basic recipe on page 194. Either make the meat sauce on page 234 or heat sauce that is already made.

Fry sausages in a medium-size skillet over medium-high heat. Do not add oil to the skillet. When ready to serve scoop out a cup of polenta, pour into dish, top with 1/2 cup meat sauce and cheese, and top again with sausage and pan drippings. Serve hot.

Serves: 4-6.

Notes: *See meat sauce recipe on page 234.
A slice of good fontina or mozzarella cheese placed over the polenta before the meat sauce is also good.

Polenta in the Morning
Polenta della Mattina

There is nothing, absolutely nothing, that can compare to polenta to warm your belly on a cold winter morning.

6 cups cooked polenta
6-8 T butter

Prepare polenta according to the basic recipe on page 194. Serve steaming hot in small custard cups. Add a pat of butter to each cup.

Yield: 6 cups.

Notes: You can add milk, cinnamon, sugar or any other topping, but the best and most traditional topping is butter.

Left-over polenta can be stored to fry later (see following recipe). Just pour polenta into a deep dish to mold, and place in refrigerator.

Polenta Pie
Polenta Pasticciata

12 (3/4-inch-thick) squares cold cooked polenta

2 cups sauce
1/2 cup freshly grated Parmesan cheese
5-6 slices mozzarella cheese (optional)
Sausage (optional)

Prepare polenta according to the basic recipe on page 194. Once made, pour into a deep-sided dish and refrigerate overnight or until cold. Prepare a sauce of your choice (see meat sauce recipe page 234).

Remove polenta from dish and cut into a dozen 3-inch squares. Sprinkle a medium-size baking dish lightly with sauce.

Place the squares over the sauce to form a layer. Cover with half of sauce and freshly grated Parmesan cheese (you also may add slices of mozzarella cheese and chunks of cooked sausage). Cover bottom layer with remaining polenta squares. Top with remaining sauce and cheeses.

Bake in oven at 350 degrees for 35 to 45 minutes. Serve hot.

Serves: 4-5.

Note: You can toast polenta squares under the broiler before assembling this dish.

Fried Polenta
Crostini di Polenta

Polenta with butter is delicious, but fried polenta is better. Today it is served as an appetizer in exclusive restaurants, often topped with a pimento or other garnish. For us it was, and still is, breakfast fare. But one can serve it with a good salad, as a snack, or on a buffet table.

6 cups cooked polenta
1-1/2 cups corn oil

Prepare polenta according to the basic recipe on page 194. Pour into a deep-sided dish and refrigerate overnight or until cold.

Remove from pan (it will come our in a firm mass). Slice into 3-by-3-by-1/2-inch thick squares.

Place medium-size iron skillet over high heat. Heat to hot. Add oil to generously cover bottom of skillet. Heat to hot. Lay sliced polenta in skillet. Fry until edges begin to brown (about 5 to 7 minutes). Turn. Fry other side (polenta is fragile, turn only once). Remove and drain on paper towel. Eat hot. If oil becomes too hot, lower heat, but polenta must fry in hot oil.

Yield: 25-30 squares.

Notes: Polenta can also be placed on a grill or in a broiler. In this case it is called *polenta ai ferri*. Allow one side to crisp, about 5 minutes, turn, and grill the second side. Nonna covered this polenta with sauce.

Sweet Semolina
Farina Dolce

Any recipe in the polenta and farina section of this cookbook can be made with farina, but this is the only recipe that originates with farina. Cornmeal is good prepared this way, too.

The recipe was given to us by our friend, Rene Moncini, whose family comes from Torino in the Piedmont where *farina dolce* is a specialty.

Farina dolce is sweet to the taste, but is not served as a dessert. Instead it is prepared as a side dish to fried veal or chicken. It is also great as a snack, or on a buffet table.

When buying farina for this dish you may purchase semolina, cream of wheat, or farina. They are all available in supermarkets.

3 cups milk
3/4 cup semolina
1/2 cup granulated sugar

1 egg yolk
1/4 cup grated lemon rind

1 egg
1 T milk
1 cup bread crumbs

1 cup corn oil

Place a large pot over medium-high heat. Add milk and allow to boil. When milk begins to bubble, add semolina. Stir well and add sugar.

Allow to cook until thick (about 10 minutes). While semolina is simmering, separate an egg and beat the egg yolk. When semolina is thick, remove from stove and quickly stir in the beaten yolk, then the lemon rind.

Grease an 8-by-8-inch dish with a little oil and pour the cooked semolina into the dish. Cover with wax paper and refrigerate until cold (about 2 hours).

When cold remove from refrigerator and cut into 3-inch squares. The squares should be more than 1-inch thick.

Beat the remaining egg with the tablespoon of milk. Dip each square into egg, then into bread crumbs. Coat generously.

Place a medium-size iron skillet over medium-high heat. Heat to hot. Add oil. Heat to hot (must fry in hot oil). Drop squares of semolina in oil. Fry until golden, turn, fry second side.

Remove from oil and allow to drain. Serve hot or cold.

Serves: 6-9.

Notes: If you use instant semolina all times change. You can sprinkle *farina dolce* with confectioners' sugar or syrup.

198

Spaghetti

Spaghetti, a round, long, thin pasta, was never served to guests in Nonna's house. It is only for the family and usually a weekday meal. The fact that its name has been elevated to mean just about any pasta serves us all right, for spaghetti, dressed up in a variety of ways, makes an excellent meal.

Spaghetti with Anchovy Sauce
Spaghetti con Acciugata

Tart and tangy, spaghetti with anchovies was often served as I was growing up. It is a good Lenten dish, but can be served any time.

1 tsp. salt
1 pound spaghetti

1/3 cup olive oil
2 oz. flat
fillets of anchovies

Place a 4-quart pot on the burner. Fill 3/4-full with water. Bring to a boil. Just as bubbles begin to appear at the bottom of the pot, add salt. When at rolling boil, add spaghetti and cook until tender or to taste (about 10 minutes). While spaghetti is cooking prepare the anchovy sauce.

Place olive oil in a small iron skillet. Place the skillet on medium-high heat. Do not overheat the oil. Add the anchovies, oil and all, and mash the fillets with a fork. Do not allow to cook.

When the spaghetti is cooked, remove from heat, drain in a colander, return to pot, add anchovy sauce and mix well. Serve immediately.

Serves: 3-5.

Spaghetti with Butter and Cheese
Spaghetti con Burro e Formaggio

This simple spaghetti dish is the origin of fettuccine Alfredo.

1 tsp. salt
1 pound spaghetti

1/4 pound butter
1/2 cup freshly grated
Parmesan cheese
Pepper, to taste

Place a 4-quart pot on burner. Fill 3/4-full with water. Bring to a boil. Just as bubbles begin to appear at the bottom of the pot add salt. When water reaches a rolling boil add spaghetti. Cook until tender or to taste (about 10 minutes). When the spaghetti is cooked, remove pot from heat, drain in a colander, return to pot, and add the butter and cheese. Mix well or until all the butter is melted. Add pepper. Serve immediately.

Serves: 3-5.

Spaghetti with Broccoli
Spaghetti con Broccoli

1 tsp. salt
1/2 pound spaghetti

1-2 cups fresh broccoli
2 T salt

2-3 T corn oil
2-3 cloves garlic
1/2 tsp. salt
1/4 tsp. pepper
1/8 pound butter
1/4 cup freshly grated
Parmesan cheese

While spaghetti is cooking prepare the broccoli. Wash and cut into pieces. Place in a large pot half filled with water and salt. Boil for 8 to 10 minutes until soft. Test with a fork. Remove and place on drain board to drain (may be placed in the refrigerator up to four days).

When ready to fry squeeze out as much liquid as possible. On a pastry board chop the broccoli into small pieces.

Place a medium-size iron skillet over medium-high heat. Heat to hot. Add oil. Peel garlic, add to oil in pan, brown, and crush with a fork until no large pieces remain.

Place the broccoli in the oil, salt and pepper to taste. Allow to brown about 15 minutes, turning often and mashing with a fork to reduce bulk.

Place a 4-quart pot on burner. Fill 3/4-full with water. Bring to a boil. Just as bubbles begin to appear at the bottom of the pot add salt. When water reaches a rolling boil, add spaghetti. Cook until tender or to taste (about 10 minutes).

When the spaghetti is cooked, remove it from heat, drain in a colander, replace in pot, add the butter and mix well or until all the butter is melted. Add broccoli, oil and all, and freshly grated Parmesan cheese. Mix well. Serve immediately.

Serves: 3-5.

Notes: In place of the broccoli you can use savoy cabbage, cauliflower, spinach, or celery for this recipe.

In Tuscany there is a special pasta called *sedanini*, which looks like pieces of celery and is specially made for this type of dish.

Spaghetti with Cinnamon
Spaghetti Bianchi con Cannella

This was one of my father's favorite meals. Very little of my father's family traditions are described in *Immigrant's Kitchen*. My father, Alfred (Freddie) Vivian, was one of a herd of children born to Peter and Ida Cavalli Vivian of Monessen. I never knew my Nonno Pete or Nonna Ida--both died before I was born. But I have fond memories of my father's brothers and sisters, all dead now except for the oldest, Helen Vivian Organtini of Norristown, Pennsylvania.

My father was an easygoing, loveable man whom, with great affection, we called, "Honey Boy." He, too, worked at Pittsburgh Steel. His family name, Vivian, was always shrouded in great mystery in our home and we never could get the story straight (we never really tried). Our cousins are called Viviani, but my father insisted that they changed their name and Vivian was the real name.

1 tsp. salt
1 pound spaghetti
1/4 pound butter
1/2 cup freshly grated
Parmesan cheese
1 T cinnamon

Place a 4-quart pot on burner. Fill 3/4-full with water. Bring to a boil. Just as bubbles begin to appear at the bottom of the pot add salt.

When water reaches a rolling boil, add spaghetti. Cook until tender or to taste (about 10 minutes).

When the spaghetti is cooked, remove from heat, drain in a colander, replace in pot, and add the butter, cheese, and cinnamon. Mix well or until all the butter is melted. Serve immediately.

Serves: 3-5.

Spaghetti with Garlic and Oil
Spaghetti Aglio e Olio

1 tsp. salt
1 pound thin spaghetti

sauce:
1/2 cup olive oil
1/2 tsp. salt
3 medium cloves garlic
Freshly ground pepper
2 T fresh parsley
1 T olive oil
1/2 cup freshly grated
Parmesan cheese

Place a 4-quart pot on the burner. Fill 3/4-full with water. Bring to a boil. Just as bubbles begin to appear at the bottom of the pot add salt. When water comes to a rolling boil, add spaghetti and stir a few times. Water will stop boiling. Return to boil, then reduce heat and simmer for 10 minutes or until done to your taste.

While spaghetti is simmering make the sauce. Place a medium-sized iron skillet on low heat. Add 1/2 cup oil and salt. Peel garlic and add to olive oil, stirring frequently until brown. Once brown crush with a fork until garlic breaks into small pieces.

Remove spaghetti from stove. Drain in a colander. Return to pot.

Pour olive oil mixture over spaghetti. Toss well and add pepper, parsley (chopped into small pieces) 1 tablespoon olive oil, and freshly grated cheese. Toss again and serve at once (oil falls to bottom of pot if allowed to stand).

Serves: 3-5.

Poultry
Pollame

When I was young Nonna had a chicken coop in the back yard, and I was forever feeding the chickens. Then one year she bought 20 live chickens and enlisted my sister-in-law Peggy and me to help her dress them. Cleaning chickens is not a pleasant job, and, as we sat under the grape arbor and chicken after chicken was brought up from the cellar where they had been killed and defeathered, we got so sick of the smell, the texture of the skin, and the minute plucking of remaining quills, that we did not eat chicken for a year. It was our loss, for it was the last time that Nonna made *galantina*. Where roast chicken was a favorite and a staple, *galantina* was one of the most unique dishes Nonna made. *Porchetta* was Nonno's specialty, *galantina* was Nonna's.

Italian chickens are corn-fed and by consensus the best chickens in Italy are from Tuscany. The Tuscan recipes are simple, easy to prepare, and heavily reliant on spices. When selecting a chicken for the following recipes, any old chicken will not do. First it must be grade A. Then it must be the proper age. A frying chicken is a young tender chicken (*pollo*) 2 to 3 months old that weighs 2 to 3.5 pounds. It is to be used for frying, just as a roaster, higher in fat and ranging from 2.5 to 5 pounds, is used for roasting. A stewing chicken, (*gallina*) more flavorful, but tougher, because it is older (10 to 18 months) when harvested, should be used for soups, stews, and sauces. A good weight for stewing chicken is 3 to 6 pounds.

Capon held noble status in our home. A capon is a neutered rooster, castrated before it is 8 weeks old, fed a fatty diet, and harvested before it is 10 months old at 4 to 6 pounds. We ate capon on every holiday until we became Americanized and ate turkey on Thanksgiving and crown rib at Christmas.

We seldom served duck, but it was definitely served on the first Sunday in October, which was the *Festa di Quarata*, the festival of our village in Italy.

Capon
Cappone

Capon, more tender than chicken, was a specialty in Nonna's home, as it was in all of Tuscany. The tender meat of the capon is far superior to chicken and the taste is richer. Capon was the meal of tradition and choice for Christmas and other holidays.

Boiled Capon with Anchovy Sauce
Cappone Lesso con Acciugata

This tasty recipe is usually made from a capon that has been used to make soup. The meat on the carcass is never discarded and is absolutely delicious served up with *acciugata*, a sauce of anchovies and capers.

1 boiled capon
Acciugata*

Remove capon from soup and allow to drain. Cut into serving pieces (legs, thighs, breast, wings, and back).

Arrange pieces of capon on a platter and cover with *acciugata* (recipe on page 230).

If you want to boil capon specifically for this dish fill a large pot with water, add an onion, carrot, stock of celery, salt, pepper and capon. Boil until capon is tender (better to make the soup on page 240 for essentially that is what you are doing).

Serves: 4-6.

Notes: *See *acciugata* recipe on page 230.
This dish can also be prepared with chicken.

Roast Capon with Fennel and Oven Potatoes
Cappone in Porchetta e Contorno di Patate

Roast capon was the main course of our Christmas dinner until we became Americanized and prepared crown ribs of beef. Although it is delicious seasoned in *porchetta*, or with oregano or rosemary, our standard was capon with sage (see the chicken recipe on page 206). This *porchetta* recipe was reserved for special occasions.

5-6 pound roasting capon
Salt and pepper

3-4 cloves garlic
3-4 slices prosciutto
3 tsp. fresh fennel seeds
3-4 sausage links (optional)

1/4 cup corn oil

5-6 potatoes (red)
Salt and pepper, to taste

Wash and clean the capon and pat dry with a clean cloth. Salt and pepper the inside of the cavity. Set aside.

Crush garlic with a kitchen mallet or handle of the knife (do not peel).

Lay prosciutto in cavity. Top with crushed garlic, fennel, then sausage (optional).

Heat the oven to 350 degrees. Generously cover the bottom of a large roasting pan with oil. Place capon, breast side up, into the roaster. Slide capon in roaster to coat back and wings with oil. Roast for 20 minutes. Turn capon breast side down. Continue roasting.

Peel and cut large potatoes into 3 to 4 pieces, small ones in half (for crunchy potatoes cut into smaller pieces). After the capon has been roasting for 30 minutes, add the potatoes. Turn all potatoes coating them with the oil in the pan. Roast for an additional 2 to 2-1/2 hours, basting the capon and turning the potatoes every 20 minutes. When almost done, salt and pepper the outside of the capon (do not salt the potatoes).

Serve with fresh garden salad, and an additional vegetable.

Serves: 4-6.

Variations: Capon can be roasted with sage, oregano, or rosemary. Use only one of these spices and eliminate the sausage and prosciutto. See chicken recipes that follow.

Chicken
Pollo

Chicken every Sunday is a treat when prepared in the variety of ways we serve it. The difficult choice is which spice to use, since all are excellent.

Roast Chicken with Sage and Oven Potatoes
Pollo Arrosto con Salvia e Contorno di Patate

Without any question, roast chicken with sage and oven potatoes was the centerpiece for 60 percent of the Sunday dinners served in Nonna's house. Once you make it you will understand why.

3-1/2 to 4-1/2
pound roasting chicken
Salt and pepper
2 T butter
8-10 sprigs fresh sage

1/4 cup corn oil
5-6 potatoes (red)

Wash and clean chicken inside and out. Dry with clean cloth. Cut away edges of wing tips and ends of legs. Salt and pepper chicken inside and out. Lift the skin off breast (do not break) and place a sliver of butter on each side of breastbone. Place a sprig of sage under skin beside butter. Place a generous sprig of sage under each wing. Fold tip under top of the wing to hold sage in place. Place several sprigs of sage in the cavity.

Heat oven to 350 degrees. Generously cover bottom of a large roasting pan with oil. Place chicken, breast side up, into the roaster. Slide chicken in pan to coat back and wings with oil. Roast for 20 minutes. Turn chicken breast side down. Continue roasting.

Peel and cut large potatoes into 3 to 4 pieces, smaller ones in half (for crunchy potatoes cut into smaller pieces). After chicken has been roasting 30 minutes, add potatoes. Turn potatoes, coating with oil in pan. Do not salt. Roast for an additional 2 to 2-1/2 hours, basting the chicken and turning the potatoes every 20 minutes.

Serve with fresh garden salad and an additional vegetable (try *aglio e olio* on pages 258-59).

Serves: 4-6 servings.

Notes: Chicken can be spiced with oregano (replace sage) or fennel (see preceding recipe) and stuffed (see following recipe). You can also make any of these flavorful recipes with chicken parts. Be sure each part has enough of the spice and follow the recipe as directed.

Stuffed Chicken with Oregano
Pollo Ripieno all'Origano

3-1/2 to 4-1/2 pound
roasting chicken
Salt and pepper
4-5 leaves fresh oregano*
2 T butter

stuffing:
1 small onion
1/4-inch-thick
slice *pancetta*
1 celery rib
1 carrot
1 tsp. fresh parsley
1/2 clove garlic

2 T corn oil
1 tsp. salt
1 tsp. pepper

4 cups bread cubes
4 T freshly grated
Parmesan cheese
1 T butter
3 eggs
1/2 cup broth
(optional)

1/4 cup corn oil
5-6 medium potatoes
(red)

Wash chicken. Dry. Cut off wing tips. Salt and pepper inside and out. Place 2 oregano leaves inside cavity. Lift skin off breast and place sliver of butter and 1/2 oregano leaf each side of breastbone.

Stuffing: Peel onion, wash, cut into quarter wedges. Cut *pancetta* into 1/2-inch pieces. Peel celery and carrot, wash, cut into 1-inch pieces. Chop parsley. Peel garlic, cut in half. Combine and grind in meat grinder or food processor (the grinder is better because it releases the juices).

Place medium-size iron skillet over medium-high heat. Heat to hot. Add oil. When hot add chopped ingredients, salt, and pepper. Saute until onions are browned, stirring often. The longer this mixture simmers, the better it tastes. It is done when it begins to stick to the skillet, about 20 minutes.

In a large bowl combine bread cubes and cheese. Melt butter, pour over bread. Beat eggs, add. Add onion mixture. Mix well. Must be moist enough to hold together. If dry, add broth or water.

Fill body cavity with stuffing. Pull skin over opening and secure with wooden skewer.

Place leaf of oregano under each wing. Fold tip under top of wing. Heat oven to 350 degrees. Cover bottom of a roasting pan with oil. Place chicken, breast side up, into roaster. Slide chicken in pan to coat back and wings. Roast for 30 minutes. Turn chicken breast side down.

Peel and cut large potatoes into 3 to 4 pieces, smaller ones in half (for crunchy potatoes cut smaller). After chicken has been roasting 30 minutes, add potatoes. Turn, coating with oil in pan. Cook additional 2 to 2-1/2 hours, basting both chicken and potatoes every 20 minutes. Turn potatoes occasionally, but do not salt. Serve with garden salad and additional vegetable.

Serves: 4-6 servings.

Notes: *You can sprinkle dry oregano. Or you can use sage in place of oregano, just as you can use oregano in the preceding recipe to replace the sage.

Chicken Galantine
Galantina di Gallina

Galantina was my Nonna's culinary masterpiece and she was often called upon to produce it for weddings when she made it either from capon or chicken. She learned the art from Amabile Sodi, her lifetime friend, who lived in the same town in Italy (Castelluccio) and came to live in the same town in America. I am sure this is not the only recipe they shared.

The art of *galantina* is to remove all bones through the neck without breaking the skin. The carcass becomes the casing for a stuffing of various meats. Nonna could make it without a mishap, and when she died in 1984 the art died with her. We cut the bird down the back and then remove the bones.

Galantina can be made with capon, chicken, duck, turkey, and even fish.

4 pound stewing chicken
2 onions
3-4 celery ribs
1 small carrot
1 tsp. salt
1 tsp. pepper

Trussing needle and cord
Large cheesecloth

8-10 cups chicken broth
(see page 241)

Although you should have a live stewing chicken to make *galantina*, while testing this recipe we used a chicken that had been frozen.

If you use a live chicken, it must be killed, defeathered, and gutted without dipping it in boiling water. If you do not have the stomach for the task, perhaps you can find a live chicken at a farm and the farmer will kill, defeather, and gut it for you. Be sure it is not placed in boiling water or the skin will not be pliable and it will be difficult to remove the bones. Removing the big feathers is the easy part, you must be sure that the small quills are also gone.

Once the chicken has been prepared wash it inside and out. Cut off the neck, wing tips, and feet. Work quickly for as the chicken sets, the skin becomes tough.

Deboning by splitting the chicken

Cut chicken in half down the back (see A).

Once chicken is split, lay on a cutting board. Begin carving the meat away from the backbone (see B).

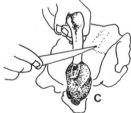

Once backbone is exposed, move to the legs. Remove the bones from the legs by cutting each leg at the joint (see C). Sever the tendon, scrape the meat from the bone, and free the bone. Twist the bone lose from the thigh and remove it. Remove thigh bones in the same manner. Next, move to the wings. Follow the same procedure as with the legs.

Turn the carcass over, begin removing the meat from the breast, scraping as close to the bone as possible (see D).

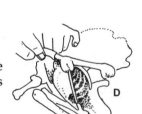

Once the bird is free from the bones lay it flat on a clean work space (see E).

stuffing:
1 onion
1 celery rib
1 T carrots
1/2 tsp. fresh parsley
1 medium clove garlic
1/4-inch-thick slice
pancetta
3 T oil
1/2 tsp. salt
1/2 tsp. pepper
1 large piece Italian
bread, decrusted
1/3 cup broth
10 oz. veal steak
3 egg yolks
1/2 tsp. salt
1/2 tsp. pepper
1 grate nutmeg

2 thick slices prosciutto
3 thick slices salted beef
tongue

Truss ends of legs and wings with heavy string, tying securely. Using needle and thread sew neck and tail openings shut. It is ready to stuff.

Put 8 quarts of water in a 12-quart pot and place over medium-high heat. Wash and peel onions, celery, and carrot. Place all chicken bones (including neck and head) in pot. Boil and skim. Add whole onion, celery, carrot, salt and pepper and bring to a boil. Lower heat, cover, and simmer for 1-1/2 hours.

Preparing the stuffing
Peel onion, wash and cut into quarter wedges. Peel celery and carrots, wash, and cut into 1-inch pieces. Chop parsley. Peel garlic and cut in half. Cut *pancetta* into 1/2-inch pieces. Combine and grind in meat grinder or food processor (the grinder is better because it releases the juices).

Place medium-size iron skillet over medium-high heat. Heat to hot. Add oil. Heat. Add chopped ingredients, salt and pepper. Saute until onions are transparent, stirring often. Saute 20 minutes. The longer this mixture simmers, the better it tastes.

Cube decrusted bread. In a small bowl combine bread cubes and broth. Allow to moisten and set aside.

Cut veal into small pieces and chop in a meat chopper, the finer the better. Place in large bowl. Add moistened bread to veal. In a separate bowl beat yolks adding salt, pepper and a single grate of fresh nutmeg. Add to veal mixture. Combine veal and onion mixtures. Blend well. Set aside.

Dice prosciutto and tongue into small pieces and set aside.

Stuffing the bird
Place stuffing in cavity of chicken. Top with slices of prosciutto and tongue (see F).

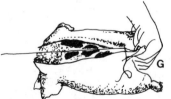

Bring the two edges of the skin together and using a trussing needle sew up all openings (see G).

210

Once openings are secure (see H), wrap the chicken in a clean thin cloth like a cheesecloth, and tie it securely (see I).

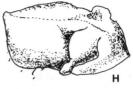

H

Remove all solid items from broth. Strain broth through sieve and return to pot. Bring to a boil.

Place the stuffed and wrapped chicken in the boiling broth. Once the broth begins to boil again lower the burner and simmer for 1-1/2 to 2 hours. Remove from burner and allow to cool for an additional hour.

I

Slicing the galantina

Remove chicken from broth. Unwrap cloth and allow to cool 30 minutes. Remove the threads. Slice like a ham (see J). Place on a large platter and serve.

J

Yield: 25-30 slices.

Note: *Galantina* is usually served as an appetizer, at table, before the first course of the meal.

Deboning through the neck

Nonna deboned her chicken through the neck. We are not skilled enough to do this, but if you want to give it a try, here's how:

Lay cleaned chicken on cutting board. Using a sharp, pointed knife, enter carcass through neck. Remove neck bone by cutting as close to bone as possible. With fingers, feel for one wing bone. Follow to joint. Make a slit at joint and work bone loose with fingers, pulling bone out from slit. Do both wings.

As you finish a section turn flesh and skin back onto carcass so that flesh will be inside out. Be sure to cut as close to bone as possible to leave as much meat as possible on bird.

Now move to breast and back. For breast, backbone, and legs follow the instructions above. Once carcass has been removed, turn chicken right side out again, and follow the stuffing and cooking instructions that precede.

Chicken on a Spit
Pollo allo Spiedo

My Nonno and Nonna enjoyed going on picnics when my mother was still a girl and I was yet to be born. These picnics were usually held on the farm of a friend and chicken on a spit was always part of the menu. This recipe is for a good size picnic, but you can do a single chicken or even a leg or breast on a charcoal grill or in the oven.

20 (3-pound)
spring chickens
Salt and pepper
1 pound butter
120 sprigs sage

3 T salt
3 T pepper
1 cup olive oil

Wash and clean the chickens inside and out. Dry with clean cloth. Cut away the edges of the wing tips. Salt and pepper each chicken inside and out.

Lift the skin off the breast (do not break the skin) and place a sliver of butter on each side of the breastbone beneath the skin of each chicken.

Place a sprig of sage under the skin beside the butter and a generous sprig of sage under each wing.

Fold the tip under the top of the wing, holding the sage in place. Place several sprigs of sage in the cavity and between the legs and the breast. Fold the legs into the skin left around the rectum.

Skewer the first bird onto the spit by piercing the bird below the wings, breast side up and facing you. Reverse the second bird so the back is facing you. Place it on the skewer upsidedown, with the wings touching the legs of the first bird. Alternate this way to assure even weight distribution. If chickens are not well balanced the spit will not turn. Place spit on fire.

In a large deep bowl combine salt, pepper and olive oil. Mix well. Tie 8 or 9 sprigs of sage together and tie them to a long stick.

Once the chickens are on the spit they must rotate constantly and the flesh must be basted. Dip the sage brush into the oil mixture and brush the chickens every 10 to 15 minutes. As the chickens cook and the wood depletes, add more wood closer to the birds bringing the heat nearer. Let grill over an open fire for 3 to 3-1/2 hours, or until golden brown.

Yield: 20 whole chickens.

Note: Nonno always said you could not roast over an open fire unless you used cherry wood.

Duck
Anitra

Duck was served for the *Festa di Quarata*, the yearly festival celebrating our village in Italy. It can also be made *galantina*, as on pages 208-11 (we never did).

Duck in Tomato Sauce with Celery
Anitra in Umido con Sedano

4-5 pound duck
1/4 cup corn oil
Salt and pepper
3-4 cloves garlic, crushed

14 oz. whole or crushed canned tomatoes
3 oz. tomato paste
1 cup broth

Celery in duck sauce*

Cut duck into serving pieces: 2 legs, 2 thighs, 2 wings, 4 pieces of breast, 2 backs. Wash and dry.

Place medium-size iron skillet over medium-high heat. Heat to hot. Add oil. Heat. Place duck in oil. Add salt, pepper and crushed garlic. To crush garlic hit it with a kitchen mallet or handle of a knife. Do not peel. Brown well to sear in juices. Lower burner. Remove duck from skillet.

Add tomatoes to juices in skillet and crush with a fork. Simmer 10 minutes. Add tomato paste. Rinse cans with 1/2 cup broth and add to mixture. Mix well. Lower heat and simmer uncovered for 15 minutes. Taste, salt and pepper if necessary.

Remove from heat and run sauce through a sieve removing pulp. Place 1 cup of sauce in a bowl and set aside to make the celery dish below. Return remainder to skillet, return heat to medium-high, simmer for 5 minutes, reduce heat and simmer uncovered for 15 minutes or until sauce begins to lose bright red color.

Add duck. Cover and simmer slowly for 30 minutes or until sauce is a brown-red and oil begins to separate and float on surface (skim if desired). Do not stir or turn. If sauce dries, add remaining broth.

Remove from skillet. Place on serving tray. Cover slightly with sauce. Place remaining sauce in gravy boat. Serve with Italian bread.

Serves: 6-8.

Fried Celery in Thin Sauce *(Sedano Fritto in Umido)*: Follow recipe on page 257 but substitute duck sauce for thin sauce. Once you have covered celery with sauce, simmer for 20 minutes. Remove from heat. Place in platter, sprinkle with freshly grated Parmesan cheese, and serve immediately.

Roast Duck with Fennel
Anitra in Porchetta

Cooking duck or chicken in *porchetta* was always a highlight of the year. The succulent aroma of fennel filled the house and made the mouth water.

Roast duck with fennel was the highlight of the homecoming festivities in Quarata. On the first Sunday in October families or children that had moved away from the town came home to festooned streets, a bike race, and concession stands loaded with good Tuscan food. Duck was roasted all day and in the evening a sit-down dinner was served in the *piazza* (main square).

4-5 pound duck
Salt and pepper

3-4 slices prosciutto
3-4 cloves garlic
2 tsp. fresh fennel seeds
3-4 sausage links
(optional)
Salt, to taste
2 tsp. pepper

Wash and clean duck and pat dry with a clean cloth. Set aside.

Place cleaned duck on a large pastry board. Rub the inside of the duck with a damp cloth and salt and pepper the inside of the cavity.

Lay prosciutto end to end covering the bottom of the cavity. Crush garlic by hitting it with a kitchen mallet or handle of a knife (do not remove skins). Sprinkle garlic over prosciutto and fennel seeds over garlic. Add the sausage (optional), stuffing the entire cavity. Secure the opening with cooking pins.

Heat oven to 350 degrees. Place roasting rack in a large roasting pan (duck makes a lot of drippings).

Place duck on rack and put into oven. Do not add oil.

Roast for at least 2-1/2 hours. Use a meat thermometer.

When almost done salt and pepper the outside of the duck and allow to finish cooking.

Serve with a fresh green salad.

Serves: 6-8.

Rice
Riso

When we were sick Nonna brewed rice. As I got older I often wondered, "Why rice?" But I have discovered that it is an Italian tradition that reaches back to the Romans, who thought rice had curative properties.

Prepared both savory and sweet and served at the beginning, middle, or end of a meal, rice, like pasta, is a staple in Italy. The recipes in this chapter, although few in number, reflect its versatility.

The most famous rice dish in Italy is *risotto,* a blend that elevates rice to a main course. It can be prepared in a number of ways and almost every region has its own variation: rice with Parmesan cheese and white wine, rice with mushrooms, or rice with tomato sauce.

Almost without exception, *risotto* is not rice topped with liquid, but rice cooked in liquid, be it broth or sauce. The difference is evident from the first taste: the rice is not coated, but the flavor has penetrated into each grain making it flavorful down to its heart.

Of the sweet recipes for rice, my favorite, and the most exotic, is the delicious rice fritter served traditionally on St. Joseph's Day. It is without equal in taste and texture.

In the United States, the best rice you can buy for Italian dishes is the imported *arborio* rice found in most Italian food stores and gourmet shops. A good long-grained rice will also do, but under no circumstances should one use instant or minute rice for Italian dishes.

Rice Fritters
Frittelle di San Giuseppe

On St. Joseph's Day, March 19, Nonna prepared rice fritters. Throughout Italy it is traditional to prepare a special sweet for St. Joseph's Day, a national holiday. The type of sweet varies from district to district. *Frittelle*, or *zeppole*, another name for the same thing, are common to regions as far afield as Sicily, Naples, and Tuscany, while the filled *bigne* or *confetti* are prominent in Sardinia and other southern provinces. There is also *sfinci* and *cassateddi*, a filled ricotta turnover. In all regions the huge frying pans come out and the town squares are rich with the aromas of frying sweets.

Rice fritters are delicate and must be made carefully or they will fall apart. *Arborio* rice, with its heavy starch content, helps to hold them together. This is not a *risotto*, but a sweet, served at the end of the meal.

3 cups milk
1 cup water
1 cup rice
2 tsp. salt
Rind of 1/2 lemon

1/2 cup granulated
sugar
2 T butter
1/2 tsp. vanilla

1 T whisky or rum
4 eggs, separated

1 cup corn oil
3/4 cup confectioners'
sugar

Place a medium-size pot over medium-high heat. Add milk and water. When liquids reach a boil add rice and salt. Stir until it reboils. Cut the lemon rind into 1/4-inch wedges and add to boiling rice. Do not stir cooking rice.

When rice is cooked remove from the burner and drain any excess liquid. Add sugar, butter, and vanilla to the warm rice and stir. Set aside to cool for 3 to 4 hours.

After rice reaches room temperature add whisky or rum, and egg yolks. The batter must be firm (see note). If runny 1/2 tablespoon of flour may be added to hold the mixture together (too much flour and the fritters will be hard). Beat egg whites separately .

Place large iron skillet on medium-high heat. Generously cover bottom of skillet with oil. Heat oil to hot. While oil is heating, fold egg whites into rice mixture. When oil is hot, drop rice mixture by spoonfuls into the oil. Fry until golden brown, turn, and finish frying other side. Drain on paper towel. Sprinkle with confectioners' sugar and serve immediately.

Yield: 24-26.

Note: Batter may be stored in refrigerator for a day, but do not add egg whites until ready to fry.

Rice with Angel-hair Pasta and/or Pine Nuts
Risotto con Capelli D'Angelo e Pinoli

5 T butter, divided
1 cup angle-hair
or pine nuts

1 clove garlic
1 cup rice
1-1/2 cups broth
1/4 tsp. salt
Freshly ground pepper
1/2 cup freshly grated
Parmesan cheese

Place a small-size iron skillet over medium-high heat. Add 1 tablespoon butter and melt. Add angel-hair and/or pine nuts (I prefer both). Allow to brown in the butter, stirring often (about 5 minutes). Do not burn. Set aside.

Melt 2 tablespoons butter in 2-quart saucepan. Peel and dice garlic, add to butter. Saute until brown. Do not brown butter. Once garlic is browned, crush with fork until it dissolves into pieces.

Add rice and stir for a minute, until butter is absorbed. Add broth and salt. Bring to boil. Cover, reduce heat. Boil 10 minutes (do not stir cooking rice). Remove from heat. Stir in remaining butter (optional), browned angel-hair and/or pine nuts (see note). Cover and allow to steam until liquid is absorbed. Add freshly ground pepper and freshly grated Parmesan cheese. Stir, turn onto platter. Serve.

Serves: 3-4.

Note: If you want angel-hair crunchy, add to rice later with pepper and cheese.

Rice Milan Style
Risotto alla Milanese

Risotto alla Milanese is *the* classic rice dish of Italy. We simply called it *risotto*, as it was the only way we made it.

2 cups meat sauce
(recipe on page 234)
2 cups broth
1 cup rice
Salt and pepper, to taste
1/2 cup freshly grated
Parmesan cheese

Place a large-size iron skillet over medium-high heat. Add meat sauce and broth and bring to a boil. Add rice, stir, bring to a boil and lower the heat.

Cover and let simmer. Do not stir cooking rice. If sauce begins to dry, add more broth. Add salt, pepper. Simmer until sauce is absorbed and rice is tender.

Add freshly grated Parmesan cheese, mix, let stand for 5 minutes, and serve.

Serves: 3-5.

Rice with Peas
Risi e Bisi

The origin of this dish is Venice during the Middle Ages. It was traditionally a heavy soup, served to the doges on St. Mark's Day, in honor of the patron saint of Venice. This is the Pelini version.

2 cups meat sauce
(recipe on page 234)
2 cups hot water (or broth)
1 cup rice

1/2 tsp. salt
1/4 tsp. pepper
2/3 cup peas

3/4 cup freshly grated Parmesan cheese

Place a large-size iron skillet over medium-high heat. Add meat sauce and hot water or broth and bring to a boil. Add rice, stir, bring to a boil and lower the heat. Cover and let simmer for 30 minutes stirring every 5 minutes.

If sauce begins to dry, add more hot water or broth. Simmer until rice is almost tender. Add salt, pepper and peas. Stir. Simmer until sauce is absorbed and rice is tender.

Add Parmesan cheese, mix, let stand for 5 minutes and serve.

Serves: 3-4.

Rice Pudding
Budino di Riso

2 quarts milk
1 cup rice

2/3 cup granulated sugar
3 eggs
1/2 tsp. salt
1 tsp. vanilla

Cinnamon, to taste

Place a medium-size pot over medium-high heat. Heat milk to boiling. Add rice and stir. Continue stirring until all milk is absorbed (45 to 60 minutes). You must stir the rice and milk so the pudding will be creamy.

Combine sugar, eggs, salt, and vanilla in a large bowl. Beat. Add 1/2 cup cooked rice to the sugar mixture. Mix well. Pour this mixture into remaining rice, blend.

Pour into individual serving dishes. Cool and sprinkle with cinnamon. Refrigerate until ready to serve.

Serves: 8-10.

218

Rice with Pumpkin Flowers
Riso con Fiori di Zucca

Fiori di Zucca means pumpkin flowers, but we have used zucchini flowers for this and the recipe on page 287 most of the time. The flower must be picked fresh in the morning when it is open. Never pick flowers with bulges, or bulbs, at the stem. These are the only flowers that will produce a fruit (a pumpkin or a zucchini).

20 pumpkin or zucchini blossoms
4 oz. prosciutto in one piece
4 T butter
2 T corn oil
15 sprigs fresh parsley
2 cups rice
4 cups broth
Salt and pepper, to taste
2 T butter
1/3 cup freshly grated Parmesan cheese
3 T pine nuts

Wash and clean blossoms, remove yellow stamen and green leaves near stem. Place on a paper towel to dry. When dry, cut into large pieces.

Cut prosciutto into 1/4-inch pieces.

Place a large saucepan over medium-high heat. Heat to hot. Add butter and oil. Chop parsley. Add prosciutto and parsley to butter and saute for 5 minutes. Add rice, saute for 4 minutes.

Heat broth to boil. Add broth to rice a little at a time, stirring until absorbed. After second cup of broth, add blossoms, salt, and pepper.

When all broth is added and rice is *al dente*, remove from heat; add butter and cheese, stir.

Place on a large serving platter and sprinkle with pine nuts. Serve hot.

Serves: 4.

Rice Torte
Torta di Riso

Rice torte was a special Easter dessert in the Pelini home. It was never served any other time.

filling:
2 cups water
Pinch salt
1 cup rice
2 T butter
1-1/4 cups granulated sugar
4 eggs
1 cup milk
Juice of 2 lemons

crust:
2 cups flour
1/2 cup granulated sugar
2 tsp. baking powder
1/4 tsp. salt

1 egg
1/2 cup shortening

Place a medium-size saucepan over medium-high heat. Add water and salt. Bring to a boil. Add rice, bring to a boil; reduce heat, cover, and allow to simmer until tender (about 15 minutes).

When rice is tender, add butter and sugar. Mix well. Cover and let cool. While rice is cooling prepare crust.

In a medium-size mixing bowl combine flour, sugar, baking powder, and salt. Mix with a fork until well blended.

In a large bowl, beat the egg, combine with shortening and add flour mixture. Combine all, mixing until well blended. Set aside.

Place half the dough on a pastry cloth or board. Dust with flour. Using a rolling pin roll out dough to fit 9-inch pie pan, and 4 inches beyond. Once rolled, fold in half, and lift into pie pan allowing excess dough to spill over sides of pan. Repeat for second pie.

In a small bowl beat eggs. Add milk. Pour into rice mixture, stirring well. Finally add lemon juice and mix again.

Pour rice mixture into pastry shells, dividing evenly between the two. Fold excess dough over top of pie leaving a 3-to-4-inch hole in the center of the pie, or trim excess dough, cut into designs and place on top of pie.

Heat oven to 325 degrees. Place pies in oven and bake for 1 hour.

Yield: 2 (9-inch) pies.

Note: The dough contains baking power, so it must be made last.

Salads, Snacks, and Sandwiches
Insalate, Spuntini, e Panini Imbottiti

In true Tuscan fashion, every salad green in Nonna's kitchen had its mate. Lettuce was married to green onions, endive and escarole to celery, and tomato to cucumber and green peppers. Nonna never combined tomatoes with lettuce. And the dressing was always a simple one: mainly olive oil and vinegar, salt and pepper, but sometimes only olive oil and pepper.

Nonna never ate romaine lettuce; it was considered too tough. And iceberg was a last resort. Instead, the young leaf lettuce picked fresh from the garden while the leaves were still a delicate green, graced our table. Bean salad was a standard, so was potato salad with olive oil and vinegar. Even dried bread was made into a salad.

Snacks were wholesome. Any "leftover" could be turned into a delicious snack, and because our table was bountiful there was always food to be eaten another day. If one peeked into an Italian lunch pail on Monday morning, it would probably include a succulent cold roast sandwich. One of the best was cold pork roast loaded with garlic and rosemary and garnished with mayonnaise and lettuce. Good lunch box sandwiches included cold spinach and lamb stew, Italian meatloaf or, of course, salami and prosciutto. Nonna never went to the store to buy a pound of luncheon meat.

Sometimes the lunch was not a sandwich at all, but fried veal or chicken, cold omelet, *schiacciata*, cod with chickpeas, pheasant with olives, or any part of the *gran fritto misto*, all with good homemade bread on the side.

My niece always says, "We're going to have a long life, look at Nonna." But I remind her that Nonna ate better than we do: no fast foods or packaged meats, no preservative, no hot dogs, and definitely no potato chips, corn chips, cheese balls, and other junk food. Nonna's favorite treat was a piece of fruit and a nibble on the hard rind of good Parmesan cheese.

Salads
Insalate

Anchovies with Onions and Parsley
Acciuge con Cipolle e Prezzemolo

So refreshing and delicious, this simple salad is not only a delight to the palate, but it is good for you.

1 T vinegar
2 cups water
6-8 whole anchovies or
12-16 anchovy fillets

4 fresh scallions
20 sprigs fresh parsley
3 T olive oil
1 tsp. vinegar
1/4 tsp. pepper

If using salted anchovies, combine vinegar and water. Wash anchovies in vinegar water. Remove, and rinse in clear water. Cut off fins and tails. Split and remove scales (if using fillets, drain oil).

Lay in a serving dish. Slice onion and chop parsley. Top anchovies with onions and parsley. Season with olive oil, vinegar, and pepper. Serve with fresh Italian bread. Do not add salt.

Serves: 3-4.

Bean Salad
Insalata di Cannellini

1 pound Great Northern
white beans*
Pinch salt
Water

Olive oil
Vinegar
Salt and pepper, to taste

If using dried beans, soak the beans overnight before boiling. Then place beans in a large pot, add salt and enough water to fill pot 3/4-full. Boil beans until tender, about 2 to 3 hours, adding additional water if necessary. Drain.

Allow to cool, and place in salad bowl. Blend with oil, vinegar, salt and pepper to taste.

Serve with smoked herring, see page 109.

Serves: 3-4.

Notes: *You may substitute canned beans for this dish, but in that case drain and wash the beans. Canned beans are softer.

Dried Bread with Parsley and Onion Salad
Panzanella

Nonna baked every week and when the bread got old and hard, in a truly Tuscan manner, she added it to soups, salads, and stews. Today we age bread especially for these special dishes. *Panzanella* is refreshing on a hot day.

5 pieces stale (hard) Italian bread
1/2 cup fresh parsley
1 medium onion
1 tsp. salt
1/2 tsp. black pepper
3-4 T olive oil
2 tsp. vinegar

Soak bread in a little water for 2 to 3 minutes (sometimes I omit this step). Cut parsley with scissors discarding tough stems. Wash and peel onion and slice as desired.

Once bread is softened, squeeze out excess moisture until it is just slightly damp. This is important for the bread must absorb the oil and vinegar.

Break bread into pieces. Add parsley, onion, salt, pepper, oil, and vinegar to taste. Toss mixture, allow to stand 15 minutes, and serve.

Serves: 3-5.

Variations: Although we never varied this dish, one may add any fresh vegetable: beans, tomatoes, even black olives. The choices are endless.

Chickpea Salad
Ceci Conditi

1 cup dried chickpeas*
Pinch salt

1 T olive oil
1 T vinegar (optional)
1/2 tsp. salt
1/2 tsp. ground black pepper

If using dried chickpeas, soak them overnight before boiling. Then place chickpeas in a large pot, add salt and enough water to fill pot 3/4 full. Cover and boil chickpeas until tender, about 2 to 3 hours, adding additional water if necessary. Drain.

Place in salad bowl and blend with oil, vinegar, salt and pepper to taste.

Serves: 4-6.

Notes: *You may substitute canned chickpeas for this dish (1 cup dried beans is equal to 1-2/3 cups cooked beans). Canned beans are softer.

Dandelion Greens and Hard-Boiled Egg Salad
Insalata di Denti-di-leone e Uova Sode

I remember picking dandelion (teeth of the lion) greens with my Dad, who loved this salad.

3-4 dandelion greens
3 eggs, hard-cooked
Olive oil
Vinegar
Salt and pepper, to taste

Clean and wash dandelion greens. Break into pieces and place in a salad bowl. Chop eggs into pieces (size is a matter of taste). Add oil, vinegar, salt and pepper to taste. Mix gently and serve.

Serves: 2-3.

Endive with Celery Salad
Insalata di Indivia e Sedano

Endive, with its prickly leaves, is a member of the chicory family. Endive and celery salad was part of the *Martedi Grasso* meal in our home (see other endive recipe on page 268).

1 head endive
3-4 celery ribs
Olive oil
Vinegar
Salt, to taste

Cut away outer leaves of endive. Wash inner leaves and allow to drain. Chop into bite-size pieces and place is bowl. Take tender inside ribs of celery, Chop into 1/4-inch slices. Mix with endive. Toss with olive oil, vinegar, and salt to taste. There is no pepper in this salad.

Serves: 2-3.

Escarole with Celery Salad
Insalata di Scarola con Sedano

Escarole can be bitter so use only the tender inner leaves for salad (see other escarole recipe on page 269).

1 head escarole
4-5 celery ribs
Olive oil
Vinegar
Salt and pepper, to taste

Wash escarole carefully and break into bite-size pieces. Cut celery into small pieces. Place in medium-size bowl. Mix well. Season with oil, vinegar, salt, and pepper.

Serves: 3-4.

Boiled Potatoes with Parsley Salad
Patate Lesse con Prezzemolo

The refreshing flavor of this Italian potato salad will make it one of your favorites, as it is ours. Nonna often served boiled potatoes with parsley salad on soup day, adding the potatoes to the broth to boil (see other potato recipes on pages 272-73).

2-3 large potatoes (red)
Water
Salt

3-4 sprigs fresh parsley
Salt and pepper, to taste
Olive oil
Vinegar

Peel and wash potatoes. Place in a medium-size pot that has been filled with water and a pinch of salt, and boil over medium-high heat (some prefer to add the potatoes to simmering broth for the last hour, but they change the flavor of the broth).

Remove potatoes. Drain and allow to cool slightly. Slice or dice potatoes to taste. Place in a large bowl. Cut parsley into small pieces with scissors. Add parsley to potatoes. Toss.

Add salt, pepper, oil, and vinegar to taste. Garlic salt is optional. Serve hot.

Serves: 4-6.

Variations: The Pelini family added 1 clove garlic cut into 3 or 4 pieces and 1 teaspoon chopped fresh basil to this salad.

Actually, like *panzanella*, any fresh vegetable can be added: tomatoes, cucumber, peppers, beans, even black olives. Anyway you try it, it is a delight and a favorite alternative to other salads.

Snacks and Sandwiches
Spuntini e Panini Imbottiti

In Italy a snack is known by a variety of names. A *spuntino*, is a little taste any time of day, while a *merenda*, is a snack in the middle of the afternoon.

Anchovy and Butter Sandwich
Panini di Acciughe e Burro

1 anchovy or
3 anchovy fillets
1 T vinegar
2 cups water
1 pat butter
1 slice Italian bread
1 sprig fresh parsley

If using salted anchovies, wash anchovy in vinegar and water. Rinse in clear water. Cut off fins and tails. Split and remove scales (if using fillets, drain oil). Spread butter on bread. Top with anchovies and leaves of parsley (large leaves are best).

Serves: 1.

Note: Makes an excellent and colorful appetizer.

Anchovies with Capers and Parsley Sandwich
Tramezzino di Acciughe con Capperi e Prezzemolo

Nonna belonged to the Italian ladies auxiliary of the NIPA and once or twice a year it was her turn to make pasta and snacks to sell on Sunday at the club house. This sandwich was a favorite. In 1938, it sold for $2.

2 cups water
1 T vinegar
5-10 anchovies in salt
or 15-20 anchovy fillets
30 sprigs fresh parsley
2 cloves garlic

3 T capers
6-7 T olive oil
5-6 Italian hard rolls,
split

Combine water and vinegar. Wash anchovies in vinegar water. Remove, rinse in clear water. Cut off fins and tails. Split and remove scales (if using fillets, drain oil).

Wash parsley and cut into bits with kitchen shears. Peel and dice garlic. Wash capers, squeeze dry and chop into coarse pieces. Combine parsley, capers, and garlic.

Line bottom of small casserole with parsley mix. Top with row of anchovies. Add 2 tablespoons oil. Continue layers. Refrigerate 2 hours or overnight. When ready to use bring to room temperature, place 3 anchovies and 1 tablespoon of parsley mixture on a hard roll.

Serves: 4.

Note: Once made, cut rolls in 1/2-inch slices and arrange on tray for a tasty and pretty appetizer.

Cold Pork Roast Sandwich with Marinated Olives
Panini di Arista Fredda con Olive Marinate

marinade:
1 cup green olives with pimentos
1/2 cup black olives
3 T pimentos
5 anchovy fillets
2 cloves garlic
4 T fresh parsley
1/2 tsp. oregano
1 tsp. lemon juice
1/8 cup olive oil
1 tsp. pepper

2 slices Italian bread or hard Italian roll
3-4 very thin slices cold pork roast with rosemary

Place olives, pimentos, anchovies, garlic and parsley in a bowl. Mix well and turn onto a pastry board. Chop into small pieces with a good knife (you can run garlic through a press), or grind in meat grinder. Return to bowl. Add oregano, lemon juice, olive oil, and pepper. Mix well. Allow to set for at least 2 hours. Can store in refrigerator for weeks.

Cut 2 slices of Italian bread (or use a hard roll). Lay on slices cold pork roast and top with 2 to 3 tablespoons olive marinade.

Serves: The olive mixture yields 1/2 cup. The remainder is enough for 1 extra sandwich.

Note: The marinade is good as an appetizer, on a buffet table, or in a hoagie or submarine sandwich. The pork sandwich was originally made without the marinade.

Hot Italian Hoagie
Panini Caldi

16 slices Italian salami
12 slices Italian cappicola
12 slices baked ham

8 slices pepper cheese

4 6-inch Italian rolls
8 large lettuce leaves
8 slices fresh beefsteak tomato
30-40 pimento olives (or olive marinade, see recipe above)

Place a large-size iron skillet on medium-high heat. Layer salami, one slice at a time, to cover bottom. Try not to overlay. Cook, turning once. Pile on side of skillet and lay in cappicola. Let cook, turn once, and pile in another side. Repeat for baked ham.

Place 4 cooked salami slices in the shape of the roll. Cover with cappicola, then ham. Repeat until you have four piles of meat in the skillet. Top each pile with 2 slices pepper cheese. Cover and cook until cheese melts.

Slice each roll lengthwise. Lay meat on bottom side of roll. Top with lettuce, tomato, and any other condiment. Slice 7 to 10 olives in half and lay on top (or use the olive marinade in cold pork sandwich recipe above). Cover with top of roll and enjoy.

Serves: 4.

Meat Sauce Sandwich
Panini con Salsa

1 good Italian bread
1/2 cup meat sauce
(recipe on page 234)

Cut the heel off a good Italian bread. Scoop out center of heel to make a hole and fill it with hot meat sauce.

Serves: 1.

Note: This sandwich is usually made while meat sauce is being prepared (see recipe on page 234).

Sausage with Onions and Green Peppers Sandwich
Panini con Salsiccia, Cipolle e Peperoni

6 sausage links
1 large onion
1 large green pepper
1/4 cup whole or
crushed canned tomatoes
1 oz. tomato paste
1/4 cup broth (or water)
Salt and pepper, to taste
6 Italian rolls

Place sausage links in medium-size skillet and sear over medium-high heat (do not add oil). When browned, remove and set aside. Cut and peel onion and pepper. Wash and cut into long, 1/4-inch-wide strips.

To juices in skillet add onions and peppers. Cover and cook until onions are transparent. Add tomatoes crushing with a fork into small pieces. Simmer 10 minutes. Add tomato paste. Rinse both tomato and paste cans with broth or water and add. Add salt and pepper to taste. Simmer 10 minutes, or until tomatoes begin to lose bright red color. Turn occasionally. If sauce begins to dry, add a little broth, but thick sauce is best.

Return sausage to skillet. Simmer 10 minutes. Sauce should be dark and oil should float on surface (skim if desired).

Slice rolls, place a sausage, several onions and peppers, and sauce on roll. Serve at once.

Serves: 6.

Prosciutto with Homemade Bread
Prosciutto con Pane di Casa

1 slice prosciutto
1 slice good Italian bread

Slice bread to desired thickness. Lay a slice of freshly cut prosciutto on top of the bread and eat. No garnish. No mayo. No tomato. Nothing. The simple taste of the thinly sliced cured ham and the fresh bread is all you need. Serve with wine.

Serves: 1.

Sauces
Salse

There are dozens of pasta sauces. *Ragu*, a sauce with meat, is known in America as *alla Bolognese* because Bologna is noted for its meat sauce. The true *ragu alla Bolognese*, is a tomato and meat sauce with cream and so important to Bologna that the recipe was codified and placed with the Chamber of Commerce.

The word *sugo* means any sauce that is derived from the juice of meat and it may or may not have chunks of meat in it. That is what we call our traditional pasta sauce with meat, *sugo*. When we have a tomato sauce without meat we called it *sugo finto* (thin or fake sauce), *sugo matto* (crazy sauce), or simply *umido* (stew).

The names of specialized sauces are often intriguing: *arrabbiata* (angry sauce) contains red hot peppers, so does *puttanesca* (sauce of the harlot). There are also rules: cheese is seldom combined with mushrooms, meatballs are never served with meat sauce, each cut of pasta has its own unique sauce, and each region, like Bologna, is known for a special combination of sauce and pasta.

But Italian sauces are not for pasta alone and are not all made with tomatoes. Tangy *acciugata* (anchovy sauce), the king of sauces in our home, is used on everything from spaghetti, boiled eggs, and boiled meats to fish and grilled T-bone steak. Bechamel, a true Italian sauce, is served as a topping in our home, but it is often used in other regions as a sauce for baked pasta.

Finally, there is *soffritto* and *battuto*, a combination of onion, celery, carrot, parsley, *pancetta*, and sometimes garlic. When fried in oil it is *soffritto*, without oil, as in broth, it is *battuto*. The most widely used mixture in our cooking, it is the base of sauces, stuffings, and soups. It produces the aroma that tells the senses something Italian is on the stove. Without *soffritto* and *battuto* there would be no such thing as an Italian kitchen.

Some specialty sauces are not found in this chapter, but in the pasta chapter and it is worth repeating one more time that if you master *soffritto* and *battuto*, the thin tomato sauce (*sugo finto*) used for pizza toppings and stews (including meat, fish, and vegetables), and a good soup stock, you have mastered the art of traditional Tuscan cooking.

Anchovy and Caper Sauce
Acciugata

The first meal I ate in Quarata was in 1967 in the great hall of our ancestral home. I had just met my Uncle Gino's family that afternoon and as I sat at the dinner table dish after dish arrived: soup with homemade pasta, *umido*, and finally grilled steak with this tangy, delicious sauce.

I was amazed. Every dish could have been prepared by my Nonna's hands. Our bond was so strong that living thousands of miles apart, we were the same. On every holiday and for every celebration our tables were heavy with foods that were called by the same names, prepared by the same methods, presented in the same order, and eaten with the same enthusiasm. By the time the *acciugata* arrived at the table I had tears in my eyes. My sense of family expanded that day. It no longer encompassed western Pennsylvania, but expanded to Tuscany, a place I had only heard about in family stories.

A similar sauce from other regions of Italy is *salsa verde*, which begins as anchovies and capers, but includes parsley, garlic, mustard, and wine vinegar. We never made it that way.

1/3 cup olive oil
2 oz. flat
fillets of anchovies
3-1/4 oz. capers
Juice of 1 lemon

Place a small iron skillet over medium-high heat. Add olive oil. Do not overheat or the sauce will be ruined. Pour in the flat fillets of anchovies, oil and all, and quickly mash the fillets with a fork until they form a paste. Remove from heat (do not allow oil to bubble, the dish will be ruined).

Rinse capers under the faucet. Squeeze. Repeat 2 to 3 times. Add to anchovies. Add lemon juice. Stir. Place in a bowl and serve (we always served this sauce in a small crystal bowl with a matching crystal ladle).

For spaghetti: Omit the capers and lemon juice. Pour over 1/2 pound cooked spaghetti, toss, and serve.

For boiled eggs: Boil eggs. Cut eggs in half. Top with *acciugata.*

For steak, boiled or baked fish, or boiled chicken, capon, and turkey: Boil or broil, top with *acciugata.*

Serves: 4-5.

Bechamel Sauce
Salsa Besciamella

Traditionally, we only used bechamel sauce for cannelloni and lasagna, but it can be combined with a variety of dishes. Bechamel is an authentic Italian sauce, not borrowed from the French, but probably borrowed by them.

2 cups milk
4 T butter
3 T flour
1/4 tsp. salt

Place milk in a small pot over medium-high heat and heat to near boiling. Do not boil or it will curdle. Place a medium-size pot over medium-high heat and while milk is heating melt butter. Do not allow to brown.

When butter is melted, add all the flour, stirring constantly. Allow to boil (bubble), but continue stirring. If the flour discolors you have overcooked it.

Remove flour mixture from heat and slowly add the hot milk a tablespoon or two at a time, stirring constantly.

When more than half the milk has been added, return to burner and add larger portions. Stir constantly and do not allow to stick. Continue stirring until consistency of heavy cream (5 to 8 minutes).

If sauce begins to bubble remove from heat. If it thins when larger portions of milk are added, stir until thick before adding more milk. When all is mixed, add a dash of salt.

Yield: 1-2/3 cups.

Note: For cannelloni on page 180, double this recipe; for grand lasagna on page 193 quadruple this recipe.

Crazy Sauce
Sugo Matto

Crazy sauce is a meatless red sauce often served on Friday and during Lent in the Pelini home. It is especially good with fresh garden tomatoes and can be used with a variety of pastas. It cooks up quickly and is a good alternative to our traditional meat sauce that takes hours to prepare.

8-10 fresh tomatoes
or 29 oz. crushed canned
tomatoes
4 T fresh parsley
2 fresh basil leaves or
1/4 tsp. dried
1 onion
1/2 clove garlic
1/8 cup corn oil
Salt and pepper, to taste

Blanch tomatoes by placing them in boiling water for a few minutes. Remove. Peel and discard as many seeds as possible. Chop tomatoes into small pieces. Chop parsley and basil. Peel and clean onion and garlic, chop fine.

Place a medium-size pot over medium-high heat. Heat to hot. Add tomatoes and cook for 15 to 20 minutes or until they have been reduced to pulp and all water has evaporated. When they begin to lose their bright red color, remove from pot and set aside.

Place medium-size pot over medium-high heat. Heat to hot. Add oil. Heat. Add onions and garlic and saute until lightly browned. Add parsley, basil, tomatoes, salt and pepper. Reduce heat and allow to simmer uncovered for 1 hour. Sauce should be brown-red with oil on surface (skim if desired).

To serve: Prepare pasta in usual manner. Once drained, add sauce. Mix well and turn onto platter. Garnish with cheese and serve.

Serves: 4.

Cream Sauce
Salsa alla Crema

3 T butter
2/3 cup heavy cream
2/3 cup freshly grated
Parmesan cheese

Place medium-size pot over medium-high heat. Add butter and melt. Add cream. Mix well and add cheese.

Remove from heat and blend into cooked pasta.

Serves: 3-4.

Variation: Add 2 ounces drained and crushed anchovies and juice of 1 lemon to cream.

232

Meatballs and Sauce
Polpette nel Salsa

In the village of Quarata when the pasta sauce is made with meat, meatballs are seldom made as an accompaniment. But taste does not always follow gastronomic rules and, when we had meatballs, which was seldom, we prepared the same sauce that we always used (see recipe on following page).

1 small onion
1/4-inch-thick slice
pancetta
2-3 celery ribs
with leaves
1 carrot
3-4 sprigs fresh
parsley
1 small clove garlic
(optional)

1/2 cup corn oil, divided
1 T pepper
1 tsp. salt

3/4 cup bread crumbs or
diced hard Italian bread
Milk to moisten
1/4 cup freshly grated
Parmesan cheese
3-4 beaten eggs
1 pound ground chuck
1/4 pound ground pork

Prepare your favorite tomato sauce (either *sugo di carne* on following page, or *sugo matto*, on page 232). While sauce is simmering prepare meatballs.

Peel onion, wash and cut into quarter wedges. Cut *pancetta* into 1/2-inch pieces. Peel celery and carrot, wash, and cut into 1-inch pieces. Chop parsley. Peel garlic and cut in half. Combine all and grind in meat grinder or food processor (the grinder is better because it releases the juices).

Place a medium-size iron skillet over medium-high heat. Heat to hot. Add 1/4 cup oil. When oil is hot add chopped ingredients, pepper, and salt. Saute until onions are transparent, stirring often. The longer this mixture simmers, the better it tastes. It is done when it begins to stick to the skillet, about 20 minutes.

Place bread crumbs in a large bowl, dampen with enough milk to moisten (do not soak) and add onion mixture, grated cheese, and eggs. Combine beef and pork, mixing well, and add to bread mixture. Mix well. If dry add more milk (or broth). Mixture must be moist.

Pick up a heaping tablespoon of mixture. Roll between hands to shape into 1-1/2-inch balls.

Place a medium-size iron skillet over medium-high heat. Heat to hot. Add remaining oil (more if necessary). When oil is hot, add meatballs and fry until golden brown. Remove from oil and drain on paper towel.

Add meatballs to simmering sauce and continue to simmer for an additional hour.

Yield : 15-18 meatballs, depending on size.

Meat Sauce
Sugo di Carne

Most cookbooks and restaurants call this type of sauce a *ragu* or *alla Bolognese*, but although Bologna is noted for its meat sauce, this recipe is Tuscan, and is as good as it gets.

It is our standard sauce for pasta including polenta, gnocchi, rigatoni, cannelloni, ravioli, and just plain spaghetti. Nonna's kitchen was never without *sugo di carne*. Each Sunday a large pot was set to brew and by the next Sunday it was all gone and she started all over again. It was her hallmark.

Tuscan *sugo di carne* begins with the by now familiar *soffritto* which serves as an ingredient for a large percentage of the recipes in this book. In the town of Lucca, also in Tuscany, cloves and nutmeg are added to *sugo di carne*.

2-1/2 pounds onions
2 cloves garlic
1/4-inch-thick slice
pancetta
3 small carrots
5-8 celery ribs
3-4 sprigs fresh parsley

1/2 cup corn oil
1 T pepper
1 T salt

3-1/2 pounds ground
chuck
3/4 pound pork sausage
8 oz. red table wine
(optional)
18 oz. tomato paste

84 oz. whole or crushed
canned tomatoes in
puree
1/2 cup broth

Peel onions, wash, and cut into quarter wedges. Peel garlic and chop into thirds. Cut *pancetta* into 1/2-inch pieces. Peel carrots and celery, wash, and cut into 2-inch pieces. Wash parsley. Combine all and grind in a meat grinder or food processor into fine pieces (the grinder is better because it releases the juices).

Place a large-size iron skillet over medium-high heat. Heat to hot. Add oil. When oil is hot, add all chopped ingredients, pepper and salt; saute until onions are browned, stirring often, about 30 minutes. The longer you cook this mixture, the better your sauce will taste. It is done when it is dark and begins to stick to the skillet.

When well cooked, add ground chuck and sausage a little at a time, shredding the meat with a fork to form small pieces. Allow to brown until meat is dark brown (about 30 minutes), stirring often so it does not stick. Add one glass of red table wine and continue to saute. Simmer for 10 minutes on medium-high heat.

When meat is done, add tomato paste to meat mixture blending well and let simmer for an additional 15 minutes.

When you add the tomato paste to the meat, place crushed tomatoes in puree in a 6-quart pot over low heat and allow to warm. Rinse both tomato and paste cans with broth or water and add to simmering tomatoes.

Remove meat mixture from skillet and add to the simmering tomatoes in 6-quart pot. Put heat on medium-high. When boiling reduce the heat; allow to simmer slowly for 3 to 4 hours. Stir often to avoid sticking. A good sauce will look dark, almost brown, and not red. It is done when oil rises to the top. Skim off excess oil.

Yield: 5 quarts.

Variations: A diced dry sausage is sometimes added to the meat. A pork rib is sometimes added to the simmering sauce. On Friday my mother would eliminate the *pancetta*, and substitute mushrooms or tuna for meat. She cut the mushrooms in half.

Note: Sauce may be stored in the refrigerator for several weeks or in a freezer for several months. It is best to store it in small containers for individual servings. If stored in freezer it tends to take on water. Reheat, bring to a boil, and simmer for 20 minutes.

Snack Idea: While the sauce is simmering in the final hour cut the heel off a good Italian bread, scoop out the dough inside, and fill the cavity with sauce.

Yields: The recipe as written makes 5 quarts of sauce. Below is a chart to increase or decrease the quantity. Unlike pasta and stuffing recipes, to reduce this sauce do not cut ingredients in half or fourths. For the best results, follow the quantities below.

	For 2 quarts:	For 2-1/2 gallons:
onions	4 medium	4 pounds
garlic	2 cloves	6 cloves
pancetta	1/2-inch-thick slice	1/2 pound
carrots	1 large	6 large
celery	4 ribs	2 whole
fresh parsley	2-3 sprigs	1/2 cup
corn oil	1/2 cup	1 pint
pepper	1/2 T	1/4 cup
salt	1 T	1/3 cup
ground chuck	1 pound	6 pounds
sausage	1/2 pound	1 pound
wine	4 oz.	16 oz.
tomato paste	10 oz.	40 oz.
tomatoes	32 oz.	1 gallon
broth	1 cup	1 quart

Sexy or Harlot's Sauce
Puttanesca

Named for the hot peppers that give it a kick, this is a delicious sauce with or without the hot taste. The amount of peppers you add is a matter of choice. We tend to keep it mild.

2 T olive oil
2 cloves garlic
2 slices prosciutto
1 fresh hot pepper or
1/4 tsp. hot pepper
flakes
10 mushrooms
(optional)
2 sprigs fresh rosemary
1/2 tsp. salt
3-1/2 cups crushed
canned tomatoes

Place a 2-quart saucepan over medium-high heat. Heat to hot. Add oil. Heat to hot. Peel and add garlic and brown. When brown crush with a fork into small pieces.

Dice prosciutto, hot pepper, and mushrooms into small pieces. The size is a matter of taste.

Add rosemary, prosciutto, hot pepper, salt, and mushrooms to hot oil with garlic. Reduce heat and simmer for 5 minutes. Add tomatoes all at once (they should make a swishing sound when they hit the hot oil).

Raise heat to high. Cover pot, bring to a boil, reduce heat and simmer for 30 minutes, stirring once in a while.

Yield: 3-1/2 cups.

Note: Serve with 3/4 pound of long thin pasta such as spaghetti or spaghettini. Top with freshly grated Parmesan cheese.

Soups
Minestre

Pasta may be the heart of the northern Italian meal, but soup is its soul. Six days a week a good soup begins our evening meal and on all holidays, from Easter to Christmas, it is soup, not pasta, that is served (actually, at Christmas we have both). Throughout my youth, once a week the big kettle was hauled out and filled with vegetables and meat to make the stock--a tradition we still maintain.

We make five basic stocks in our kitchen: beef, capon, chicken, chicken and beef, and a mixed holiday stock with a medley of meats. Eventually the chicken and beef broth with an ox tail thrown in for added taste became our favorite. We never eat soup on the day it is made in order to let it set and gel so we can skim away the fat.

Out of that clear liquid come meals of boiled meat, broth for stews, bean soups, minestrone, and bowl after bowl of clear liquid gold in which a small *pastina* (soup pasta) is cooked. Brought to the table piping hot, soup is always accompanied by freshly grated Parmesan or Romano cheese.

If soup has a thin broth it is a *minestra,* if thick, a *zuppa,* and if made with vegetables it is a minestrone. Bean soups are *zuppa.* They are a Tuscan specialty and are wonderful winter fare. They are thick, hearty, and flavorful and sure to become a favorite in your home as they are in ours.

No Italian cookbook is complete without a good vegetable soup, a minestrone, and we have our Tuscan version. Minestrone is a summer favorite when fresh vegetables enhance the flavor. We always serve it heaping with freshly grated cheese.

Soups for special occasions include cappelletti, a homemade stuffed pasta; wedding soup, rich in greens; *passatelli,* homemade pasta passed through a machine; and *pasta grattata,* grated homemade pasta dropped into boiling broth. They are an elegant addition to a meal.

In times past, soup was always the first course of our meal, but today we often make it the meal itself.

Stock Broths
Brodo Consumato

The secrets to a good stock are fresh ingredients, ample time, and straining the vegetables into the stock after they are cooked. The longer you cook broth, the better it is and the stock that exits the refrigerator as a jelly is a prize.

For excellent broth use bones and meat. A good soup bone is the knee joint of the cow. Once the pot is on the stove and all the ingredients are simmering away, a lid is put on the pot to stop the liquid from dispersing into jets of steam, and additional water is never added. Finally, when the stored broth comes out of the refrigerator, the fat that has risen to the top is discarded.

For delicate broths small pastas *(pastina)* are used: peppercorns called *acini di pepe;* tubular *ditallini,* miniature cousin to larger *diti* used in heavier soups and with sauces; little dots of pasta called *manfrugil;* rice-shaped bullets of *orzo;* small squares of *quadrucci;* and *tripolini,* small eggbows. For holidays *cappelletti,* tiny stuffed hats, sisters of the larger ravioli, are a must.

Pastina is never, never, never cooked in the entire quantity of broth and stored away. It gets mushy. Rather a fresh batch is brewed at each meal using the stock in the refrigerator, just enough for the folks at hand.

The time needed to cook *pastina* in broth is determined by the amount of heat. The lower the heat the longer it takes: medium low, 8 to 10 minutes; very low, 15 to 20 minutes. The amount of *pastina* for soup is a matter of taste: 1 quart of broth to 1/2 cup *pastina* is our rule.

Beef Broth
Brodo di Manzo

1-1/2 pounds beef shank
1 whole beef knee bone*

3-4 onions
3-4 carrots
3-4 celery ribs and leaves
3-4 sprigs fresh parsley
1 T salt
1/2 T pepper
2-3 very ripe tomatoes or canned whole tomatoes

Fill a 6-to-8-quart pot 3/4-full of water and set on a burner at high heat. Add beef shank and knee bone. Bring to a boil. When boiling, skim off impurities that come to the top of the broth. Keep skimming until clear. The more you skim the clearer your broth will be. Some people actually throw this water away, add new water, and begin again. Once the liquid is boiling, lower the heat to medium, but be sure the liquid continues to simmer.

Clean and cut onions into quarters. Pare and cut carrots into thirds. Clean and cut celery into thirds. Wash parsley. Add all to pot. Add salt, pepper and ripe tomatoes. Make sure the pot continues to simmer.

Cover with a lid to avoid loss of liquid. Lower heat so that broth simmers slowly. Simmer for 4 hours or until the meat falls away from the bones. Allow to cool.

238

When the broth cools to room temperature remove all solid items from broth. Strain broth through a sieve. Place all vegetables in the sieve and place the sieve over the pot of strained broth. Crush the vegetables through the sieve into the broth until only a small amount of pulp remains. Discard pulp.

Jar the broth in individual serving containers. Refrigerate until ready to use. Broth may be stored in the refrigerator for up to a week, or frozen for a month or more.

When ready to use, remove broth from refrigerator and immediately lift the fat which has settled on the top and discard. If broth has turned into a gel, you will have excellent soup.

Yield: 4-6 quarts.

To serve: Place 1 quart broth in a 2-quart pot. If you are using only a portion of a jar of broth, be sure to shake the jar well before removing the stock for heavy vegetable particles settle to the bottom. Bring to a boil. Add 1/2 cup *pastina* of choice, reduce heat to low, cover and simmer for 15 to 20 minutes or until *pastina* is cooked to taste. Serve at once with freshly grated Parmesan cheese.

Serves: 3-4.

Notes: One more reminder to never add water to boiling broth while cooking. This will dilute the broth and destroy the flavor.

*Beef knee bones are available in the meat department at your local market.

After the broth is made, cut up beef and make into any of the boiled dishes in the Meat/Beef section of this book on pages 116-17.

Capon Broth
Brodo di Cappone

5-6 pound stewing capon

3-4 onions
3-4 carrots
3-4 celery ribs and
leaves
3-4 sprigs fresh parsley
1-1/2 T salt
1/2 T pepper
2-3 very ripe tomatoes
or canned whole
tomatoes

Fill a 10-to-12-quart pot 3/4-full of water and set on a burner at high heat. Add capon. Bring to a boil. While boiling, skim off impurities that come to the top of the broth. Keep skimming until clear. The more you skim, the clearer your broth will be. Some people actually throw this water away, add new water, and start again. Turn heat down, simmer.

Clean and cut onions into quarters. Pare and cut carrots into thirds. Clean and cut celery into thirds. Wash parsley. Add all to pot. Add salt and pepper and ripe tomatoes. Make sure the pot continues to boil. Cover with lid to avoid loss of liquid. Lower heat so that broth simmers slowly. Simmer for 4 hours or until the meat falls away from the bones. Allow to cool.

When broth is at room temperature, remove all solid items from broth. Strain broth through a sieve. Place all vegetables in the sieve and place the sieve over the pot of strained broth. Crush the vegetables through the sieve into the broth until only a small amount of pulp remains. Discard pulp.

Jar the broth in individual serving containers. Refrigerate until ready to use. Broth may be stored in the refrigerator for up to a week, or frozen for a month or more. When ready to use, remove from refrigerator and immediately lift fat which has settled on the top of the container, and discard. If broth has turned into a gel, you will have excellent soup.

Yield: 5-7 quarts.

To serve: Place 1 quart broth in 2-quart pot. If using only a portion, shake jar well before removing stock because vegetable particles settle to bottom. Bring to a boil. Add 1/2 cup *pastina* of choice, bring to a boil, cover, reduce heat and simmer for 15 to 20 minutes. Serve at once with freshly grated Parmesan cheese.

Serves: 3-4.

Notes: One more reminder to never add water to boiling broth while cooking. Water dilutes broth and destroys flavor. Cut capon and serve with *acciugata*, (see recipe on page 204).

Chicken Broth
Brodo di Gallina

5-6 pound stewing
chicken

3-4 onions
3-4 carrots
3-4 celery ribs and
leaves
3-4 sprigs fresh parsley
1-1/2 T salt
1/2 T pepper
2-3 very ripe tomatoes
or canned whole
tomatoes

Fill 10-quart pot 3/4-full of water and set on a burner at high heat. Add chicken. Bring to a boil. While boiling, skim off impurities that come to the top of the broth. Keep skimming until clear. The more you skim, the clearer your broth will be. Some people actually throw this water away, add new water, and start again. Turn heat down, and simmer.

Clean and cut onions into quarters. Pare and cut carrots into thirds. Clean and cut celery into thirds. Wash parsley. Add all to pot. Add salt and pepper and ripe tomatoes. Make sure the pot continues to boil. Cover with lid to avoid loss of liquid. Lower heat so that broth simmers slowly. Simmer for 4 hours, or until the meat falls away from the bones. Allow to cool.

When broth is at room temperature, remove all solid items. Strain broth through a sieve. Place all vegetables in the sieve and place the sieve over the pot of strained broth. Crush the vegetables through the sieve into the broth until only a small amount of pulp remains. Discard pulp.

Jar broth in individual serving containers. Refrigerate until ready to use. Broth may be stored in refrigerator for up to a week, or frozen for a month or more. When ready to use, remove from refrigerator and immediately lift the fat which has settled on the top of the container, and discard. If broth has turned into a gel, you will have excellent soup.

Yield: 4-6 quarts.

To serve: Place 1 quart broth in a 2-quart pot. If you are using only a portion, shake jar well before removing soup because vegetable particles settle to the bottom. Bring to a boil. Add 1/2 cup *pastina* of choice, bring to boil, cover, reduce heat and simmer for 15 to 20 minutes or until *pastina* are done. Serve at once with freshly grated Parmesan cheese.

Serves: 3-4.

Notes: Cut up chicken and serve with *acciugata* (see recipe on page 230).

Holiday Broth
Brodo per la Festa

1-1/2 pounds beef shank
1 whole beef knee bone*
1/2 soup chicken
3-4 pieces ox tail
2 turkey wings

8-10 onions
6-8 carrots
8-10 celery ribs and
leaves
3-4 sprigs fresh parsley
3 T salt
2 T pepper
4 very ripe fresh
tomatoes
or 8 oz. whole canned
tomatoes

Fill 20-quart pot with 15 quarts water and set on burner at high heat. Add beef shank, knee bone, chicken, ox tail, and turkey wings. Bring to boil. While boiling, skim off impurities that come to top of broth. The more you skim, the clearer your broth will be. Some people throw this water away and add new water. Lower heat to medium, but be sure pot continues to boil.

Clean and cut onions into quarters. Pare and cut carrots into thirds. Clean and cut celery into thirds. Wash parsley. Add all to pot. Add salt, pepper and ripe tomatoes. Make sure pot continues to boil. Cover with lid to avoid loss of liquid. Lower heat so that broth simmers slowly. Simmer for 4 to 4-1/2 hours or until meat falls from bones. Cool.

When it is at room temperature remove solid items from broth. Strain broth through a sieve. Place vegetables in sieve and place sieve over pot of strained broth. Crush vegetables through sieve into broth until little pulp remains. Discard pulp.

Jar broth in individual serving containers. Refrigerate. May be stored in refrigerator for a week, or frozen for a month or more. When ready to use, remove from refrigerator and immediately lift the fat which has settled on top and discard. If broth has turned into a gel, you will have excellent soup.

Yield: 2-1/2 to 3 gallons.

To serve: Place 1 quart of broth in a 2-quart pot. If using only a portion of a jar, shake well before removing soup. Bring to a boil. Add 1/2 cup *pastina* (matter of taste), bring to boil, cover, reduce heat and simmer for 15 to 20 minutes or until *pastina* are done. Serve at once with freshly grated Parmesan cheese.
Serves: 3-4.

Notes: One more reminder to never add water to boiling broth. It dilutes broth and destroys flavor.
*Beef knee bones and ox tails are available at local markets. A good meal is the boiled ox tail. If it is not falling off the bone it will be tough.

Soups from Broth
Minestre dal Brodo

Once the basic stocks from pages 238-42 are made, they can be used as a base for a variety of good tasting soups.

Cappelletti in Broth
Cappelletti in Brodo

Every holiday meal in our home begins with a good stock filled to overflowing with homemade cappelletti and topped with freshly grated Parmesan or Romano cheese. It is our favorite.

2 quarts holiday broth
80 cappelletti
1/2 cup freshly grated
Romano or Parmesan
cheese

Place a 4-quart pot over medium-high heat. Heat to boiling. Do not remove cappelletti from freezer until broth is at the boil; then slowly add cappelletti (see recipe on pages 182-83) to boiling broth. Stir with a wooden spoon a few times. Broth will stop boiling. Return to boil, reduce heat, cover, and simmer for 15 minutes or until done to your taste.

Place in large tureen and bring to the table while still hot. Serve with freshly grated Romano or Parmesan cheese.

Serves: 4-8.

Italian Lemon Soup
Minestra al Limone

1 quart broth
1/2 cup *pastina*
(optional)

4 eggs, separated
Pinch salt
Juice of 2 lemons

Place a 3-quart pot on high heat. Add broth, bring to a boil, and, if using *pastina*, add (see types of pasta on pages 30-31). Cover, reduce heat, and allow to simmer about 10 to 15 minutes or until *pastina* is done. Remove from stove.

Separate the eggs and beat the egg whites until stiff. Add yolks and pinch of salt to whites and beat well. Slowly add 2 cups broth to the egg mixture and continue to beat. When the eggs and broth are well mixed pour into remaining broth and *pastina*. Heat, but do not boil (it will poach the eggs). When ready to serve, squeeze lemon juice into the broth.

Serves: 4.

243

Wedding Soup
Minestra di Scarola

Escarole soup, as the name reads in Italian, is a traditional wedding soup in the south of Italy. It was a favorite in Arnold Pelini's wife Rose's family and became a part of our kitchen tradition when she joined the Pelini family. The first time I tasted it was at their wedding.

1 large head escarole
3 cups water

2 T fresh parsley
1/4 cup freshly grated Romano cheese
1 cup freshly grated Parmesan cheese
1/4 pound ground beef
1/8 pound ground veal
1/8 pound ground pork
1/4 tsp. salt
1/8 tsp. pepper
1/4 tsp. oregano
1/4 tsp. basil
1 egg
1/4 cup bread crumbs
4 quarts chicken, beef, or holiday broth

Wash escarole under cold running water. Be sure to open the leaves to get out any hidden grit.

Place a large-size pot over medium-high heat. Add water and escarole and boil for 10 minutes or until done. Drain and allow to cool. When cool chop into small pieces and set aside.

While escarole is cooling, chop parsley into fine pieces and grate cheeses.

In a large mixing bowl combine beef, veal, pork, parsley, cheeses, salt, pepper, oregano, basil, egg, and bread crumbs. Mix well and shape into 1/4-to-1/2-inch balls.

Place broth in 6-quart pot over medium-high heat and bring to a rolling boil. Add meatballs, cover, and simmer for 5 minutes. Add escarole, lower heat, and simmer an additional 10 minutes. Serve with additional freshly grated Parmesan cheese.

Serves: 10-12.

Notes: If you want to add a small *pastina*, add 1/2 cup 2 to 3 minutes after adding meatballs (see pages 30-31 for types of *pastina*).

The success of this soup is a good stock. Do not use broth from a can. Make one of the good stocks at the beginning of this chapter.

Dropped and Passed Soups
Minestre Cadute e Passate

Three types of soup are created by dropping homemade pastas into boiling broth: *stracciatella*, meaning "torn to rags," where the mixture is like a batter and is slowly drizzled into the boiling soup; *passatelli*, where the ingredients are passed through a thick sieve by the same name; and *pasta grattata*, where the fresh pasta is grated into the stock using the wide side of the cheese grater.

Italian Egg Drop Soup
Stracciatella

Stracciatella, "torn into rags," is a favorite soup for babies. It is easy to make once the basic stock is made.

2 eggs
Salt
2 tsp. flour
5 T Parmesan cheese

1 quart chicken, beef, or holiday broth

Beat eggs in a small bowl. Add salt, stir in flour, add cheese and beat until it becomes a smooth batter.

Place a medium-size pot over medium-high heat. Add chicken or beef stock and bring to a boil. When soup is at rapid boil, take a spoonful of batter and drizzle it into the broth a little at a time.

Stir for 2 to 3 minutes. Batter should cook into long strings. Serve hot with additional freshly grated Parmesan cheese.

Serves: 4.

Notes: You can add *pastina* to this dish if you wish (see selection on pages 30-31). Prepare broth, add 1/2 cup (matter of taste) *pastina*, bring to boil, cover, reduce heat, and when done to taste, add batter.

245

Passed Soup Tuscan Style
Passatelli alla Toscana

Passatelli is a form of Italian cooking where a stuffing is prepared and then passed through a thick sieve called a *passatelli* directly into simmering broth. The base is a mixture of eggs, bread crumbs, and Parmesan cheese. A variety of ingredients are added depending on the region.

The *passatelli* iron is not easy to find, even in Italian stores, and if you want one you must look through Italian food catalogs until you find one. Although similar to a potato masher, we have never been able to successfully use the masher to replace the *passatelli* iron.

3 eggs
6 T freshly grated
Parmesan cheese
6 T dry bread crumbs
3/4 tsp. grated lemon
rind
1/2 tsp. salt
1-1/2 tsp. corn oil

1-1/2 quarts broth,
chicken, beef, or holiday

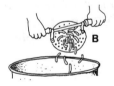

Break eggs into a medium-size bowl. Beat well. Add cheese, bread crumbs, lemon rind, salt, and oil. Blend (should be the consistency of dry, mashed potatoes). Knead.

Form mixture into a flat pancake, wrap in wax paper, and cool in the refrigerator for at least 4 hours, but preferably overnight.

When ready to use, place broth in a medium-size pot over medium-high heat. Bring to a boil. When broth is boiling, remove pancake from refrigerator. Unwrap and place on a pastry board.

Hold the *passatelli* iron in both hands and rock it over the pancake, pressing firmly. Pieces of the pasta will pass through the holes like very small sausages (see A).

Lift the iron and place it over the boiling soup. Scrape pasta into the soup (see B). Continue to rock the iron over the pancake and drop the pasta into the soup until all is used. You may have to reshape the pancake toward the end.

Work quickly for when the pasta rises to the surface of the boiling broth, it is cooked. Serve with additional freshly grated Parmesan cheese.

Serves: 4-5.

Grated Pasta Soup
Pasta Grattata

This is an excellent, weighty pasta soup with a wonderful flavor, made often and with gusto in Nonna's kitchen. We lost the skill, but the Pelini family did not, and this is their recipe. However, we are happy to report that *pasta grattata* has become a regular addition to our kitchen once again.

2 eggs
2/3 cup freshly grated
Romano cheese
1/4 tsp. salt
1 to 1/2-2 cups flour

1 quart broth, chicken,
beef, or holiday

Break eggs into a medium-size bowl. Beat well. Add cheese and salt. Mix well.

Slowly begin to add flour. When dough is manageable and not too sticky, turn onto floured board. Knead, adding flour, until it will not absorb any more flour (about 20 minutes).

Shape into a pancake. Wrap in wax paper. Refrigerate overnight, or for at least 4 hours.

When ready to use, place broth in a medium-size pot over medium-high heat. Bring to a boil. When broth is boiling, remove pasta from refrigerator, unwrap, and place on a pastry board.

Using a regular cheese grater, grate on the thick (slow) side. Grate all the pasta.

Scrape pasta into the soup. Work quickly for when the pasta rises to the surface of the boiling broth, it is cooked (about 5 minutes).

Serve with additional freshly grated Parmesan cheese.

Serves: 3-4.

Bean Soups
Zuppa di Fagioli

Tuscans were not called *Toscani mangiafagioli* (bean eaters) for nothing. The wonderful thick bean soups of Tuscany are hearty, flavorful treats that can grace both an elegant table and a humble cottage and be at ease. Nonna often made *minestra di fagioli*, without the *pancetta* on Friday or during Lent, as the first (and sometimes only) course to a meatless meal.

Great Northern White Bean Soup
Zuppa di Cannellini

There are two main bean soup recipes presented here. The first is Elizabeth's adaptation of the original recipe brought to America by Sandrina and Nonna. The second is the original Tuscan recipe.

2 (2-pound, 8-oz.) cans Great Northern White Beans
4-6 cups broth (can use water)

2-3 fresh tomatoes or 1/3 cup whole or crushed canned tomatoes

3 large onions
1/4-inch-thick slice *pancetta*
2 carrots
4-5 celery ribs and leaves
Sprig fresh parsley

1/4 cup corn oil
1 T pepper
2 T salt

Place beans into 4-quart pot over medium-high heat. Rinse cans with a little broth and add to pot. Add remaining broth (for thick, thick soup use 4 cups, thinner soup 6 cups). Bring to a boil. Lower heat, cover and simmer. After 10 minutes add tomatoes. Allow to simmer 30 minutes.

Peel onions, wash, and cut into quarter wedges. Cut *pancetta* into pieces. Peel carrots and celery, wash, and cut into 2-inch pieces. Wash and chop parsley. Combine all and grind in meat grinder or food processor into fine pieces (grinder is better because it releases the juices).

Place a large-size iron skillet over medium-high heat. Heat to hot. Add oil. When oil is warm, add all chopped ingredients, pepper, and salt and saute until onions are transparent (about 20 minutes), stirring often. Add to bean mixture. Let simmer for 10 minutes. Remove from stove and pour into a blender a little at a time. Liquefy. Return to pot, return to stove, cover, simmer for additional 1-1/2 to 2 hours.

Serve with freshly grated Parmesan cheese or a wedge of lemon, not both.

Yield: 4-5 quarts.

1 pound Great Northern White Beans (dried)
8 cups water
1 tsp. salt
Dash pepper

Original Tuscan Bean Soup: Soak beans overnight in enough water to cover. Drain. Combine beans with water, salt and pepper. Bring to a boil, cover, reduce heat and simmer 2-1/2 to 3 hours.

2 T corn oil
2 cloves garlic
1/2 tsp. dry rosemary
or 1 sprig fresh
1/2 cup crushed
canned tomatoes

Place medium-sized skillet over medium-high heat. Add oil. Heat. Peel garlic and add. Saute until golden. Remove and add rosemary and tomatoes. Simmer 5 minutes. Liquefy beans in a blender and add to 4-quart pot. Strain and liquefy tomatoes and add to beans. Add 3 to 4 cups water. Simmer over low heat for 1-1/2 to 2 hours. Stir often. **Yield:** 2-1/2 to 3 quarts.

Pasta and Beans *(Pasta Fagioli):* Although pasta is not needed for this hearty soup, if you wish to use pasta use heavy *ditallini*, elbows, or cut up spaghetti. Never add pasta to entire stock unless you intend to serve all of it. After liquefying, return soup to burner, bring to a boil, add 2 cups pasta (quantity is matter of taste). Lower heat, cover, and simmer for 15 minutes or until pasta is cooked to taste.

Bean Soup with Ham Bone *((Zuppa di Fagioli con Osso del Prosciutto):* Use 1/2 a ham or prosciutto bone or 1 ham hock, 2 cups diced ham. Place a large pot over medium-high heat. Add bone and barely cover with water. Bring to a boil. Discard water and repeat process. Drain and set aside until soup is ready.

Prepare soup as in first recipe, but eliminate salt. After liquefying, return to stove, bring to a boil, add bone and meat, cover, and simmer for an additional 1-1/2 to 2 hours. Serve with grated Parmesan cheese.

Bean Soup with Stale Bread and Green Onions *(Pappa ai Fagioli):* In Italy, this soup is known by a number of names including *ribollita*, *zuppa frantoiana*, and *pappa ai fagioli*. It is a specialty of the olive harvest. As oil is in its first pressing, the soup is in the pot. Good Tuscan bread is steeped in oil and placed in the bottom of a deep bowl, topped by soup. 4 cups bean broth, 4 slices hard Italian bread, 5 to 6 scallions. Make bean soup from first recipe. Lay slice of bread in bottom of soup dish. Pour hot soup over bread. Steep 10 minutes. Serve with green onions.

Lentil Soup *(Zuppa di Lenticchie):* This same basic recipe is used to make lentil soup, just substitute lentils for beans. Garnish each serving with dash of cumin and squeeze of lemon juice.

Chickpea Soup with Egg Noodles
Zuppa di Ceci con Pasta

As children my brother and I called chickpea soup Santa Claus soup because we only had it on Christmas Eve.

48 oz. canned chickpeas*
1-1/2 cups broth (or water)

1/4 cup fresh rosemary sprigs
2 large cloves garlic
2 T fresh parsley
1/2 cup celery ribs and leaves
1 small carrot
Salt and pepper, to taste

1/4 cup corn oil
1/4 cup whole or crushed fresh or canned tomatoes

2-1/2 cups wide pasta (optional)

Parmesan cheese or lemon wedge

Place a 4-quart pot over medium-high heat. Add chickpeas (including liquid), reserving 1 cup, and 1-1/2 cups broth or water. Bring to a boil. Add rosemary, cover, lower heat, and allow to simmer slowly for 30 minutes. While simmering chop garlic, parsley, celery, and carrot in a meat grinder or food processor (the grinder is better because it releases the juices). There are no onions in this soup.

Place a medium-size iron skillet over medium-high heat. Heat to hot. Add oil. Add garlic mixture, salt, and pepper to oil. Saute 20 minutes. The longer you cook this mixture the better the soup will taste. Simmer until vegetables are dark and begin to stick to the skillet (about 20 minutes). Add tomatoes, mash them into small pieces. Simmer slowly an additional 10 minutes.

Add vegetable mixture to simmering chickpeas. Continue to simmer for an additional 30 minutes. Remove from stove and puree in blender at high speed. Return to pot and simmer slowly for about 1 to 1-1/2 hours.

About 15 minutes before serving add the remaining whole chickpeas. Some people prefer to eat *ceci* soup without pasta. If so, serve and garnish with Parmesan cheese or wedge of lemon.

To combine with pasta add 1 cup wide pasta per quart of soup, cook 15 minutes or to taste, and serve with freshly grated Parmesan cheese or wedge of lemon, not both.

Yield: 2 to 2-1/2 quarts.

Notes: This is a thick soup and gets thicker as it sits. To thin, add additional broth. Can be stored in refrigerator for up to a week, in freezer for a couple of months. Do not add pasta to broth to be stored.

*To use dried chickpeas, soak 1 cup dried overnight then boil until tender (up to 4 hours), and add at least 1 cup of this liquid to the broth. Canned chickpeas are softer.

Vegetable Soups
Minestrone

Thick bean soup is not the only vegetable soup we prepare. Fresh vegetables of all kinds make good soups and we enjoy them year round.

Garden Soup
Minestrone dell'Orto

Fresh garden vegetables are the best to use in this soup. In the past all the ingredients were taken from Nonno's garden. Today, we do not have a large garden and make the soup from store-bought vegetables.

1 onion
1 celery rib
1/4 cabbage
2 carrots
2 fresh tomatoes
2 potatoes (red)
1 zucchini
2 T fresh parsley
1 T fresh basil*

2 T corn oil
1/2 pound Swiss chard

1 tsp. salt
1 tsp. pepper
1/2 cup rice

Wash and peel all vegetables; chop all vegetables into bite-size pieces.

Place a 10-to-12-quart pot over medium-high heat. Add oil and when warm, add chopped onions. Saute onions until transparent, then add remaining vegetables and herbs, saving the Swiss chard for last. Add enough Swiss chard to fill the pot to the top (chard will reduce dramatically).

Cook until all vegetables are soft, stirring often. Once soft, add enough water to cover vegetables, add salt and pepper and cook 2 to 3 hours.

Remove vegetables from broth with a sieve. Puree vegetables in a blender or food processor. Return puree to broth in the pot.

Add rice, bring to a boil, cover with a lid, reduce heat, and simmer until rice is done.

Yield: 3-4 quarts soup.

Note: *If you do not have fresh basil, eliminate it from this soup.

Classic Vegetable Soup
Minestrone

2 cans (2-pound, 8-oz.)
Great Northern White
Beans
2 quarts water

3 cups broth (water)
2-3 medium-size fresh
tomatoes or 1/3 cup
canned

3 large onions
1/4-inch-thick slice
of *pancetta*
2 carrots
4-5 celery ribs
with leaves
Sprig fresh parsley
1/4 cup corn oil
1 T pepper
1 T salt

3 medium potatoes (red)
1/2 pound fresh green
beans
1/2 small head cabbage
10 oz. fresh spinach
2 zucchini
4-6 oz. whole or crushed
fresh or canned tomatoes

Place beans into a 4-quart pot. Rinse can with a little broth and add remnants to pot. Add remaining broth. Place pot over medium-high heat and bring to a boil. Lower heat, cover, and allow to simmer. Peel tomatoes and after 10 minutes, add to pot. Allow to simmer for 1 hour.

While beans are simmering, peel onions, wash, and cut into quarter wedges. Cut *pancetta* into pieces. Peel carrots and celery, wash, and cut into 2-inch pieces. Wash and chop parsley. Combine all and grind in a meat grinder or food processor into fine pieces (the grinder is better because it releases juices).

Place a large-size iron skillet over medium-high heat. Heat to hot. Add oil. When oil is warm add all chopped ingredients, pepper, salt and saute until onions are transparent, about 20 minutes, stirring often. The longer you cook this mixture the better your soup will taste. Add to soup. Let simmer for 10 minutes. Remove soup from stove and pour into a blender. Liquefy. Return to stove, bring to a boil, cover, reduce heat, and simmer.

Peel and dice potatoes; cut green beans into pieces, chop cabbage and spinach, and dice zucchini. Add all to pot and allow to simmer for 30 minutes. Crush second batch of tomatoes and run through a blender. Add to soup, cover with a lid, and simmer for an additional 1-1/2 hours.

Serve with freshly grated Parmesan cheese.

Yield: 3 quarts.

Notes: If you wish to add pasta, use a heavy noodle and add for the last 15 minutes. If you wish to add meat, add 1/4 pound beef shank or 2 chicken legs with beans. When cooked, remove meat, break into pieces, discard fat, skin, and bones and add.

Other Soups
Altre Zuppe

Baccalà Soup
Minestra di Baccalà

Baccalà soup was a specialty of Mrs. Sansone, the mother of Vivian's husband Tom.

10-12 oz. dry *baccalà* (cod)
Water

1 onion
4 potatoes (red)

1/4 cup corn oil
4 fresh tomatoes or
16 oz. whole or crushed canned tomatoes
1/4 tsp. pepper

3 cups broth

Buy a dry strip of *baccalà* from an Italian store. Soak in cold water for 2 days, changing the water each day. Remove, rinse well in running water. Peel and dice onion and potatoes.

Place *baccalà* in large-size pot. Add water to cover and boil for 10 minutes, or until water is clear. Drain and cool. Do not cut up; it will break up itself.

Place a large-size iron skillet over medium-high heat. Heat to hot. Add oil. Heat to hot. Add onions and saute until transparent (7 to 10 minutes). Do not brown. Add tomatoes and pepper and bring to a boil; reduce heat to medium-low, cover, and simmer for 10 minutes. Add broth. Simmer 20 minutes. Add *baccalà* and continue to simmer for an additional 10 minutes. Add potatoes and simmer an additional 30 minutes. Let stand one hour before eating. Cod is salty, add salt only if necessary.

Serves: 6-8.

Potato Soup
Minestra di Patate

2 potatoes (red)
1 onion

1 T corn oil
1/4 tsp. salt
Dash pepper
3 oz. tomato paste
4 cups water
1/2 cup spaghetti

Wash, pare, and cube potatoes. Peel onion and chop into fine pieces. Place a medium-size pot over medium-high heat. Heat to hot. Add oil. Heat to hot. Add onion and saute until soft. Add potatoes, salt and pepper. Toss and allow to cook 5 minutes. Add tomato paste and water. Bring to boil, cover, reduce heat, simmer for 1 hour. If soup has reduced too much add more water.

Break spaghetti into small pieces and add to soup. Cook 10 minutes or until tender. Serve.

Serves: 4.

Cream of Tomato Soup
Minestra di Pomodoro Cremoso

2 onions
2 T corn oil

6-8 fresh tomatoes
2 T tomato paste
1-1/2 tsp. salt
3/4 tsp. pepper
1-1/2 cups water
2 cups milk

Peel and chop onions. Place a medium-size iron skillet over medium-high heat. Heat to hot. Add oil. Heat. Add onions and saute until transparent (about 7 or 8 minutes). Do not allow to brown.

Place tomatoes in a pot and cover with boiling water. Allow to blanch for 2 to 3 minutes and then drain and remove the skins. Chop tomatoes into pieces and add to onions. Reduce heat, cover, and simmer for 10 to 15 minutes.

Add tomato paste, salt, and pepper. Simmer 5 minutes. Add water. Simmer another 10 minutes.

Remove from skillet and puree in blender. Add milk (if too thick add more milk). Serve at once.

Serves: 4.

Tomato and Bread Soup
Pappa al Pomodoro

In this delicious Florentine soup we fry the bread before soaking it in the soup, so it need not be "hard as a rock."

12 firm tomatoes
3 cloves garlic

1/2 cup corn oil
5 sprigs fresh sage
1 tsp. salt
1/2 tsp. pepper

6 slices stale bread
1/4 tsp. salt
1/4 tsp. pepper
2 quarts broth
8-10 T Romano cheese
Parsley, to garnish

Wash and peel tomatoes and dice into fine pieces. Peel garlic. Set aside.

Place a large-size iron skillet over medium-high heat. Heat to hot. Add oil. When oil is hot add peeled garlic, chopped sage, salt and pepper. When garlic begins to brown crush with a fork.

Add bread to skillet, brown both sides. Be sure it absorbs some garlic and sage. Remove bread from skillet. Place tomatoes in the same skillet. Allow to come to a boil. Add broth, additional salt and pepper, cover, simmer for 40 minutes.

To serve: Place 1 slice browned bread in soup bowl. Cover with soup. Let set 5 minutes. It will become mushy (and delicious). Add cheese and garnish with sprig of parsley. Serve.

Serves: 4-6.

Vegetables
Le Verdure

Fresh garden grown vegetables created a bonanza of delightful eating from early spring to late autumn as day after day Nonno brought the freshly picked tomatoes, onions, lettuce, peppers, and zucchini to the table. "Eat your vegetables!" never had to be said, for our vegetables were tasty, spicy, and carefully selected to blend with the rest of the meal.

Among the first foods cultivated by early man, vegetables were introduced as an integral part of the daily meal by the Florentines in the Middle Ages. One vegetable that is poorly represented in this book, but should not be, is the cardoon (*cardi*), a plant that looks somewhat like a celery. Cardoons were definitely a part of our cooking in Italy and were fried, stewed, and, when young, eaten raw; but they were not readily available in the United States and disappeared from our culinary list.

By far, the largest number of recipes in this chapter belong to the zucchini, a vegetable whose Italian name has been incorporated into the English language. The zucchini is the most versatile of Italian vegetables. Its flower is delicately fried and its fruit is boiled, broiled, fried, stuffed, stewed, grilled, or eaten raw.

We use the carrot as an ingredient in recipes, but never serve it as a dish by itself. Spinach, kale, and Swiss chard are used mainly as stuffings and fillers in our kitchen, and are represented by few independent recipes, but cooked celery and escarole hold a noble place in Tuscan cooking and are represented in the recipes that follow.

Of the various ways of preparing vegetables, frying is our specialty, so important to our diet that the art and its recipes are given a separate chapter which includes fried vegetables, meats, and fish.

Fried Vegetables in Thin Sauce
Verdure Fritte in Umido

A very special vegetable dish that begins with most of the fried vegetables presented in the chapter of the *gran fritto misto,* but joins them with a tomato sauce, is *fritto in umido,* which takes perfection beyond reality. It can be used for green beans, cabbage, cauliflower, celery, fennel, or Swiss chard and is an excellent accompaniment to meat in thin sauce or a roast. Celery or fennel is always served with duck, cauliflower with pork, green beans and cabbage with beef. Swiss chard is never eaten fried in batter alone, but always fried and made in thin sauce.

Pick one:
1 pound green beans
1/2 cabbage
1/2 head cauliflower
1/2 celery
1 fennel
1 Swiss chard

Fried Green Beans *(Fagiolini Fritti):* 1 pound fresh green beans. Snap off about 1/4-inch from each end of the bean and discard. If you like the beans long leave as is, or snap into 2 or 3 pieces. Place in a large pot and wash with running water. Place a medium-size saucepan over medium-high heat. Add water and a pinch of salt. Add green beans and boil for about 10 minutes or to taste. Drain and allow to cool. Fry according to recipes on pages 283 and 288, then finish with thin sauce recipe on page 257.

Fried Cabbage *(Cappuccio Fritto)* or **Fried Savoy** *(Verza Fritta):* Use 1 head cabbage. Wash cabbage and cut in half. Slice each half into 1/2-inch slices and cut each slice into smaller serving pieces. Place a medium-size iron skillet over medium-high heat. Add enough water to fill the skillet. Add a pinch of salt and bring to a boil. Gently place each piece of cabbage in boiling water and cook until tender. Cabbage tends to fall apart so boil a few at a time. Remove carefully and set on paper towel to drain. Do not stack. Fry according to recipe on pages 283 and 288, then finish according to thin sauce recipe on page 257.

Fried Cauliflower *(Cavolfiore Fritto):* Wash the cauliflower and cut in half. If extra large, cut again. Place in a large pot half filled with water and a pinch of salt. Boil for 8 to 10 minutes until soft. Test with a fork. Remove and place on drain board to drain (may be placed in the refrigerator for up to 4 days). Fry according to recipes on pages 283 and 288, then finish according to thin sauce recipe on page 257.

Fried Celery (*Sedano Fritto*), **Fried Florentine Fennel** (*Finocchio Fritto*), **or Fried Swiss Chard** (*Bietola Fritta*): Use 2 to 3 ribs fresh celery, fennel, or Swiss chard (pick one, do not mix). Clean and wash ribs. Peel off tough strings by grabbing lose strings at bottom of rib, holding between thumb and a paring knife, and pulling. Cut rib into 4-inch pieces. Place small pot over medium-high heat. Add ribs. Add water until 1-inch above ribs. Bring to a boil. Add 1 teaspoon salt and boil until tender, about 5 to 10 minutes depending on the size of the vegetable. Drain and cool. May be stored in refrigerator for up to 3 days. Fry according to recipes on pages 283 and 288, then finish according to thin sauce recipe below.

Thin Sauce

Fried vegetables
2 T olive oil or pan drippings*
1 clove garlic
1-1/4 cups whole or crushed canned tomatoes
3 oz. tomato paste
1/2 cup broth
Salt, to taste
Pepper, to taste
5-6 pats butter
4 T freshly grated Parmesan cheese

Parboil vegetable of choice and fry according to the recipes on pages 283 and 288. Once fried, remove vegetables from skillet and set aside. Wipe skillet, add oil or pan drippings. Heat to hot. Peel garlic, dice into thirds, and add. Brown garlic crushing with a fork into small pieces. Add tomatoes to juices in skillet crushing with a fork into small pieces. Cover and simmer 8 to 10 minutes. Add tomato paste. Rinse both tomato and paste cans with 1/2 cup broth or water and add to mixture. Simmer 20 to 25 minutes, or until tomatoes lose their bright red color. Taste, add salt and pepper if necessary.

Remove from heat and run through a sieve pushing pulp through sieve with a spoon or fork. Throw remaining pulp away.

Place fried vegetables in skillet, dot with butter and freshly grated Parmesan cheese. Return sauce to skillet, covering vegetables well. Do not turn or stir. Simmer slowly for 15 minutes, or until sauce is brown-red and oil begins to separate and rise to the surface (skim if desired). Remove from heat.

Place in platter, sprinkle with more freshly grated Parmesan cheese, and serve immediately.

Serves: 4, as a side dish.

Notes: Time for tomatoes to simmer varies with type of tomato.

*Pan drippings from any of the roasts in this book make an excellent substitute for oil.

257

Fried Vegetables with Garlic and Oil
Verdure Fritte con Aglio e Olio

One more delicious way to fry vegetables is in garlic and oil. Vegetables that are superb prepared in this manner are broccoli, cabbage, savoy cabbage, and cauliflower.

These are excellent side dishes for roasts. In fact, the best way to prepare them is to use the savory pan drippings from the roast in place of oil. When I am on one of my many diets I spray the skillet with vegetable spray. Although never as good as oil or pan drippings, it is still delicious as a treat on an otherwise bland diet.

Pick one:
1/2 bunch broccoli
1/2 head cabbage
1/2 head savoy cabbage
1/2 head cauliflower

1 tsp. salt

Broccoli: Wash broccoli and break into small bunches. Cut off extra leaves and discard; then peel the tough part from the stem and discard.

Place in a large pot half filled with water and dash of salt. Bring to a rapid boil. Add broccoli, cover, turn off burner, steep for 5 to 6 minutes.

Remove and place on drain board to drain (may be placed in refrigerator for up to 4 days). Continue as described on page 259.

Cabbage (*Cappuccio*) **or Savoy Cabbage** (*Verza*): Savoy is a delicious winter cabbage found in any supermarket. To prepare either cabbage, wash and cut in half. If extra large, cut again.

Place in a large pot half filled with water and a dash of salt. Boil for 8 to 10 minutes until soft. Test with a fork.

Remove and place on drain board to drain (may be placed in the refrigerator for up to 4 days). Continue as described on page 259.

Cauliflower (*Cavolfiore*): Wash the cauliflower and cut in half. If extra large, cut again.

Place in a large pot half filled with water and a dash of salt. Boil for 8 to 10 minutes until soft. Test with a fork.

Remove and place on drain board to drain (may be placed in the refrigerator for up to 4 days). When ready to fry take 1 to 2 pieces of boiled cauliflower and chop into small pieces. Continue as described on page 259.

2 T olive oil or pan
drippings from roast
2-3 cloves garlic
1/2 tsp. salt
1/4 tsp. pepper

To fry in garlic and oil:

Do not combine vegetables. Select one. Par-boil as directed on preceding page. When ready to fry take a bunch of boiled vegetable and squeeze out as much liquid as possible.

On a pastry board chop the vegetable into small pieces, the smaller the better.

Place a medium-size iron skillet over medium-high heat. Add oil, or pan drippings from a good roast.

Peel 2 to 3 cloves of garlic, add to oil in skillet, brown, and crush with a fork until no large pieces remain.

Place the chopped vegetable in the oil, salt and pepper to taste (test by taste before adding salt because pan drippings may already be salty).

Allow to saute about 15 minutes, turning often and mashing with a fork. Serve as a side dish.

Yield: 4, as a side dish.

Fresh Artichokes
Carciofi Freschi

The artichoke, a member of the thistle family, is a descendent of the cardoon. Known in ancient Rome, it was introduced to the world from the sun-drenched hills of Sicily and continued to spread until it became the centerpiece of the Renaissance table. Today it is grown in fields called *carciofaie* all along the Italian coast. In the spring dozens of artichoke festivals are held throughout Italy, where the artichoke continues to be revered as a king among vegetables. When in season, it is always a part of the *fritto misto* and you will find no better recipe for fried artichokes than the one listed in that chapter (see page 287). There is also a recipe for artichoke omelet on page 168.

Except in the fried version, where the entire leaf is eaten, the edible part of the artichoke is the heart at the bottom of the fruit between the stem and choke and the fleshy part at the bottom of each leaf. To eat, pick off a leaf, put the end in your mouth, and pull the leaf through your teeth leaving the fleshy part in your mouth.

To Clean an Artichoke:

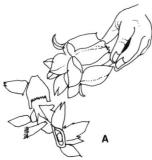

Wash all artichokes well in cold water.
Clean by removing hard outer leaves (see A).

A

Cut off stem (see B).

B

Cut tips off leaves (see C).

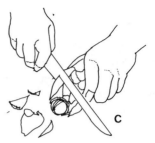

Spread to expose center of artichoke (see D).

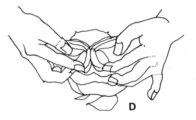

Remove pointed and hairy parts in center of artichoke (choke).
To loosen the leaves hit the side of each artichoke on a drain board three or four times.

Wash by placing artichoke in fresh water to which a pinch of salt and a teaspoon of lemon juice has been added.

Drain upsidedown on drain board.

Artichoke flesh discolors if not used quickly.

Stuffed Artichokes
Carciofi Ritti Ripieni

My mouth waters every time I think of this delicious dish. It is a meal in itself and a great luncheon idea. We enjoy serving it on Friday, after a hearty dish of bean soup. But it is also elegant enough to grace our Easter meal.

3 artichokes

Wash and prepare artichokes as described on pages 260-61.

1 small onion
1/4-inch-thick slice *pancetta*
1/2 celery ribs
1/2 small carrot
1 tsp. fresh parsley
1 clove garlic

Peel onion, wash and cut into quarter wedges. Cut *pancetta* into 1/2-inch pieces. Peel celery and carrot, wash, and cut into 1-inch pieces. Chop parsley. Peel garlic and cut in half. Combine all and grind in meat grinder or food processor (the grinder is better because it releases the juices).

3 T corn oil
1/2 tsp. pepper
1/2 tsp. salt

Place a medium-size iron skillet over medium-high heat. Heat to hot. Add oil. When oil is hot add chopped ingredients, pepper, and salt. Saute until onions are transparent, stirring often. The longer this mixture simmers, the better it tastes. It is done when it begins to stick to the skillet, about 20 minutes.

1 cup bread crumbs
4 T freshly grated Parmesan cheese

In a large bowl mix bread crumbs and grated cheese. Add onion mixture. Mix well. Mixture must be moist enough to hold together. If dry, add water or broth.

Olive oil or water

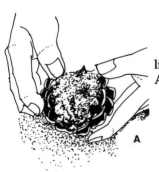

Dry each artichoke. Sprinkle inside with a little oil. Spread outer leaves and stuff the center (see A) of the artichoke.

A

Spread second layers of leaves one at a time and stuff with mixture (see B), then stuff the third layer. Continue until all artichokes are stuffed.

B

Place artichokes upright (see C) in steamer or deep saucepan. Cover the bottom of the pan with water and sprinkle a little oil over each artichoke.

Cover and steam cook for 1-1/2 to 2 hours. Check water level every 15 minutes, and, if necessary, add more water.

Serves: 3-6.

Fresh Asparagus
Asparagi Freschi

The asparagus is an ancient vegetable and member of the lily family. It also has diuretic and laxative properties. In other words, it is good for you. When buying asparagus look for a rich green color and closed tips.

To cook fresh asparagus trim bottom of stalks and leave fresh tips (about 8 inches long). Place a deep, narrow pot (a glass coffeepot will do nicely) over medium-high heat and add 2 cups water and 1/2 tsp. salt. Add asparagus so that the delicate tips are above the water line and the stalks of asparagus are upright. Cover and cook about 12 minutes. Asparagus is excellent dressed with oil, vinegar, salt, and pepper, but also delicious fried (see page 288).

Asparagus with Anchovy Sauce
Asparagi con Acciugata

1 pound asparagus
1 bay leaf
4 hard-cooked eggs
*Acciugata**
Lettuce to line platter

Cook asparagus as described above, but add a bay leaf to the water. Drain and chill.

Boil eggs to taste. Drain, peel and cut in half lengthwise.

Place a lettuce leaf on a salad plate. Top with asparagus and eggs. Cover with *acciugata.*

Serves: 4.

Note: Recipe for *acciugata* is on page 230.

Fresh Green Beans
Fagiolini Freschi

I cannot count the number of times I saw Nonna sitting under the grape arbor in her back yard snapping the ends off freshly picked green beans. Every time I do it myself, I think of her.

Green beans, another gift to the New World from Italy, are a part of the *fritto misto* and are excellent in thin sauce (see recipes at beginning of this chapter). There is also a wonderful green bean appetizer recipe found on page 47.

To clean green beans:

Snap 1/4-inch off each end of the bean and discard. If you like beans long leave as is, or snap into 2 or 3 pieces. Place in large pot and wash with running water. Place a medium-size saucepan over medium-high heat. Add enough water to cover the beans and a pinch of salt. Add beans, boil 5 to 10 minutes or to taste. Drain and allow to cool.

Green Bean Salad
Insalata di Fagiolini Freschi

1/2 pound fresh green beans
Pinch salt
1 clove garlic
Salt, pepper, to taste
3-4 T olive oil
1-2 tsp. vinegar

Prepare beans as above. While beans are boiling, peel garlic and crush with the broad side of a heavy knife. When beans are cool, place in a salad bowl, add salt, pepper and peeled, crushed garlic. Toss. Add oil and toss again. Add vinegar and give the beans a final toss. Serve.

Serves: 3-4.

Green Beans in Tomato Sauce
Fagiolini al Pomodoro

1 pound fresh green beans
2 large very ripe fresh tomatoes
1 clove garlic

1/4 cup corn oil
1/4 tsp. salt
Dash pepper

Clean beans. Wash and drain. Place medium-size pot over medium-high heat. Fill with water. Bring to a boil, blanch tomatoes, remove, and skin. Cut into small cubes. Peel garlic.

Place medium-size iron skillet over medium-high heat. Heat to hot. Add oil. Add peeled garlic and allow to brown. Crush with a fork into small pieces. Add beans to oil. Allow to blister for few minutes. Add tomatoes, salt, pepper, and stir.

Cover, simmer for 50 to 55 minutes, until beans are tender and tomatoes lose bright red color.

Serves: 3-4.

Fresh Broccoli
Broccoli Freschi

Broccoli, rich in vitamins A and C, was developed from the cabbage in, of course, Italy. It was known in ancient Rome and was introduced to America by the Italian immigrants of this century. When selecting broccoli avoid bunches whose buds have turned yellow.

To prepare, wash the broccoli and break into small florets. Cut all extra leaves and discard, then peel the tough part from the stem and discard. Place in a large pot half filled with water and 1 teaspoon salt. Bring to a boil. When at rapid boil, turn off burner, cover, and allow to steep for 10 minutes. Remove and place on drain board to drain (may be stored in the refrigerator for up to 4 days). Broccoli is a part of the *fritto misto*. It is also excellent drizzled with butter or sauteed in garlic and oil (see recipe on pages 258-59).

Broccoli with Mushrooms
Broccoli con Funghi

10 oz. broccoli
1/2 pound fresh
mushrooms
2 large cloves garlic

2 T corn oil

Pinch salt
Pinch pepper

1/4 cup freshly grated
Parmesan cheese

Prepare broccoli as described above. Remove florets from large, thick stems of broccoli.

Clean and slice the mushrooms and set aside. Peel garlic and slice into small pieces.

Place a medium-size iron skillet over medium-high heat. Heat to hot. Add oil, and when hot add garlic. Saute 1 to 2 minutes until garlic is brown, then crush garlic with a fork into small pieces.

Add broccoli stems and saute 2 to 3 minutes stirring constantly. Add florets and saute 2 to 3 minutes stirring constantly. Finally add the sliced mushrooms. Continue to stir. Season with salt and pepper to taste.

After 3 minutes remove from stove. Arrange in a serving dish and sprinkle with freshly grated Parmesan cheese. Serve at once.

Serves: 3-4.

Eggplant
Melanzane

Eggplant comes in a variety of shapes and sizes. The most common is deep-purple and bulbous, but it can be white and tubular, or green and long like a zucchini. We always use the purple variety. In addition to the recipes presented here, you can stuff eggplant according to the recipes for stuffed zucchini that follow.

Preparing the eggplant:

Cut top and bottom stems from eggplant, remove outer skin and slice into 1/4-inch slices. Place in large pot, add water and pinch of salt. Allow the eggplant to soak. As the water turns brown, drain, add more water and more salt. Do this 3 or 4 times to blanch out the bitterness. Drain and pat dry.

Fried Eggplant
Melanzane Fritte

1 eggplant
1/2 cup corn oil
Salt, to taste

Prepare eggplant as described above. Place medium-size iron skillet over medium-high heat. Heat to hot. Add oil (eggplant requires a lot of oil).

When hot, drop eggplant into oil (oil must be hot or the flesh will absorb all the oil). Repeat until skillet is full. Do not stack. Salt and allow to fry until golden brown; turn, fry second side.

Remove from skillet and place on a paper towel to absorb extra oil. Serve hot.

Serves: 6-7, as a side dish.

Baked Eggplant with Tomatoes
Melanzane con Pomodoro al Forno

1 medium eggplant
1/2 cup fresh parsley
1 clove garlic
1/2 tsp. salt
1/4 tsp. pepper
1 cup crushed
canned tomatoes
or 2 ripe tomatoes
1 tsp. corn oil

Wash. Remove top of eggplant. Dry and cut lengthwise into halves. Score each half several times and place in a broiler for 2 to 3 minutes or until the tops start to brown.

Wash and finely chop parsley. Peel and chop garlic. Place eggplant in casserole, cover with parsley, garlic, salt and pepper. Spoon tomatoes over eggplant (for fresh tomatoes, cut each into two horizontal pieces, and place juice side down on eggplant).

Drizzle with oil. Bake at 350 degrees for 1-1/4 hours. Do not add liquid.
Serves: 2.

Eggplant Parmesan
Melanzane alla Parmigiana

1 fried eggplant

2 cloves garlic
1-1/4 cups whole or
crushed canned
tomatoes
3 oz. tomato paste
1/2 cup broth
Salt and pepper

4 oz. mozzarella cheese
1/2 cup freshly grated
Parmesan cheese
5-6 pats butter

Prepare eggplant and fry as described on page 266. Remove from skillet and set aside. Peel garlic. Add to oil in skillet. Brown and crush with a fork into small pieces. Add tomatoes to the juices in the skillet, crushing with a fork into small pieces. Lower heat, cover, simmer 8 to 10 minutes.

Add tomato paste. Rinse both tomato and paste cans with broth or water and add to mixture. Simmer 20 minutes, or until tomatoes begin to lose bright red color. Taste; add salt and pepper if necessary.

Cut mozzarella into 1-inch squares. Grate Parmesan cheese. Make piles of each on a pastry board.

Place a layer of fried eggplant along the bottom of a square (8-by-8-by-2-inch) baking dish. Do not overlap. Place 9 squares of mozzarella in a checkerboard pattern. Sprinkle 1 teaspoon of Parmesan over the mozzarella.

Arrange a row of eggplant on top of the first. Add mozzarella and Parmesan. Continue alternating eggplant and toppings until all eggplant is layered in dish.

Finally pour tomato sauce over eggplant, then top generously with remaining mozzarella and Parmesan.

Heat the oven to 350 degrees and bake for 30 to 45 minutes. Remove from oven, cover with foil and allow to stand 10 minutes.

Before serving cut eggplant into 9 square pieces: 3 cuts lengthwise and 3 cuts width-wise. Serve with a steel spatula.

Serves: 9.

Notes: Eggplant Parmesan is an alternative to lasagna and accompanied by a fresh garden salad makes a delicious meal. It is also a good dish for a buffet.

You can top this dish with bechamel sauce (see recipe on page 231).

Fresh Endive
Indivia Fresca

Nonno planted endive and escarole in August and picked it in October. Just before picking it was tied tight to blanch the inside leaves. After blanching, it was picked and stored for good eating all winter. The outer leaves were cooked and stored, to be used in wedding soup, or as a cooked side dish. The inner leaves were used in salad (see recipe on page 224).

Endive Parmesan
Indivia alla Parmigiana

1 pound endive
Pinch salt
2 cloves garlic
3 T corn oil

1-1/4 cups whole or
crushed canned
tomatoes
3 oz. tomato paste
1 cup broth
Salt and pepper, to taste

1 cup bread crumbs
1/2 cup freshly grated
Parmesan cheese

Wash endive carefully and remove long, tough outer leaves. Place a large-size pot over medium-high heat. Fill half full with water and a pinch of salt. Add endive. Boil until tender, about 10 minutes. Drain, allow to come to room temperature, and squeeze out additional moisture.

Peel garlic. Place a medium-size iron skillet over medium-high heat. Heat to hot. Add oil. When oil is hot, add garlic and allow to brown. When brown, crush with a fork into small pieces.

Add tomatoes to the juices in the skillet, crushing the tomatoes with a fork into small pieces. Simmer 8 to 10 minutes.

Add tomato paste. Rinse both tomato and paste can with broth or water and add to mixture. Reduce heat, cover, and simmer 20 minutes, or until tomatoes begin to lose their bright red color. Taste, add salt and pepper if necessary.

Remove from heat and run tomatoes through a sieve pushing pulp through sieve with a spoon or fork. Throw remaining pulp away.

Place a layer of cooked endive in a 9-by-9-inch casserole dish. Pour 1/3 of tomato mixture over endive. Sprinkle with 1/3 of bread crumbs and freshly grated Parmesan cheese. Repeat for remainder of endive and top with sauce, bread crumbs, and cheese. Bake in 350-degree oven for 45 minutes.

Serving: 6.

Fresh Escarole
Scarola Fresca

Escarole looks like a cross between bibb lettuce and endive. It is good in salads, soups, and stuffings. This unusual recipe comes from Norma Iervoline, one of our testers. The Pelini family has been enjoying it for years (see escarole salad recipe on page 224).

Stuffed Escarole
Scarola Ripiena

1 head escarole

1 clove garlic
6 anchovy fillets
1/4 cup pine nuts
5-6 oz. pitted black
olives
1/2 cup bread crumbs
1/4 cup freshly grated
Parmesan cheese
2 T olive oil

Wash escarole under running water, opening the leaves to clean the inside (do not break leaves). Turn upsidedown and drain on paper towel. Allow to dry.

Peel and chop garlic into fine pieces. Chop anchovies and pine nuts into small pieces. Drain black olives and chop into small pieces.

Combine garlic, anchovies, and pine nuts in a small bowl. Add bread crumbs and grated cheese, then oil and chopped olives (do not add salt as anchovies are salty enough). Mix well.

Place escarole on a pastry board. Spread mixture on each leaf, then gather leaves together and tie them at top with a string. If not secure, wrap string loosely around body.

Place a medium-size high pot (a glass coffee pot is good) over medium-high heat. Add 2 inches of water. Place escarole in pot so that it stands up. Bring water to a boil, cover with a lid, and allow to steam for 30 minutes, or until tender (you can also place escarole in a steamer).

Remove escarole from pot, lay on pastry board, allow to cool for 30 minutes, and cut into slices.

Yield: 7-8 slices.

Fresh Mushrooms
Funghi Freschi

When I was growing up I always felt the mushroom, especially fried, was our secret and was a bit resentful when fried mushrooms began to appear on menus in restaurants and cocktail bars. I felt vindicated when they never tasted as good as ours.

The mushroom is a fungus without roots, stems, leaves, seeds or reproductive cells. There are over 44,000 varieties of wild mushrooms in the world and only a little over 30 are poisonous. But 30 is enough for one to be very careful when going mushroom hunting. Today, as a result of pollution and deforestation, the wild mushroom is in trouble and not as abundant as it once was. In fact, in central Europe many species are now extinct.

When buying mushrooms look for unbruised caps with under sides that are dense and not opened. These are the freshest. The shelf life of a mushroom is short, so buy in small quantities. Some cookbooks and TV chefs recommend brushing mushrooms with a brush to take off any dirt instead of washing them. But we always washed them; in fact, we sometimes peeled the tops. You decide what is best for you.

Fried mushrooms are the centerpiece for the *gran fritto misto* (see recipe on page 289). There is also an excellent stuffed mushroom recipe on page 46.

Mushrooms in Garlic and Butter
Funghi con Aglio e Burro

1/2 pound mushrooms

2 T butter
2 cloves garlic
Salt and pepper, to taste

Take one mushroom at a time and cut off the very tip of the stem and remove any blemishes on the crown (you may wish to peel the top layer off the crown). Slice each mushroom lengthwise into 4 or 5 pieces.

Place a medium-size iron skillet over medium-high heat. Heat to hot. Melt butter in skillet. Add garlic. When garlic is brown, crush with a fork into small pieces. Add mushrooms, salt, and pepper to taste. Lower heat and saute for 5 minutes.

Serves: 3-4.

Fresh Green Pepper
Peperoni Freschi

Many people find green peppers hard to digest, but if you rub the pepper with a little oil and place it under a broiler for a few minutes, you can peel off the outer skin with a paring knife. Then the indigestible part is gone. Additional recipes are green peppers in an omelet on page 169 and green pepper with sausage sandwich on page 228.

Stuffed Peppers
Peperoni Ripieni

Peppers in all varieties--red, yellow, green, even jalapeno--are found in markets nationwide. The best peppers to use for this recipe are the small, long green peppers called Italian Elle or cubanelle (narrow) found in most supermarkets. This recipe is also good for stuffed, elongated white eggplant, small zucchini, and small tomatoes.

10-12 small peppers

1 clove garlic
1/2 tsp. fresh parsley
1/2 tsp. fresh basil
3 slices Italian bread
1/2 cup milk

1 egg
1 pound ground round
1/2 tsp. salt
1/4 tsp. pepper
1/3 cup freshly grated
Romano cheese

Corn oil

Wash peppers, remove tops, scrape out seeds and white inner ribs. Set aside.

Peel and chop garlic. Chop parsley and basil. Break bread into small pieces, moisten with milk (it should absorb all the milk).

In a large bowl combine garlic, egg, meat, parsley, basil, salt, pepper, and grated cheese. Mix well. Finally add bread. Mix well.

Stuff each pepper. Rub a little oil between your hands and rub the outside of the pepper with oil.

Place on an oiled cookie sheet and bake at 400 degrees for 25 minutes, turning every 5 to 6 minutes. Peppers should be brown. Reduce oven temperature to 350 degrees and bake for an additional 45 minutes.

Serves: 6-8.

Note: This is a good item for a buffet table or to serve as an appetizer.

Potatoes
Patate

Potatoes are delicious no matter which way you serve them: roasted, fried, mashed, stewed, boiled, or baked. We prefer red potatoes: slightly more expensive, but sweeter. For boiled potatoes see the potato salad recipe on page 225; for stewed potatoes see potatoes with pork steak or sausage on pages 151 and 153.

Double Baked Potato
Patate Doppie al Forno

4 potatoes (red)
8 pats butter

4 T butter
1/2 cup milk
1 tsp. salt
Paprika
4 tsp. freshly grated
Parmesan cheese

4 pieces aluminum foil

Wash each potato and pat dry. Place each on aluminum foil. Add pat of butter and seal foil around each potato. Bake in 350-degree oven for 30 to 45 minutes depending on size of potato.

When potato is done remove from oven and unwrap. Cut off top of each potato. Scoop out inside trying not to break the skin. Place all pulp in a bowl and add butter, milk, and a pinch of salt. Whip potatoes and spoon back into skins. Lay potatoes on baking dish. Sprinkle with paprika and Parmesan cheese. Return to oven, set oven on Broil. Broil on high for 5 to 6 minutes or until crusty. Serve at once.

Serves: 4.

Fried Potatoes, Onions, and Peppers with Rosemary
Patate Fritte con Peperoni, Cipolle e Rosmarino

This is a good dish for breakfast, brunch, or a buffet.

3 large potatoes (red)
2 large onions
2 large green or red bell peppers
1/4 cup corn oil

1 T rosemary
1/2 tsp. salt
Dash pepper

Clean, peel and dice potatoes, onions, and peppers into 3/4-inch pieces, the smaller the better. Place a large-size iron skillet over medium-high heat. Heat to hot. Add oil.

When oil is hot, add potatoes. Fry for 10 minutes. Keep on high heat until potatoes begin to turn brown, then add onions, peppers, rosemary, salt and pepper. Reduce heat and cover with a lid. Allow to steam until done.

Yield: 4-6.

Variation: Add diced salami or sausage.

Mashed Potatoes Italian Style
Pureà di Patate all'Italiana

4 potatoes (red)
1/4 tsp. salt

3/4 cup milk
5 pats butter

4 T freshly grated
Parmesan cheese
4 T pine nuts

Wash potatoes, peel, and dice into 1-inch pieces. Place a medium-size pot on medium-high heat. Add water, potatoes, and salt. Bring to the boil, then simmer until potatoes are done.

Remove from stove and drain. Place potatoes in a mixing bowl. Add milk and butter and blend until all lumps are gone.

Remove potatoes from mixer and add cheese and pine nuts. Blend together and serve.

Serves: 4.

Roast Potatoes
Patate al Forno

Our favorite potatoes. This recipe appears with all the roasts in this book, including pork, veal, lamb, and beef, but potatoes made this way are delicious and so much a part of our cooking that we have repeated the recipe here.

4 large potatoes (red)

1/4 cup corn oil or pan drippings
1/4 tsp. sage, fennel, or rosemary
Salt
Pepper

Wash and peel potatoes. Cut into 4 or 5 pieces (for crunchy potatoes cut into smaller pieces).

If roasting potatoes with a roast, after the roast has been roasting for 30 minutes, add potatoes. Turn, coating them with the oil in the pan. Cook for an additional 2 to 2-1/2 hours, basting and turning every 20 minutes.

If preparing the potatoes without a roast, place peeled and cut potatoes in a roasting pan, add pan drippings from a good roast and roast as above.

If you do not have pan drippings, add oil, your favorite spice (fennel, sage, or rosemary), salt, and pepper; roast as indicated.

Serves: 4.

Note: It is the pan drippings and spices that make these potatoes so good. The better the roast, the more satisfying the potatoes.

Garden Tomatoes
Pomodori dall'Orto

Tomatoes arrived in Italy in the 16th century, long after pasta. They came from South America and the Italians called them *pomi d'oro*, golden apples. But the story of their migration does not end there. When the Italian immigrants brought them to the United States in the 1800s they were soundly rejected. It was not until the 1860s that the tomato became an acceptable food in the United States.

Nonno always planted tomatoes. Each spring we went to a special hot-house to buy the tomato plants. Once the plants were a foot high, poles were placed beside each one, and the vine tied so the plant would grow straight and tall.

The first tomatoes were ready by early July. Oh, how proud Nonno would be when he brought the first tomato to the table. Then all the delicious fresh tomato recipes would come out and day after day we enjoyed these truly "golden apples."

While writing this book I planted my first tomato patch (I could hear Nonno laughing each evening as I watered and tended the plants). Although we had only eight plants, we got dozens and dozens of tomatoes. It was with great satisfaction that I picked them each evening.

Tomato, Green Pepper, and Cucumber Salad
Insalata di Pomodori, Peperoni, e Cetrioli

2-3 garden fresh tomatoes
1 large green pepper
1 large cucumber

dressing:
Olive oil
Vinegar
Salt, pepper

Wash the tomatoes, remove the green stems, cut in half and each half into 4 or 5 wedges. Wash the green pepper, cut in half and remove all seeds and pods, cut lengthwise into wedges. Peel the cucumber, cut lengthwise and slice crosswise into pieces. Place all in a large deep dish and add dressing to taste (we always enjoyed oil, vinegar, salt and pepper, but lemon can be substituted for the vinegar).

Serves: 4-5.

Note: For people who find peppers hard to digest, a helpful hint is to peel the outer skin off the pepper. Rub it with oil and place it under a broiler for a few minutes. Then peel the skin off the pepper with a paring knife. The indigestible part is gone.

Garden Tomatoes and Basil
Pomodori al Basilico

Without fresh garden tomatoes this dish is ordinary.

1 garden fresh firm
tomato
1 tsp. fresh basil
2 T olive oil
1/2 tsp. salt
1/4 tsp. pepper
1 T vinegar (optional)

Wash the tomato, remove the green stem, cut in half, and each half into 4 to 5 wedges. Place in a bowl. Add the basil first, spreading it over all the tomatoes. Toss and let sit for 5 minutes. Add oil, salt, and pepper to taste. Vinegar is optional.

Serves: 2.

Fresh Tomatoes on Italian Bread
Struffa Struffa

Generations of our children have enjoyed this hearty open-faced sandwich. They all love it and the family lore that accompanies the making.

1 garden tomato, very
ripe
2 slices fresh Italian
bread
Salt, pepper
Olive oil

Slice the tomato in half. It must be very ripe for this dish. Rub half of tomato on bread leaving a pinkish color and a few seeds. Add salt, pepper and a little oil. Use second half of tomato for second slice of bread. Serve immediately.

Yield: 2 portions.

Stuffed Tomatoes
Pomodori Ripieni

10 ripe firm tomatoes
1/4 cup fresh parsley
4 fresh leaves basil
1 clove chopped garlic
1-1/2 cups fresh bread
crumbs
Salt and pepper, to taste
1/2 cup freshly grated
Parmesan cheese
Corn oil

Wash tomatoes and remove stems. Slice in half and remove seeds leaving interior pulp. Chop parsley and basil. Peel garlic and chop fine.

In a large bowl combine parsley, basil, garlic, bread crumbs, salt and pepper, and grated cheese. Stuff tomato halves. Place tomatoes on oiled baking dish and bake at 350 degrees for 30 minutes or until tomatoes are tender.

Yield: 20 tomato halves.

275

Fresh Zucchini
Zucchini Freschi

Zucchini, native to Italy, is a staple of Italian gardens and is served in so many different ways that it is hard to believe all the dishes come from the same vegetable. It should never be allowed to grow too large or too long, but served young and tender at about 7 to 9 inches long and 1-1/2 inches in diameter.

The zucchini and its flower are a special part of the *gran fritto misto* (see the recipes on page 287).

Zucchini, Onion, and Tomato Stew
Zucchini, Cipolle, e Pomodoro Stufati

2 medium zucchini
2 medium onions
4-5 very ripe tomatoes
2 T corn oil
1/4 tsp. salt
1/4 tsp. pepper
2 T tomato paste

Peel and wash zucchini and cut into 1-1/2-inch cubes. Peel and wash onions, cut in half and then into 1/8-inch wedges. Blanch tomatoes remove skin, and cut into pieces.

Place a medium-size skillet over medium-high heat. Heat to hot. Add oil. Heat to hot. Add onion. Simmer for 10 minutes, or until onions are transparent. Add zucchini, salt, and pepper. Simmer for 10 minutes and add tomatoes. Crush tomatoes with a fork. Add paste, stir; simmer.

Cover, lower the heat, and allow to simmer for at least an hour, until tomatoes lose their bright red color. Stir often. Serve with fresh Italian bread.

Serves: 6-8, as a side dish.

Boiled Zucchini
Zucchini Lessi

Whenever the soup is simmering on the stove and there are fresh zucchini in the garden, this refreshing, low-cal dish is conjured up.

2 medium zucchini
Salt, pepper, to taste
Olive oil
Vinegar

Wash zucchini and remove stems. Place in simmering soup and boil for 1 hour. Remove and place in colander; let drain for 10 to 15 minutes. Split lengthwise, let stand 10 minutes. Drain off any liquid. Dress with salt, pepper, oil, and vinegar to taste.

Serves: 4.

276

Zucchini with Cheese
Zucchini alla Parmigiana

2 zucchini
4 T butter
1/8 tsp. salt
1/8 tsp. pepper
3 T fresh parsley
1 tsp. basil
1/2 cup freshly grated
Parmesan cheese

Wash zucchini, peel, and slice into thin slices. Place a medium-size iron skillet over medium-high heat. Add butter and melt. Add zucchini, cover, reduce heat, and saute until brown, about 20 minutes. Add salt and pepper, parsley and basil. Simmer 5 minutes.

Remove from skillet and place on serving tray. Sprinkle generously with Parmesan cheese. Stir and serve.

Serves: 2 (this is not a mistake, zucchini reduce).

Zucchini in White Wine
Zucchini con Salsa di Vin Bianco

2 zucchini
1 small onion

4 T butter
1/2 cup white wine
3/4 tsp. salt
1/8 tsp. pepper
2 T fresh parsley
1 large leaf fresh basil

Place a medium-size pot over medium-high heat and parboil zucchini, skins and all (about 5 to 7 minutes depending on size).

Remove from water, drain, and let cool. Wash and peel onion and chop into fine pieces.

Place a medium-size iron skillet over medium-high heat. Add butter and melt. Add onions and saute until onions are transparent. Add wine, salt, pepper, parsley, and basil.

Slice parboiled zucchini into 1/4-inch slices. Add to skillet and cook for 15 to 20 minutes or until tender.

Serves: 4.

Zucchini with Bread Stuffing
Zucchini Ripieni di Pane

In addition to zucchini, this recipe can be made with eggplant, tomatoes, or peppers.

2 onions
1 clove garlic
1/4-inch-thick slice
pancetta
1 small carrot
2-3 celery ribs
2-3 sprigs parsley

2 T corn oil
1 tsp. pepper
2 tsp. salt
2 medium zucchini

2 cups bread crumbs
1/4 cup freshly grated
Parmesan cheese
2 eggs
1/8 cup corn oil

Peel onions, wash, and cut into quarter wedges. Peel garlic and chop into pieces. Cut *pancetta* into small pieces. Peel carrot and celery, wash, and cut into 1-inch pieces. Chop parsley. Combine all and grind in a meat grinder or a food processor into fine pieces (the grinder is better because it releases the juices).

Place a medium-size iron skillet over medium-high heat. Heat to hot. Add 2 tablespoons oil. When oil is warm add all chopped ingredients, pepper, and salt. Reduce heat, cover, and saute until onions are transparent, stirring often.

Cut zucchini in half lengthwise. Scoop out the center leaving about 1 inch of pulp. Chop scooped out pulp into small pieces and add to the already cooking onion mixture. Cover and simmer about 20 minutes, stirring often. The longer you cook this mixture the better your stuffing will taste. It is done when the vegetables are dark and it begins to stick to the skillet.

When cooked, remove from skillet and combine with bread crumbs and grated cheese. Beat the eggs and pour over the mixture. Mix well. If dry add a little broth or water.

Fill both halves of the zucchini with the mixture. Grease baking dish with a little oil and place zucchini halves side by side in the dish.

Bake in 350-degree oven for 1 hour.

Serves: 4-5.

Zucchini with Meat Stuffing
Zucchini con Ripieno di Carne

2 onions
1/4-inch-thick slice
pancetta
2-3 celery ribs
1 small carrot
2-3 sprigs parsley

2 large zucchini
1/4 cup corn oil
1 T pepper
1 T salt

1/2 pound ground beef
1 cup bread crumbs
1/4 cup freshly grated
Parmesan cheese
2 eggs, beaten

1/4 cup corn oil
2 cloves garlic
1-1/4 cups whole or
crushed canned tomatoes
3 oz. tomato paste

1/2 cup broth

Peel onions, wash, and cut into quarter wedges. Cut *pancetta* into small pieces. Peel celery and carrot, wash, and cut into 1-inch pieces. Chop parsley. Combine all and grind in meat grinder or food processor into fine pieces (the grinder is better because it grinds into fine pieces and releases the juices).

Cut zucchini in half lengthwise. Scoop out the center leaving about 1 inch of pulp. Chop scooped out pulp into small pieces and add to onion mixture.

Place a medium-size iron skillet over medium-high heat. Add 1/4 cup oil. When oil is hot add all chopped ingredients, pepper, salt. Cover, lower heat and saute, stirring often, until onions are transparent, about 20 minutes. The longer you cook this mixture the better the stuffing will taste. Remove from skillet and set aside.

When cooked remove skillet from heat and add ground meat, bread crumbs, grated cheese and beaten eggs. Mix well. Fill the zucchini halves with the mixture and place them in a greased baking dish.

Place a medium-size iron skillet over medium-high heat. Heat to hot. Add 1/4 cup oil. Heat. Peel garlic and add to oil. Allow to brown and crush with a fork into small pieces. Add tomatoes, crushing with a fork into small pieces. Bring to a boil, reduce heat, cover and simmer 8 to 10 minutes. Add tomato paste. Rinse both tomato and paste cans with 1/2 cup broth (or water) and add to mixture. Cover and simmer 20 minutes, or until tomatoes begin to lose bright red color.

Remove from heat and run through a sieve pushing pulp through sieve with a spoon or fork. Throw away remaining pulp. Taste, add salt and pepper, if necessary.

Pour tomatoes (see note) over stuffed zucchini. Bake in 350-degree oven for 1 hour.

Serves: 4-5.

Note: You can substitute 2 cans tomato soup for the tomato mixture, but don't tell Elizabeth.

279

Notes

Grand Mixed Fry
Gran Fritto Misto

If there is a more delicious dish in the world, I do not know it. Serving up a great mound of fried meats, fish, and vegetables sprinkled with fresh lemon and eaten with a fresh green salad was an event of paramount importance in Nonna's house. The word would go forth, "We are having *fritto misto* on Sunday," and the anticipation was almost unbearable. If someone in the family had made plans, they were changed, or the friends were invited to join us in this eating orgy. We served *fritto misto* as often as possible: as the holiday meal for Holy Saturday, as a favorite request for birthdays, and on summer picnics, hauled in bushel baskets filled to the brim. When a particular vegetable came in season it was, "We are having artichokes with the *fritto misto*," and it was a solemn moment, almost a time to tremble with delight, but certainly a time for a big smile.

Fritto misto is prepared throughout Italy. It is so popular that *friggitorie* exist throughout the country, selling nothing but fried foods. Today fried vegetables have been discovered by American restaurants and are offered doused in liquid cheese.

Fritto misto is prepared in three different ways, depending on the type of food. It is either dipped in batter, dredged in flour and egg, or pressed into bread crumbs. The meats include veal, lamb, and chicken. The fish include cod, halibut, smelts, shrimp, oysters, and squid. The vegetables are the most exotic items on the Italian menu: artichokes, asparagus, green beans, cauliflower, celery, eggplant, Florentine fennel, mushrooms, zucchini (pumpkin) flowers, and zucchini. God help the cook that does not know which meat must be pressed in crumbs, which vegetable is dipped, or which fish is dredged. This is a secret as important as the cut of pasta or the quality of bread. So here it is, so special it deserves a chapter by itself.

Frying Food
Cibi Fritti

The best way to fry food is with an iron skillet, a *padella di fritto*. We have a variety of sizes, one for every possible use. Unfortunately, by today's standards, you need plenty of oil when frying. The skillet should be filled 1/4-to-1/2-inch full with good vegetable oil (we use corn oil). We never use olive oil to fry our food.

Place the skillet on medium-high heat and heat until hot. Add oil to cover the bottom. Heat to hot, but not to smoking. Food that is fried in cold or warm oil will absorb the oil and be greasy. A good way to test the oil is to drop a small piece of meat or vegetable into the oil. If it begins to bubble with small bubbles around the food, it is ready. If it bubbles too vigorously, it is too hot.

Never stack food in the frying pan. Be sure each piece has ample space around it. Lay the food into the hot oil and allow to brown on one side. Turn only once. If food sticks to the bottom of the skillet the oil is not hot enough or there is not enough oil. Let it be, for when it is cooked it will free itself.

If you are frying a large quantity of food the oil will become depleted and begin to foam. It will have to be replenished. Remove the last piece of cooked food, drain existing oil, wipe the skillet with a paper towel, return it to heat, add new oil. Heat and continue frying.

Always place fried food on a paper towel after removing from the frying skillet. This allows excess oil to drain.

Batter
Pastella

The amount of batter needed for various vegetables depends on the size of the vegetables, just as the amount of oil depends on the size of the skillet. If additional batter is required, do not add to existing batter, but begin fresh.

2 eggs
1 T olive oil
2 tsp. water
Salt to taste
3 T flour

Beat eggs in a medium bowl. Add oil, water, and salt. Mix well. Slowly add flour. Mix until it forms a smooth thin paste. Prepare the batter ahead so that it can rest.

Place a large-size iron skillet on medium-high heat. Heat to hot. Add oil to generously cover bottom of the skillet. Heat to hot. Dip food into the batter, coat well. If batter does not adhere to food, add more flour to batter.

Place in hot oil. Brown one side, turn, brown other. Drain on paper towel. Eat immediately.

If you need more batter, do not add to the prepared batter, but start anew.

Dredged in Flour
Infarinati

When you use flour, roll the food in the flour first, then in the egg.

1 cup flour
2 eggs
1-1/2 tsp. salt
3/4 tsp. pepper

Corn oil

Place flour on board or in flat dish. Gently roll each piece in flour, coating generously. Place on another flat dish, do not stack. Beat eggs, salt, and pepper in a flat bowl. Set near stove.

Place medium-size iron skillet over medium-high heat. Heat to hot. Add oil. When oil is hot, dip floured food in the beaten egg, coating generously. Drop immediately into hot oil. Repeat until skillet is full. Do not stack.

Allow to fry until golden brown, turn, and allow the other side to brown. Remove from skillet one at a time and place on a paper towel to absorb extra oil. Continue until all is fried. Serve hot with a wedge of lemon.

If brown flour accumulates in the oil, you used too much flour and fried too hot.

Pressed in Bread Crumbs
Cibi in Pan Grattato

When you use bread crumbs, dip the food in the egg, then in the crumbs.

1 cup bread crumbs
1/4 cup freshly grated
Parmesan cheese
2 eggs
1 tsp. salt
1/2 tsp. pepper

Corn oil

Never use bought or seasoned bread crumbs. Save stale Italian bread until hard. Grate on a cheese grater. Add grated cheese to crumbs and mix well.

Beat eggs in flat dish, add salt and pepper. Dip food into beaten egg, turn, and coat well.

Place a medium-size iron skillet over medium-high heat. Heat to hot. Add oil. Heat to hot.

Press egg-dipped food onto bread crumbs, turn, press again. Drop immediately into hot oil. Do not stack.

Fry until golden brown, turn, fry second side. Remove from skillet and place on a paper towel to absorb extra oil. Continue until all is fried. Serve hot with a wedge of lemon.

Fried Meat Medley
Fritto Misto di Carne

Fried meat is the linchpin of the mixed fry. And the best meats are chicken and veal. Always a favorite whether served in the *fritto misto* or alone, our unadorned chicken recipe stands far above all the heavily spiced fast-food varieties. Ambrosia is the best way to describe our excellent, excellent, fried veal. Bushels of both were cooked and taken on picnics and the only thing that came back were the crumbs. They are easy to prepare and delicious to eat. Simplicity is the secret--no garlic, no spice--simple and uncomplicated Tuscan food.

Batter Dipped
Pastella

Fried Brains (*Cervello Fritto*): Use batter prepared as described on page 282 with 1-1/4 pounds beef, lamb, or calf's brains, corn oil, wedge of lemon.

Prepare batter. Wash brains. Pour a small amount of boiling water over brains and remove covering membrane. Cut into serving pieces.

Place medium-size iron skillet over medium-high heat. Heat to hot. Add oil to cover bottom of skillet. Heat to hot. Drop a piece of brain into batter. Turn to coat well. If batter is too thick, add additional water and mix. If too thin, add more flour. Place in hot oil. Repeat. Fry until golden brown, turning once. Serve at once with wedge of lemon.

Serves: 4-6.

Note: Brains fry quickly, so do not over cook. Very good if served piping hot with fried mushrooms or fried artichokes.

Dredged in Flour
Infarinati

Fried Chicken (*Pollo Fritto*): Use the recipe for dredge on page 283 with 1 chicken fryer cut into pieces and 1 large lemon cut into wedges.

Wash all pieces of chicken, remove extra skin and fat, and drain. Dredge chicken as described in recipe on page 283.

Place a large-size iron skillet over medium-high heat. Heat to hot. Coat bottom generously with oil. When oil is hot, dip a piece of the floured chicken into the egg, coating generously. Drop into hot oil. Repeat until skillet is full. Allow to fry until golden brown, turn, and brown. Remove from skillet one at a time and place on a paper towel to absorb extra oil. Continue until all is fried. Serve hot with lemon wedges.

Serves: 6-8.

Fried Baby Lamb Chops or Ribs *(Costolette di Abbacchio Fritte):* Use 8-10 baby lamb chops or ribs, 3-4 eggs, 1 cup flour, salt, pepper, corn oil, 1 large lemon cut into wedges. Prepare the chops or ribs by cutting away any extra fat and gristle. Dredge in flour as described on page 283.

Place a medium-size iron skillet over medium-high heat. Heat to hot. Add oil. When oil is hot, dip a floured lamb chop into the beaten egg, coating generously. Drop immediately into hot oil. Repeat until skillet is full. Do not stack. Allow to fry until golden brown. When the chops are golden brown turn, and allow the other side to brown. Remove from skillet one at a time and place on a paper towel to absorb extra oil. Continue until all chops are fried. Serve hot with lemon wedges.

Serves: 5-8.

Fried Baby Lamb's Head *(Testina di Agnellino Fritto):* Use 1 baby lamb's head, water, 2 eggs, salt, pepper, 1/3 cup flour, corn oil, 1 large lemon cut into wedges.

Clean lamb's head by removing excess skin. Cut off ears. Remove eyes and brains. Place a large-size pot over medium-high heat. Add enough water to cover. Then add a pinch of salt. Boil lamb's head for 10 to 15 minutes. Remove from water and allow to cool. When cool, remove all meat from the bones. Discard bones. Cut meat into serving pieces. Dredge meat in flour as described in recipe on page 283.

Place a medium-size iron skillet over medium-high heat. Heat to hot. Add oil. Dip floured meat into egg a piece at a time and drop into the hot oil. Fry at a high temperature and brown on both sides. Remove and set to drain on a paper towel. Serve hot with lemon wedges.

Serves: 4-6.

Pressed in Bread Crumbs
Cibi in Pan Grattato

Breaded Veal Steak *(Vitello Impannato):* Use 2 slices veal steak, 4 eggs, 2 cups unflavored bread crumbs, 4 T freshly grated Parmesan cheese, 1 tsp. salt, 1/2 tsp. pepper, corn oil, 1 large lemon cut into wedges.

Prepare the veal cutlet by cutting away extra fat and gristle. Lay on a board and pound with kitchen mallet (or the rib end of a large knife) to tenderize. Beat egg with pinch of salt. Combine bread crumbs and cheese. Cut each steak into 4 or 5 pieces. Dip in beaten egg and press into bread crumbs as described in second recipe on page 283.

Place large-size iron skillet over medium-high heat. Heat to hot. Add oil. When oil is hot, add cutlets. Repeat until skillet is full. Do not stack. Allow to fry until golden brown. When cutlets are golden brown, turn and allow other side to brown. Remove from skillet one at a time and place on a paper towel to absorb extra oil. Continue until all the veal is fried. Serve hot with wedges of lemon.

Serves: 4-6.

Fried Fish Medley
Fritto Misto di Pesce

Just as there is a mixed fry of meats or vegetables, the Italian table has a mixed fry of fish. The batter and dredging methods are the same. We never used bread crumbs for fish.

Dredged in Flour
Infarinati

Fried Cod, Halibut, Oysters, Shrimp, or Smelts *(Baccalà, Passera di Mare, Ostriche, Gamberetti, or Eperlano Fritti):* The final course of the Christmas Eve meal. Use 1 pound fish, 1 cup flour, 3 beaten eggs, salt (for dried cod prepare as directed on page 103, omitting salt), pepper, corn oil, wedge of lemon.

Clean fish. Wash carefully and place on a paper towel to drain. Dredge with flour as described in first recipe on page 283.

Place a medium-size iron skillet over medium-high heat. Heat to hot. Add oil. When oil is hot, dip floured fish in the beaten egg, coating generously. Drop immediately into hot oil. Repeat until skillet is full. Do not stack. Allow to fry until golden brown. When golden brown, turn, and allow the other side to brown. Remove from skillet one at a time and place on a paper towel to absorb extra oil. Continue until all the fish are fried. Serve hot with a wedge of lemon, a good salad, and Italian bread.
Serves: 4-6.

Fried Squid *(Calamari Fritti):* Use 1 pound squid, 2 eggs, 1 cup flour, salt, pepper, corn oil, lemon wedges. If the squid is fresh you must clean it very well to remove all the inedible parts, especially the sack that holds the ink.

The skin is coated with a tough outer film that can be removed by rubbing it gently with your hands. Cut off the head, then remove tentacles from head. They are good eating. Cut into pieces and set aside. Remove insides through the opening left by the head. Clean the body, but do not slit. Be sure to remove the inner lining carefully. Wash the inside in cold water, then cut it into rings similar to onion rings.

Place flour with a dash of salt and pepper on a large work space and stir. Gently roll each piece of squid in the flour, coating generously. Beat eggs with a dash of salt. Set all near stove.

Place a large-size iron skillet over medium-high heat. Heat to hot. When hot, add oil. When oil is hot, dip a piece of the floured squid in the beaten egg, coating generously. Drop immediately into hot oil. When the pieces are golden brown, turn, and brown second side. Remove and drain. Serve hot with fresh lemon wedges and a good green salad.
Serves: 4-6.

Mixed Vegetable Medley
Misto di Verdure Fritte

Batter-dipped and dredged vegetables fried to a golden brown form a major part of the *fritto misto*, a meal fit for a king in its variety and quantity.

Batter Dipped Vegetables
Verdure con Pastella

There are two ways to prepare the vegetables for the *fritto misto*: dipped in a batter or dredged in flour and covered in beaten egg.

Fried Zucchini Flowers *(Fiori di Zucca Fritti)*: Use 12 pumpkin or zucchini flowers, 2 eggs, 1 T olive oil, 2 tsp. water, salt, 3 T flour, corn oil. Delicate and tasty, fried pumpkin or zucchini flowers are an exotic treat served for only a few weeks every year. You cannot find these flowers in groceries; they must be picked fresh from the garden in early morning and cooked for dinner that day. The flowers bloom before the fruit. Flowers with bubbles near the stem will produce zucchini or pumpkins and are never picked. Although we call the flowers pumpkin flowers in Italian, we seldom prepared pumpkin flowers, but used zucchini flowers instead.

Prepare batter as described on page 282. While batter is resting carefully clean the fragile blossoms. Remove the yellow stamens as gently as possible so as not to tear the blossoms. Remove the green leaves near the stem. Clip the stem. Gently wash the blossoms, shake, and lay on a paper towel to dry. When ready to fry, dip flowers into batter one at a time, coating generously and place in hot oil. If batter is too thin, add flour. Eat immediately.
Yield: 12 fried flowers.

Fried Zucchini *(Zucchini Fritti)*: Use 1 large zucchini, 2 eggs, 1 T olive oil, 2 tsp. water, salt, 3 T flour, corn oil. Wash and peel skin from zucchini and slice into thin slices like a cucumber (we never cut zucchini into strips). Prepare batter as described on page 282. Dip the zucchini into the batter, coating well, and place in the hot oil. If batter is too thin, add more flour. Brown on one side, turn, and finish browning on the other. Drain on paper towel. Eat immediately.
Serves: 3-4.

Dredged Vegetables
Verdure Infarinati

To cook dredged vegetables, place flour with a dash of salt and pepper on a large work space and stir. Gently roll each piece of vegetable in the flour, coating generously. Beat eggs and a dash of salt. Set all near stove.

Place a large-size iron skillet over medium-high heat. Heat to hot. When hot add oil. When oil is hot, dip a piece of the floured vegetable in the beaten egg, coating generously. Drop immediately into hot oil. When the pieces are golden brown, turn, and brown second side. Remove and drain. Serve hot with fresh lemon wedges and a good green salad.

Fried Artichokes *(Carciofi Fritti):* Use 2 fresh artichokes, 1 cup flour, 2 eggs, salt, pepper, corn oil, wedge of lemon. Clean artichokes as described on pages 262-63. Cut each in half lengthwise. From each half cut 5-6 wedges. Check each wedge for prickly centers and if any remain, remove them. Roll in flour, dip in beaten egg, and fry.
Serves: 4-6.

Fried Green Beans *(Fagiolini Fritti):* Use 1 pound fresh green beans, 1 cup flour, 2 eggs, salt, pepper, corn oil, wedge of lemon. Snap off about 1/4-inch from each end of the bean and discard. If you like the beans long leave as is, or snap into 2 or 3 pieces. Place in a large pot and wash with running water. Place a medium-size saucepan over medium-high heat. Add water and a pinch of salt. Add green beans and boil for about 10 minutes or to taste. Drain and allow to cool. Gather 5 to 6 beans into a bunch and dip the bundle in flour, then the beaten egg, coating generously. Place in hot oil. Continue as described in preceding recipes.
Serves: 4-6.

Fried Cabbage *(Cappuccio Fritto):* Use 1 head cabbage, 1 cup flour, 2 eggs, salt, pepper, corn oil, wedge of lemon. Wash the cabbage and cut in half. Slice each half into 1/2-inch slices, then cut each slice into smaller serving pieces. Place a medium-size iron skillet over medium-high heat. Add enough water to fill the skillet. Bring to a boil. Gently place each piece of cabbage in boiling water and cook until tender. Cabbage tends to fall apart so do a few at a time. Remove carefully and set on paper towel to drain. Do not stack. Dredge each piece of cabbage in flour and continue as described in preceding recipes.
Serves: 4-6.

Fried Cauliflower *(Cavolfiore Fritto):* Use 1 cauliflower, 1 cup flour, 2 eggs, salt, pepper, corn oil, wedge of lemon. Wash cauliflower and cut in half. If extra large, cut again. Place in large pot half filled with water and dash of salt. Parboil 5 minutes until soft. Test with a fork. Remove and place on drain board to drain. Allow to cool (or will break up). Break off florets and gently roll each piece in the flour, coating generously. Continue as described in preceding recipes.
Serves: 4-6.

Fried Celery *(Sedano Fritto):* Use 2-3 ribs fresh celery, 1 cup flour, 2 eggs, salt, pepper, corn oil, wedge of lemon. Clean and wash celery ribs. Peel off tough strings by grabbing lose strings at bottom of rib, holding them between thumb and a paring knife, and pulling. Cut into 4-inch pieces. Place small pot on stove over medium-high heat. Add celery. Add water until an inch above celery. Bring to a boil. Add salt and boil until tender, about 5 to 10 minutes depending on the size of the pieces. Drain and cool. Gather 3-4 boiled pieces together. Squeeze together to form a group. Roll in flour and continue as on page 287. **Serves:** 4-6.

Fried Eggplant *(Melanzane Fritte):* Use 1 eggplant, 1 cup flour, 2 eggs, salt, pepper, corn oil, wedge of lemon. Cut top and bottom stems from eggplant, remove outer skin, and slice into 1/4-inch slices. Place in large pot, add water and pinch of salt. Allow the eggplant to soak. As the water turns brown, drain, add more water and more salt. Do this 3 or 4 times to blanch out the bitterness. Drain and pat dry. Dredge in flour and continue as described on page 287.
Serves: 4-6.

Fried Florentine Fennel *(Finocchio Fritto):* Fennel, used by Prometheus to shield the source of fire, looks like celery, but has a bulbous bottom and tastes like anise. In season in the fall, we serve it raw with *pinzimonio,* or fried in the *gran fritto misto.* Use 1 fennel, 1 cup flour, 2 eggs, salt, pepper, corn oil, wedge of lemon. Wash fennel. Cut away ribs and save for another time. Use only the bulbous bottom. Slice into wedges like artichoke on page 288. Continue as described on page 287.
Serves: 4-6.

Fried Mushrooms *(Funghi Fritti):* Use 8 oz. fresh mushrooms, 2 eggs, 3 T flour, salt, pepper, corn oil, wedge of lemon. Take one mushroom at a time, cut off the tip of the stem and remove blemishes on crown (you may wish to peel the top layer off crown). Mushrooms should be button size for frying and if they are too large, cut into halves or quarters. Allow to drain. Beat eggs in a deep bowl. Place flour in a brown paper bag. Salt and pepper slightly. Shake well. Place all mushrooms in bag and shake very well until all are coated. Dip each mushroom in egg individually. Fry as described on page 287.
Serves: 4-6.

Pressed in Bread Crumbs
Cibi in Pan Grattato

Fried Asparagus *(Asparagi Fritti):* Use 1 pound fresh asparagus, 1 cup bread crumbs, 2 eggs, 4 T water, salt, pepper, corn oil, wedge of lemon. Place water in a large skillet. Bring to a boil with 1 tsp. salt. Add washed asparagus, cover and let cook until tender, about 12-18 minutes, depending on size. Drain. Roll asparagus in crumbs, pressing firming on both sides (crumbs will not cover entirely). Place a medium-size iron skillet over medium-high heat. Heat to hot. Add oil. Beat eggs with water, salt and pepper to form a wash. Dip asparagus in egg, roll in crumbs again, and drop immediately into hot oil. Brown on all sides.
Serves: 4-6.

Bibliography

Ainsworth, Catherine Harris. *Italian-American Folktales*. Buffalo: Clyde, 1977.

Barolini, Helen. *Festa, Recipes and Recollections of Italian Holidays*. New York: Harcourt Brace Jovanovich, 1988.

Boni, Ada. *Italian Regional Cooking*. New York: Bonanza Books, 1965.

Bugialli, Giuliano. *Giuliano Bugialli's Classic Techniques of Italian Cooking*. New York: Simon and Schuster, 1982.

Bugialli, Guiliano. *Guiliano Bugialli's Foods of Tuscany*. New York: Stewart, Tabori, Chang, 1992.

De Medici, Lorenza. *De Medici Kitchen*. San Francisco: Collins, 1992.

De Medici, Lorenza. *Florentine: A Tuscan Feast*. New York: Random House, 1993.

De Medici, Lorenza. *Heritage of Italian Cooking*. New York: Random House, 1990.

De Medici, Lorenza. *Tuscany, the Beautiful Cookbook*. San Francisco: Collins, 1992.

Del Conte, Anna. *Gastronomy of Italy*. New York: Prentice-Hall Press, 1987.

Field, Carol. *Celebrating Italy*. New York: William Morrow and Company, 1990.

Field, Carol. *The Italian Baker*. New York: Harper and Row, 1985.

Hazen, Marcella. *The Classic Italian Cookbook*. New York: Ballantine, 1973.

Hazen, Marcella. *Essentials of Classic Italian Cooking*. New York: Knopf, 1992.

Hooker, Katherine. *Byways in Southern Tuscany.* New York: Charles Scribner's Sons, 1918.

Malpezzi, Frances M. and William M. Clements. *Italian-American Folklore.* Little Rock: August House, 1992.

Pezzini, Wilma. *The Tuscan Cookbook.* New York: Atheneum, 1978.

Romer, Elizabeth. *The Tuscan Year: Life and Food in an Italian Valley.* New York: Atheneum, 1985.

Root, Waverley. *The Food of Italy.* New York: Atheneum, 1971.

English Recipe Index

A

Almond Cookies, 86.
Anchovies with Capers and Parsley Sandwich, 226.
Anchovies with Onions and Parsley, 222.
Anchovy and Butter Sandwich, 226.
Anchovy and Caper Sauce, 230.
Anise Cookies, 87.
Antipasto, 42.
Apple Pie, 94.
Artichoke Omelet, 168.
Asparagus Omelet, 168.
Asparagus with Anchovy Sauce, 263.

B

Baccalà Soup, 253.
Baked Eggplant with Tomatoes, 266.
Basic Omelet, 168.
Basic Polenta, 194.
Batter Dipped Fried Brains, 284.
Bean Salad, 222.
Bean Soup with Ham Bone, 249.
Bean Soup with Stale Bread and Green Onions, 249.
Bechamel Sauce, 231.
Beef Broth, 238-39.
Beef Rounds with Stuffing, 122.
Beef Rounds without Stuffing, 123.
Beef Rump in Red Sauce with Celery, 124.
Beef Rump in Red Sauce with Spinach, 125.
Beef Rump in Red Sauce with String Beans, 126.
Biscotti, 88.
Blood Pudding, 158.
Blue Cheese and Green Olive Spread, 44.
Boiled Beef, 116.
Boiled Beef with Potatoes, 116.
Boiled Capon with Anchovy Sauce, 204.
Boiled Meat Patties, 117.
Boiled or Broiled Cod with Chickpeas, 103.
Boiled Potatoes with Parsley Salad, 225.
Boiled Zucchini, 276.
Bows, 89.
Brain Fritters, 158.
Braised Blue Pike, 102.
Bread Stuffing, 67.
Breaded Veal Steak, 285.
Brigidini, 90.
Broccoli with Mushrooms, 265.

C

Calf's Liver and Onions, 127.
Camomile Tea, 54.
Capon Broth, 240.
Cappelletti in Broth, 243.
Cappuccino, 53.
Cheese Omelet, 168.
Chestnut Cake with Rosemary and Pine Nuts, 81.
Chicken Broth, 241.
Chicken Galantine, 208-11.
Chicken Liver Canape, 44.
Chicken on a Spit, 212.
Chickpea Salad, 223.
Chickpea Soup with Egg Noodles, 250.
Classic Pizza, 76-77.
Classic Schiacciata, 74.
Classic Veal Scaloppine, 138.
Classic Vegetable Soup, 252.
Cod in Sauce with Onions, 104.
Cod in Sauce with Sage and Garlic, 105.
Cod with Sweet and Sour Sauce, 106.
Cold Pork Roast Sandwich with Marinated Olive, 227.
Crazy Sauce, 232.
Cream of Tomato Soup, 254.
Cream Pie, 95.
Cream Pudding, 96.
Cream Sauce, 232.

D

Dandelion Greens and Hard-Boiled Egg Salad, 224.
Double Baked Potato, 272.
Dried Bread with Parsley and Onion Salad, 223.
Duck in Tomato Sauce with Celery, 213.

E

Easter Bread, 68-69.
Easter Pie, 171.
Eggplant Parmesan, 267.
Endive with Celery Salad, 224.
Endive Parmesan, 268.
English Cream, 97.
Escarole with Celery Salad, 224.
Espresso, 52.

F

Fettuccine Alfredo, 188.
Fettuccine Carbonara, 188.
Fettuccine with White Clam Sauce, 189.
Fish Stew, 107.
Foolproof Pie Crust, 94.
Fresh Fruits, Nuts, and Cheeses, 98.
Fresh Peaches with Red Wine, 98.
Fresh Pork Belly in Porchetta, 146.
Fresh Tomatoes on Italian Bread, 275.
Fried Anchovy Bread, 72.
Fried Artichokes, 288.
Fried Asparagus, 289.
Fried Baby Lamb Chops, 285.
Fried Baby Lamb's Head, 285.
Fried Brains, 284.
Fried Broccoli with Garlic and Oil, 258.
Fried Cabbage in Thin Sauce, 256.
Fried Cabbage with Garlic and Oil, 258.
Fried Cabbage, 288.
Fried Cauliflower in Thin Sauce, 256.
Fried Cauliflower with Garlic and Oil, 258.
Fried Cauliflower, 288.
Fried Celery in Thin Sauce, 257.
Fried Celery, 288.
Fried Chicken, 284.
Fried Cod, 286.
Fried Dough with Sugar, 71.
Fried Eggplant, 266.
Fried Eggplant in Batter, 289.
Fried Fish Medley, 286.
Fried Florentine Fennel, 289.
Fried Florentine Fennel in Thin Sauce, 257.
Fried Food Dredged in Flour, 283.
Fried Food in Batter, 282.
Fried Food Pressed in Bread Crumbs, 283.

294

Italian Recipe Index

297

General Index

A

Acciugata, see anchovy and caper sauce.
Acini di pepe, 7, 238.
Aglio e olio,
    broccoli, 258.
    cabbage, 258.
    cabbage, savoy, 258.
    cauliflower, 258.
    with spaghetti, 202.
Albertini, Carlo (Cirli), 6, 20.
Aliquippa, 4, 14.
Amaretti, 21, 22, 95.
Amaretto di Saronno, 51.
Amico, Mrs, 72, 181.
Anchovies, 24, 46, 72.
    with onion and parsley
        salad, 222.
Anchovy and Caper Sauce, 46,
    230.
    recipe, 108.
    with asparagus, 263.
    with capon, 204.
    with halibut, 108.
    with hard-boiled eggs, 46.
    with spaghetti, 199.
    with grilled steak, 121.
Anchovy bread, fried 72.
Angel-hair, with rice, 217.
Angele, Margaret (Peggy), 4.
Anise, 28.
Antipasto, 42.
Appetizers, 41-49.
    antipasto, 42.
    blue cheese and olives, 44.
    chicken liver, 44.
    hard-boiled eggs with
        anchovy and caper sauce,
        46.
    hot bath (*Bagna Calda*), 42-
        43.
    marinated green beans,
        artichokes, and
        mushrooms, 47.
    milt and chicken liver, 45.
    oil, salt and pepper dip, 47.
    prosciutto with cantaloupe
        or figs, 48.
    stuffed mushrooms, 46.
    tomato canape, 48.
    white canape, 49.
Apple, pie, 94.
Apples, 18.

April, 13.
Arezzo, 2, 7, 17-18, 115.
Arista, 148.
Arno River, 115.
Arrabbiata, 229.
Artichoke
    to clean, 260-61.
    omelet, 168.
    marinated, 47.
    stuffed, 262-63.
    fried, 288.
Asparagus
    with anchovy sauce, 263.
    fried, 289.
    omelet, 168.
August, 17.

B

Baccalà, see cod.
Bagna calda, 41, 42-43, 47.
Bands, musical, 17.
Basil, 8, 28.
Batter, for frying, 282.
Battuto, 37, 229.
Bean Soups, 248-50.
see also soups.
Beans, green, 14.
    fried, 288.
    fried in sauce, 256.
    in tomato sauce, 264.
    marinated, 47.
    salad, 264.
    with beef in red sauce, 126
Beans, white
    salad, 222.
    in soups, 248-50.
    with pork chops, 150.
    with ham, 249.
    with pasta, 249.
Bechamel sauce, 229, 231.
    with lasagna, 193.
Beef, 115-128.
    boiled, 116.
        meat patties, 117.
        with potatoes, 116.
    broth, 238-39.
    grilled steak, 121.
    in red sauce
    with celery, 124.
    with spinach, 125.
    with string beans, 126.
    meatloaf, Italian style, 118.
    roasts, 120.
        pot roast, 119.
        standing rib, 120.
    rounds (*brasiole*)

    with stuffing, 122.
    without stuffing, 122.
    stew, 122.
Befana, 10.
Beverages, 51-62.
    cappuccino, 51.
    espresso, 52.
    tea, 54.
    wine, 55-62.
        table wine, 56-59.
        half wine, 60.
        prop wine, 60.
        holy wine, 61.
Bindi, 2.
    Domenico (Menco), 3, 11.
    Laura, 3.
Biscotti, 15, 16, 88.
Blood pudding, 158.
Blue cheese, see Gorgonzola.
Bocce, 1, 14.
Boiled
    capon, 204.
    cod, 103.
    beef, 116-17.
    potatoes for salad, 225.
Boilers, copper, 10.
Bollito misto, 38.
Bologna, 8.
Bonchi, 14.
    Anselmo, 4.
Bottega, 5, 52.
Brain
    fritters, 158.
    fried, 284.
Breads, Schiacciate, and Pizzas,
    63-78.
Bread, 8, 10.
    crumbs, 24.
    dried with parsley and
        onion salad, 223.
    fried, 8.
    garlic (*fett'unta*), 66.
    homemade, 62-63.
    pizza, 76-78.
        classic, 76-77.
        seafood, 77.
        vegetable, 77.
        white, 78.
    schiacciata, 74-75.
        classic, 74.
        Sandrina's oiled , 75.
        with grapes, 74.
    stuffed 72-73.
        fried anchovy, 72.
        sausage in a
            blanket, 73.
    stuffing, 67.

299

302

Notice

If you are desperate to find a treasured Italian family recipe, let us hear from you--maybe we can help. Write a description of the dish, tell us what region of Italy, and if the dish was prepared for a special occasion. We will try our best.

If you have a special recipe you want to share with us, send it along. Be sure to include region of Italy and family lore related to the recipe.

In either instance, all we ask is permission to use the material you send us in a publication when, and if, we do another *Immigrant's Kitchen*.

Send to:
Immigrant's Kitchen
Trade Routes Enterprises
518 Fourth Street
Monessen, Pennsylvania 15062

Notes